Climbing
The Corporate
Matterhorn

Climbing

The Corporate Matterhorn

James A. Newman
Vice-Chairman
Booz, Allen & Hamilton, Inc.

Roy Alexander
Editor-in-Chief
Marketing Times

John Wiley & Sons
New York • Chichester • Brisbane • Toronto • Singapore

83542

Library of Congress Cataloging in Publication Data:

Newman, James A.
    Climbing the corporate Matterhorn.

    Includes bibliographical references and index.
    1. Executives.   2. Management.   3. Success in
business.   I. Alexander, Roy, 1925–   .   II. Title.

HD38.2.N49 1985   658.4'09   84-15357
ISBN 0-471-80764-8

Printed in the United States of America

10 9 8 7 6 5 4 3 2

To JoAnn

Without her understanding
and help many relationships
in this book would have
ended quite differently

FOREWORD

CLIMBING to the top of the corporate mountain takes considerable doing. When I first entered the fascinating world of management, I knew I had much to learn. Advice books existed, of course, but most covered what to do *after* you reached the top. I found sparse comment on how to actually get there.

I wish I could have found management counsel from seasoned campaigners like Jim Newman of Booz, Allen & Hamilton. Jim's knowledge of management practice is encyclopedic. Over the years, several of us have suggested that Jim Newman's comments be immortalized. Now he's done it in *Climbing the Corporate Matterhorn*. What's more, it's all preserved in his famous old-shoe tone. Because of Jim Newman's collaboration with Roy Alexander, a business journalist who believes useful information should also be entertaining, *Matterhorn* reads like a first-rate adventure novel. Imagine shrewd insight on getting there that's fun to read!

The pages come alive with managers solving problems and learning from mistakes as they climb upward. But what I find unique to my experience is the *way* he tells the aspiring climber how to get there—where to start, what educational tools he or she must have, how to get a job and a better job, how to deal with difficult bosses, where to get good advice, and how to *think* like a manager (especially important, how to make sure you have *time* to think).

Looking back on my own advancement needs, I can tell you without reservation: This is a golden resource for men and women who want to climb the Corporate Matterhorn. And I can tell you further that I've learned valuable lessons reading it here and now.

This book serves society. This is the age of the manager. We need more movers and shakers than ever before to solve the productivity problems so necessary to survival and advancement of the company, the nation, and the free market system that makes it all possible.

If you must earn your wings every day in management, this book is for you. Read it, savor it, keep going back to it. You'll find it indispensable.

FRANK BORMAN
Chairman and CEO
Eastern Airlines

Miami, Florida
October 1984

Preface

IN this book, the authors draw upon some 70 years of direct experience in the business community—crossruffed with observations of career climbers in literally thousands of forward, backward, and sideways movements. We draw morals from success, near-success flawed by often simple fatal error, and failure on the grand scale.

Just so you'll know who's talking: When we tell I-was-there experiences, we're drawing on the personal background of James A. Newman in his many years of advising top management at Booz, Allen & Hamilton, the premier management consulting firm. He is the *I* in this book.

When we relate experiences in the third person as we do throughout, we are often reflecting the personal investigations of Roy Alexander in his business reporting and editing for *Marketing Times* and for clients of The Alexander Company, his communications firm.

When we talk about what *we* feel or advise, we're reflecting the joint opinion of the authors.

In some cases, we use actual names of people and companies. In other instances, we have changed names to spare the innocent and, even more so, to protect the guilty.

The best of fortune in your push upward.

JAMES A. NEWMAN
ROY ALEXANDER

New York, New York
October 1984

Acknowledgments, Sources, and Recommended Reading

Basic acknowledgment, of course, is our debt to hundreds of professional managers—sometimes irascible, often difficult, never lacking in variety—who provided the grist for this opus. Their reward, far above our power to augment, has already been documented in the book.

Should you want to tap individual added spigots of insight into this amorphous management mass, here are useful clues:

1. *Creative Management,* by William Marsteller, Crain Books, 740 N. Rush Street, Chicago, offers much common sense and humor on what makes a *sensible* manager.

2. *Dr. Whitt N. Schultz,* articulate author and speaker on creative thinking and self-management, is at Richard/Allen/Winter,

Ltd., 222 Wisconsin Avenue, Lake Forest, Illinois. He offers a free list of his booklets and advisories.

3. *William V. McDonnell,* sales/marketing VP at Honeywell's residential division, originally spoke on *Conducting the Management Orchestra* before Sales and Marketing Executives of Atlanta. A version of his talk later appeared in *Marketing Times.*

4. *David Ogilvy,* reachable via Ogilvy & Mather, Inc., 2 East 48th Street, New York, New York, is a prolific author on management. Ask Jackie Kilgour in his office for a list of Ogilvy books and articles.

5. Lois Wyse, most recently author of *The Six Figure Woman* (good reading for men, too), has produced several quite good management advisories. Ask for a list of her books from Wyse Advertising, 505 Park Avenue, New York, New York.

6. For more on women managers, see *The Effective Woman Manager* (John Wiley & Sons: 1980) by Nathaniel Stewart.

7. *Earl D. Brodie,* 465 California Street, San Francisco, California, is a trenchant, often acerbic, disturber-of-the-peace in small business management. His comments are often provocative. Ask for a free sample of his newsletter.

8. Climbers fascinated (or horrified) by the problem of *understanding* the boss should ask Dr. Bob Mezoff (ODT Associates, Box 134, Amherst, Massachusetts) for free seminar outlines.

9. Walter Keichel III writes a regular *Fortune* column called *Office Hours.* He's entertaining, sometimes outlandish, often perceptive. Read him regularly to your advantage.

10. Andrew S. Grove, president of Intel, has written *High Output Management* (Random House: 1983)—useful to climbers interested in inside-out management strategy and tactics.

11. If you'd like to jump into office politics with both feet, read *Winning at Office Politics* (Van Nostrand Reinhold: 1981) by Andrew J. Dubrin.

12. Charles Percy's Horatio Alger-like story is detailed in *Charles Percy: Strong New Voice from Illinois* (Harris-Wolfe & Co., Jacksonville, Illinois) by Martha Cleveland.

13. Salesmanship, covered lightly in this book as a discipline of marketing, is treated in detail in *Secrets of Closing Sales* (Prentice-Hall: 1983) by Charles Roth and Roy Alexander. It may be helpful in instructing your sales force.

14. To indulge your fascination with the Erratic Genius (treated several times in this book) read *Marion Harper: An Unauthorized Biography* (Crain Books: Chicago) by Russ Johnston. Highly readable and instructive.

Final acknowledgments go to colleagues of the authors. Connie Jason, managing editor of *Marketing Times,* made invaluable contributions to this book's order and usefulness. Our editor, Michael J. Hamilton, editorial supervisor, Robert G. Golden, and production supervisor, Mary Daniello, proved perspicacious and patient beyond all abnormal reason. Word processing, transcribing, and typing were managed expertly by Linda Sullivan, Evril Thompson, and Scott Hill.

With this much diligence at hand, we'll probably be at a loss to explain the inevitable gremlins and type-lice that attack the printed work of deserving authors!

J.A.N.
R.A.

Contents

PART ——— 1

Equipping Yourself to Climb

CHAPTER 1

Take It from the Top

AT one time, movie stars and athletes supplied most of our celebrity needs in Western civilization. Today, business executives are often equally well known. Lee Iacocca visits us nightly on the TV screen. Victor Kiam tells us he likes the shaver so much he bought the company. Frank Borman reminds us about earning our wings each day. We follow the domestic and corporate shifts of William Agee and Mary Cunningham. We read of the goings and comings of Walter Wriston at Citicorp and we see the unmistakable spire of Walter's whistle—the slanted-roofed Citicorp building in midtown Manhattan.

We're also aware of their money, again like the top jock or screen idol. People know Lee Iacocca gets $795,000 plus a bonus that pushes his yearly income to $1 million.

"Pretty soft touch," they say. Yet, reality's something else again. The contrast between a top corporate official and an outstanding football star (Hershel Walker gets $5 million for a three-year contract) or baseball star (signing a five-year contract for $1 million a year) is great. It's a vastly different world.

The actor or TV news personality moves into a glamor mode early on because of physical capability, acting ability, or a fascinating face or body. Tom Brokaw, my fellow jogger in Cornwall, Connecticut gets $500,000 a year. Barbara Walters gets $1 million.

When these performers are interviewed, we learn how long and hard they worked to make The Big Time. What? Five or ten years? Compare that to the time (often 20 to 40 years), training, and hard work of climbing the Corporate Matterhorn before a candidate reaches the CEO's spacious corner office.

In more candid moments, performers also admit luck played a great role. They're right! The nation could produce 50 on-camera presenters competitive with Dan Rather (and I find Rather very pleasing and competent). But it's a function that can be replicated.

I do not believe we can produce 50 candidates competitive with Rawleigh Warner, CEO of Mobil Oil, or Jean Riboud, the head of Schlumberger. The selection process that's been going on for years has sifted out the best person for the job. At dozens of checkpoints up the slope, the climber gets evaluated and re-evaluated against fellow climbers. Each time some strivers are eliminated.

So luck is not a factor in a successful climb up a corporate peak. The corporate climb is much more responsive to applied intelligence (carefully honed and developed via hard work, long hours, single-mindedness, and determination). It's a difficult, demanding, rigorous task. There's no easy formula in this book or elsewhere. In fact, after examining the requirements, you may decide not to make the trip. That's a legitimate view. There are many ways to be gainfully employed and happy without entering the competition.

If, on the other hand, you are a *rara avis* dedicated to unusual achievement—and you have ability and energy to back it up—this book will help you. We will cover getting on the climb team, ascending to each new height, and surviving the shakeout that occurs at each day camp on the slope. And we'll cover rewards to the successful climber (great), and the glamor (considerable).

This competition involves 150 million people—the entire population of the private sector, probably 60 or 65 percent of the nation's total workforce. Yet only a few hundred reach the summit of gigantic business Matterhorns. Each one who does achieve it reaches the rarified heights one step at a time.

There's no quick fix here. Today's achievers dedicated themselves to a long, steady, difficult climb years ago. No business career is an overnight sensation.

The daily regime alone is awesome. The CEO of a large manufacturer often works 76 hours a week—twice as much as his employees on the production line. So much for the CEO's "soft touch." Moreover, the CEO has been logging in a lot of time like that for many years— or he wouldn't be in the corner office.

John DeLorean, regardless of his recent problems, worked 12 to 14 hours a day straight through weekends in his climb at Pontiac and the same earlier at Packard—not uncommon hours for a real climber.

The climb also functions as a giant sorting and sifting machine. The future CEO passes a winnowing process at each ledge. The survivors are more than plenty good—they're absolutely tops, the very best. Some are *nefariously* good, some are *deviously* good.

Some like DeLorean appear to get sunstroke or snowblindness along the way. But most are well adjusted. I can't imagine an ill-adjusted person making this climb. It requires top mental and physical health—coupled with powerful motivation.

In the 1840s, wagon masters said of covered wagon pioneers leaving Missouri for Oregon: "The cowards never started. The weak died along the way." That, like this business climb, was a tough trip for tough people. Everyone cannot *start*. Certainly not everyone can finish.

Henry Ford II, when asked if his son was destined to be a big wheel at Ford Motor Company, said: "If he wants to, I'd like to see him do it. If he doesn't want to, I'd like to see him *not* do it. Depends on whether he's willing to be married to the company or not. He may not be. A lot of people aren't. Those that aren't shouldn't try it."

Will to do is vital. As corporate managers, we've learned what *we* think about a candidate is much less important than what *he* or *she* thinks. On paper a fellow may be a logical candidate of Hi-Tech Manager. But he's got to be dedicated and willing to put in 14-hour days. Only he knows if he has the push—and he may not know until he starts out.

On a climb, a series of bosses must keep giving you a chance at the peak slope. So choosing good bosses is an asset, when you can manage it. Often you cannot. When you get a boss that's less than helpful, you've got to find another way around the problem. By definition, the successful climber passes a number of former bosses on the way up.

In making the climb, as we'll show you, you must be very good about controlling yourself. On a day-to-day basis, you'll experience a tremendous range of emotions. You must overcome terrible frustrations. At times, you'll need to be ruthless.

Sometimes you get the impression the large company CEO is not human, a computer mind with ice-water veins. You're right. These are not ordinary people. The average guy or gal will never make it. Leo Durocher said: "Nice guys finish last." We add: "Average guys don't finish first."

This quality is sometimes called the *killer instinct.* Anything that gets in the way must be removed. There's also a benign side to it: a green beret combat colonel can be quite fatherly in looking after his men. We'll talk about both sides of the quality.

We'll isolate early characteristics required for the climb. As basic equipment, you need to take along brains, aggressiveness, and strong drive. Being a genius is not required, however. An MIT study found that students in the highest rank in grade averages never became top leaders in the real world. They often become head of the laboratory or top scientists.

When on campus, astute corporate recruiters don't look for the straight A students. They look for the B students who have been very active in campus activities. In sports and student government. On student publications. On debate teams.

And you must be willing to work. House Speaker Tip O'Neill reserved decision about President Reagan until he found out Reagan works only two and a half hours a day. "Not enough time," in Tip O'Neill's view, "to do a big job." O'Neill believes in work—particularly for Republicans.

We'll also show the importance of stick-to-itiveness. As CEO, you push a strong conviction even when all the odds are stacked against you. If it's right, don't worry about it being popular. But when you push these visceral feelings, you've got to be right at least 50 percent of the time. Otherwise, you and your convictions will be headed down the slope. Tough requirements? You bet.

On top of that, each day you must reassess priorities—not by what you'd prefer doing—but by what will make the greatest corporate contribution. View each day as a new problem—regardless of what you did yesterday. Ask yourself what's shifted, what's changed, what's different. Then start all over again.

Unexpected change tests your flexibility under fire. We will talk about how to cope with change that's even more varied in the real world. The person who says "Everything'll be all right as soon as it all settles down" won't make it. Things never settle down.

Not that you're climbing a trouble-free slope. *Au contraire:* it's full of booby-traps. If you're a native-born scrapper, that's fine. But realize this salient fact: climbing the Corporate Matterhorn is a fight—all the way—from day one. It's a real battle. It's fun when you win. It's traumatic when you slide back (as you will from time to time). It's fascinating in many ways. But to make it, you must enjoy the fray. The calm peace-seeker will not reach the summit.

Given the rigors of the trip, why should anyone want to go? The rewards are enormous. The CEO is a global traveler. He consorts with high officials of government, the movers and shakers of society. He can afford palatial estates in the tropics (for winter living) and the north woods (for summer time). He is attended by a retinue of aides and lieutenants worthy of a caliph of ancient Baghdad. His power (Henry Kissinger called power the ultimate aphrodisiac) is greater than presidents of dozens of smaller nations. He has within his ability the opportunity to genuinely change society for the better. As Teddy Roosevelt said of the White House: "It's a bully pulpit." Many CEOs are celebrities, eagerly sought after by talkshow hosts and social lionesses alike, all of which is gasped at by the gaping public. So, in addition to all the reasons *you* know, we'll cover why people make the climb.

Everything on earth comes at a price, and corporate success—without exception—calls for long hours, heavy and often inconvenient travel, and days and weeks away from family, with not-uncommon alienation and domestic problems that go with it. Many candidates balk at the price and we'll discuss the tradeoffs.

We're not recommending corporate climbing to everyone. We recommend it *if* you're suited and enjoy the good fight. And *if* you're an activist. The name of the game is action—above all. The expression "do something even if it's wrong" applies to corporate management. You must act. Throughout this book, we'll keep putting you on the activist track.

This book is for the *continuing* climber. Sure, it's important to know when you should realistically drop out of the expedition. Seasoned managers must tell people they haven't got what it takes. But they don't spend a lot of time telling them how to look someplace else. Neither will we. Our focus is on the climber that stays on the upward slope.

CHAPTER
────────── **2**

Evaluating the Requirements: Do You Really Want to Go?

THE shattering telephone call came from my German partner. "John Murray, the automotive manager, has just committed suicide!"

"What happened?" I shouted.

"He's been operating under severe pressure," my partner said. "Very uptight. Lot of trouble with his new job. The division's results were sliding. Heat from the home office. His wife was unhappy: no friends in Germany. Their four-year-old child was sick and his wife couldn't communicate properly with the hospital. The combination was evidently too much for him."

In a state of shock, I hung up and dropped everything to make arrangements. Even though I've had far too many tragic calls over the years, I've never become accustomed to them—not anymore than the combat soldier accepts death of his friends.

But lethal stress is all-too-common in management. Real physical dangers exist as well (kidnapping has become a problem of late). Take the perils into account before you elect to climb the Corporate Matterhorn. Now's the time to review what's expected of you—body and mind—and then decide if you really want to go.

Workaholics Encouraged

For openers, you must dedicate yourself to the task, not just this week, this month, or this year, but until you reach the peak. By total commitment, we mean 10- to 12-hour days, 6 or 7 days a week.

Abraham Krasnoff's Long Island-based Pall Corporation had the highest percentage growth of any of the nation's shareholder-owned companies in the past decade. And 63-year-old Krasnoff still rises at 4 a.m. to begin sifting through paper work. He can't remember taking a vacation.

Your vacations usually include work. And you'll adjust your vacation schedule six times until it fits business needs. At the vacation site, you'll be interrupted with telephone calls from the office.

You'll need to cope with real home-business conflicts:

"Jack, I know it's important for your division to lead the company this year. But you and I are coming to a fork in the road here at home. Harry and Morris are getting impossible. They miss their father—both the companionship and the discipline. You're going to have to choose: which is more important?"

How often has this scene been played! It's a long-run drama. You'll need to handle it. A manager's principal commodity is time. And time demands are insatiable. The inventive managers find a way to serve both business and family. But it's far from easy. Be sure you're confident about this conflict before you start.

KNOW THYSELF

Socrates said "know thyself" and it's still sound advice. Before you start the trip, evaluate your mental ability and, even more important, evaluate how you utilize it.

Do you have a management mind that realistically evaluates your abilities before taking on a new assignment? You must.

Can you analyze problems and come up with workable solutions? Are you insatiably curious about little and big things? About why people and organizations work or fail to work! Do you have a sense of urgency and hatred of delay? Or do you, as President Abraham Lincoln said about his troublesome general, McClellan, have The Slows?

Burleigh Gardner, when at the University of Chicago, conducted a comprehensive study of characteristics of successful executives. He found critical factors occurring in this order: (1) intelligence, (2) judgment, (3) motivation, (4) determination, (5) people sensitivity.

He also identified a surprising sixth characteristic: most successful executives enjoy working with their hands (be it carpentry, masonry, gardening, painting, or sculpture).

Examine these qualities one by one.

Intelligence.   Without I.Q., your climb will be difficult (not impossible, if a few characters I've known are any indication). If you aren't bright, you'd better have a superabundance of all the other requirements.

Judgment.   This is difficult to evaluate and even harder to predict; it is an essential commodity. Judgment is the ability to arrive at a sound conclusion from a given action—in a situation where delay is often disastrous. You must comprehend the variables and weigh them properly before undertaking a course of action.

Judgment also means understanding people—knowing how far you can push them, and at what point they crack.

In job interviews, I often present the applicant with a set of business facts—then give him or her 15 minutes to come up with a written analysis of what to do about them. The time pressure is important (it always exists for the corporate climber) and there's always a shortage of facts. You must exercise best judgment from information *at hand.* And your decisions had better be good most of the time.

How would you fare under those conditions? Ask an experienced friend to give you such a test. You may find it quite indicative.

One pollster surveyed a cross section of CEOs to see what qualities they revered most in their fellows. The findings: quick decision-making.

Motivation.   When you're staggering ahead in a howling blizzard and the obstacles seem insurmountable, you must have courage and determination to press onward.

When I was president of Exeter Academy in Exeter, New Hampshire, the board met to talk about a second capital fund drive. After carefully listening to our conservative advisors, I stood up and said: "Let's set our goal at $30 million."

One trustee screamed: "You're out of your mind! We've just raised $15 million nine years ago!"

"Impossible target," said another.

"Nope," I said. "$30 million. We can do it."

Finally after considerable debate, we set $26 million as target. Most of the trustees were dubious. What was the end result five years later? You guessed it: We raised $26.5 million! You get what you expect to get!

Many times I've seen this repeated in business among managers with conviction and purpose. Where would emerging hi-tech businesses be today if their leaders crumbled before each obstacle? How many staid companies have been rejuvenated by strongly motivated leaders? Look at Jack Welch of G. E. or Jim Robinson of American Express or Walter Wriston of Citicorp.

And remember, aspiring climber: to get out in front of the pack you must be a self-starter and an inspirer of others. Many times you'll look at your team and say: "If only they didn't need to be prodded into action!" But they do need both the carrot and the stick. And that's why a leader is needed.

Determination.   The planner with the will to succeed prevails over the plodder. As a rising manager, expect conflict. Be prepared to convince others: it goes with the territory. If you don't like argument, if you find adversity difficult, rethink your plan of joining the climbing team. Maybe you'd be happier on a plateau—as a teacher or an artist.

Would Lee Iaccoca have succeeded without determination? Could Sir Michael Edwardes have turned around British Leyland when faced with two horrendous problems—low executive pay and strong unions? Could middle managers (heading product groups or divisions for Procter & Gamble or Gillette or Johnson & Johnson or General Electric) help their companies become leaders without determination?

No. Motivation is critical.

People Sensitivity.   Proper understanding and handling of people is probably the most important single requirement. To many analysts, management keeps coming back to people smarts. Eliza Collins, a *Harvard Business Review* editor, places people skills at the top of the list in importance:

> *Today, making it in management begins with self-knowledge, the capacity to grow and withstand stress, and the ability to deal with conflicting emotions, both on and off the job.*

Sure, you get help from personnel departments and management development committees and, in certain industries, resource planners. But arms and legs or computer models aside, the ultimate job of assessing, directing, and handling subordinates rests 100 percent in your lap, old buddy or old gal.

If you do it right, your mission may succeed. If you don't do it right, you will surely fail.

Now before we go too far, understand this: I'm not plumping for that mythical quality called *leadership*. Or that miraculous ability to make people follow the Pied Piper. I *am* talking about the everyday requirements of handling and managing people.

Start with the easiest part: if you have lazy slobs who must be goaded every inch of the way, get rid of them. So much for that.

But what about the out-and-out bastards who make life miserable for everybody—including you—people that are nonetheless creative and productive. Well, here's where you evaluate the trade off. If you decide you need these multitalented hardcases, you're elected to handle them. (And if you're still with us later, we'll tell you *how*. Right now, you're gauging the climb and whether you should make it.)

Codifyinɢ ᴛʜᴇ Mᴀɴᴀɢᴇᴍᴇɴᴛ Mind

Other experts dig out other success factors—with some overlap. A college conducted a study of prominent alumni and published the characteristics that occurred most often:

People-Smarts.   Skill in people selection and a knack for motivating people of different viewpoints.

Sloganeering.   Ability to reduce desirable policies to simple values (Thomas J. Watson's *Think,* for example).

Productive Deviousness.   The ability to get around people and problems when initially blocked.

Directed Energy.   High levels of creativity and energy coupled with a pronounced confidence in making this output productive.

Time Parsimony.   High achievers guard time jealously so they get about an hour a day to do as they please (often to merely sit and think).

Health Awareness.   This conserves body and mind for unusually high output. This means avoiding drugs, excessive alcohol or nicotine, sugar or salt—with emphasis on exercise.

Flexible Work Schedule.   This allows achievers to capitalize on arising opportunity. They hire others to handle repetitious tasks and concentrate on creative work that stretches the mind.

Structured Associations with People.   These make people feel good about themselves.

Lifelong Learning.   Orientation via reading, classes, seminars, discussion groups. Eagerness to learn is constant.

Early Risers.   These types of people are usually early-in-day achievers.

Nature-Oriented.   Eager to participate in the natural wonders of the universe.

Fix-It-Nature.   This is reflected in their most common hobby: handcraft or home shop work. *Interest:* building things and making them work.

Such are the characteristics common to successful managers. No formula is perfect, of course; that's why we give you several. But many items on that list fits dozens of CEOs that I know personally. Several of these traits are worth considering separately—which we will do.

When you see how many managers are inadequate in desired traits, you get a better understanding of why such a small percentage make it to the rarefied air. Even possessing these characteristics and the energetic conviction to apply them, you must know *where* you're going. Take continuing inventory of situations—including yourself. Develop confidence. If you think you are beaten, you are. Pick the best people to help you. Put square pegs into square holes. Be a deeply involved player. Go the extra mile. Display firmness and conviction along with compassion. Respect your peers and gain their respect. Keep score carefully. Give lots of credit to others. Be constantly hungry for knowledge.

All this sounds like impossible specs, you say! Maybe. But next time you meet an impressive CEO, check him or her out. You'll find many a CEO qualifies on a rather astounding number of these points. Think about it!

Leadership: Sense and Nonsense

Now before we leave the requirements and get into the management mind, let's go back to what leadership *isn't*—it'll help you to shed the excess weight (you need to climb as unencumbered as possible).

You probably assume a manager is a good leader, as is often the case. However, avoid mumbo-jumbo on the subject. Harvard's Abraham Zalenik, for instance, worries a great deal about *transformational* vs. *transactional* leadership. In *The New York Times* he analyzes leadership by *ego, superego,* and *id.* This hoorah is a waste of time.

Others hail the leader as a *keeper of the corporate culture,* in the popular new phrase. Corporate culture is evidently a set of shared values that get reflected in behavior and, in the best cases, furthers everyone's pursuit of a common end. Corporate culture, some of these seers feel, is the creation of a strong leader who hammers away at a message to his organization for years.

Well, I'm amused at the way stale wine gets hawked in new bottles. Sure, a good CEO decides what his company stands for—and then makes sure it does *that.* Seems to me the same quality was once called *corporate image,* before that term got over-used. This is the way it adds up: You'd be well advised to avoid these transient fads and stick to common sense and sound practice, which never go out of style.

Still other gurus say leadership is synonymous with vision. They cite Citicorp's Walter B. Wriston as a prime example of vision. I know and admire Wriston and it's hard to deny he has vision.

But an effective CEO is *supposed* to plan ahead, *expected* to be an architect of change in large or small arenas. Forward-planning is hard to do well. But the many effective CEOs who do it are impatient with this verbal agonizing. You should be, too. Learn to recognize double-talk when you encounter it.

What Top Contenders Lack

Now that you've seen the ideal makeup of the management mind—and no candidate can possibly measure up to *all* standards—look at some notable lacks among CEOs and CEO-aspirants.

Morgan W. McCall, Jr. and Michael M. Lombardo (Center for Creative Leadership, Greensboro, North Carolina) studied derailed managers and dug out qualities that threw them off track:

☐ Insensitive to others: abrasive, intimidating, bullying style. Sometimes this means a cold, aloof, arrogant manner.

☐ Betrayal of trust.

☐ Overly ambitious: thinking of next job, playing politics.

☐ Specific performance problems with the business.

☐ Overmanaging: unable to delegate or build a team.

☐ Unable to staff effectively, or to think strategically, or to adapt to boss with different style.

☐ Overdependent on advocate or mentor.

Beware of Simplistic Formulae

Beware of simplistic formulae about what makes a good manager—formulae often put forth by writers without management experience. Bruce Horowitz writes in *Dun's Business Monthly* that great CEOs understand their own shortcomings and learn to compensate for them. I disagree.

The hell-for-leather CEO is a pusher and driver of himself and others. He's moving much too fast to worry about his shortcomings. Besides, his ego generally doesn't allow him to think too disparagingly of himself—he's just not that kind of person.

Horowitz cites a study of 41 top executives. The most successful ones, he concludes, play to their strengths and build a staff that covers their weaknesses.

Well, they *might* do this instinctively. But I doubt if they do it deliberately. They don't figure it out, they're driving too hard. Publicly they probably don't admit to shortcomings. (Privately they may.)

Horowitz sees this as a cold calculated planned approach to career betterment. I see successful climbers as aggressive and enthusiastic and single-minded. But not that calculatingly analytical.

This kind of pronouncement is typical of the researcher or academic sitting on the sidelines watching the game—rather than somebody actually in the fray.

Horowitz goes on to say common CEO flaws are *arrogance, insecurity, lack of foresight,* and *inability to cope with business setbacks* and *faulty people selection.* He's just outlined problem characteristics of the human species—particularly its leaders.

I also issue similar warnings about other highly touted management advisories—including the current fad book, *In Search of Excellence.* Its conclusions, when you get right down to them, are: Do it simpler and faster. And four of the top 14 companies in *In Search of Excellence* were disaster areas a couple of years after the book came out. *Oversimplifying brings trouble.*

There are a great many amateur psychologists out there commenting about business. Take their offerings with a ton of salt. John DeLorean's case has been widely discussed. One favorite theory is that he's insecure and is trying to focus attention on himself—even attention on his failures and scandals. This is hogwash. A person with an ego like John DeLorean's isn't *ever* going to *try* to fail for any reason.

College professors get themselves quoted widely on management topics. Watch them, too. Eugene Jennings of Michigan State University recently said that, in the 1950s and 1960s, the CEO was expected to only solve the day's problems—let tomorrow take care of itself. But in the 1980s, he says the CEO must be more future oriented. I could just as easily make a case the other way, but I won't. "All generalizations are false—including this one."

Obviously Jennings didn't read *In Search of Excellence,* which advises you to forget about strategic plans and settle down doing the things faster today.

These formulae are all suspect.

If a business and its CEO are successful and growing vis-à-vis competition and market share, you can be sure that both long-term functions (such as forward planning and sensitivity to the public) and short-range functions (such as reacting to a competitor's new product) are being handled effectively. What appears to be a judgment call is often the result of a private detailed investigation.

Other suspect comments come from outside the field of management. I have great regard for the Menninger Clinic as a medical facility. But when doctors start analyzing management styles—based on their experience with patients—I part company with them. One Menninger doctor says some executive patients lack the ability to get satisfaction working *through* others. They can't adjust to being a *planner* rather than a *doer*, he says, and quotes one manager: "I used to work 12 hours a day but now I can leave the office at 2:30 in the afternoon and nobody cares."

Well, the world often suffers from infusions of nonsense—up to and including that comment. The driving manager that has risen by working 12 hours a day doesn't go home at 2:30 p.m. He has so many things to do that his problem is constantly setting priorities.

Most top leaders in business or government are never short of ideas. Dozens of projects are churning in their minds. I've worked for bosses who could think of more things in ten minutes than I could get done in three weeks of steady work. It's always a matter of setting priorities. So when a doctor says a manager goes home at 2:30 p.m., el medico has his wires crossed. Or he's not talking about a real manager.

For your sake as well as ours, we won't cover even half the nonsense written about what the CEO is and ought to be. But you, with samples in hand, can keep a weather eye out for balderdash—a good exercise for a manager at any level.

Finally, before you say "I'm on" to the expedition, look at the odds. You must believe you're a rare bird, indeed, to make the top. One analyst says it takes 10,000 first-level managers to make a single division head, 500 division heads to sift out one president, and four presidents to allow one chairman. You must look at these odds and say: "Okay, I still want a shot at it."

Summary: Climber Specs

There you have it, potential climbers, a mulligan stew of reasons why you may want to make the climb—offset by a lot of reasons why you may want to stay home or set less-than-topside goals. We're pointedly avoiding telling you *how* to climb each crag at this stage and just what the challenge *is*. If you decide to string along with us (and we hope you do) and if you're realistic about the requirements, we'll be delighted to offer comments from the coach's box as you gain altitude. It's a great trip for the mentally tough, physically fit candidate blessed with applied gray cells.

The sifting-out process has already begun. Fall in! We're moving up the slope!

CHAPTER 3

Education: Basic Equipment for the Climb

A one-armed man *could* become a baseball pitcher. A runner with one short leg *could* become an ace at the 440-yard dash. A stutterer *could* become a radio announcer. But none of these are *likely*.

A corporate climber without college education *could* claw his or her way to the top. But, in this day and time, it's unlikely. In The Gilded Age a century ago, men without high school sat at the helm of large companies. Today college is assumed and the real question is: What *advanced* work have you done? And what is your plan for *continuing* education?

It is not the knowledge you gain in college—although that's damned important—it's the stigma if you don't try. That's part of the pre-selection process. College is considered so essential today that if you don't figure out a way to get there, you're documenting characteristics that work against you.

Nor is the problem over if the non-college person lucks out and gets a good starting job. Suppose you make a good record and want to move to another firm. The evaluators at the new company immediately go back into your background and out comes the college problem again. So you must have college. But there are many ways to get it.

Say you're out of high school and have figured out a way to attend day classes toward a degree. If that means you must work while on campus, all the better. Work is a plus when the corporate recruiter calls. Try to make your part-time work contribute toward your management goals.

If you're working now and cannot afford to attend full time, take evening courses toward a degree. If you aren't content with the education you already have—*and you'd better not be*—take evening work. View education as a continuing lifelong process.

An excellent two-week summer course is a productive way to spend your vacation—and many companies will help finance this for employees. So further your career-climbing credentials. Get education and keep getting it. (You can be sure your competitors headed up the slope *will*.)

At such courses, reflecting the need to constantly re-evaluate priorities, computerized management games start you out with a given set of circumstances. Then they'll ring a bell and say:

"This product has been taken off the market."
"You've got a strike in your Indiana plant."
"You're being investigated by the FTC."

CollEGE: WhERE?

Should you attend a small community college or large university? Or somewhere in between? A name or non-name place? A case can be made for attending a large university, that microcosm of society. It has real-life competition: students vying for top jobs in campus activities and striving for top grades. A university is a rehearsal for the real world. Classmates who survive will be the real movers in society.

That's the case for the university—but I don't agree with it. For undergraduate work, I believe a small college with high academic standards is best.

The years between 14 and 20 are very formative in a young person's life. Dump impressionable students into a large university and a certain number get lost. They don't grab hold of anything. They just get swept up in the currents.

"But isn't that survival of the fittest?" a colleague asked. "Isn't that also part of the selection process?"

That may be. But I've seen good candidates fail to develop on a large campus. You get identity in a smaller setting. Sometimes that's very important. I favor going to a smaller place where you'd get more individual attention and more individual opportunity.

Ivy League vs. Non-Ivy League

Recognizing the explosion in universities in all locations, is there any longer that much significance to attending an ivy league school? The hard answer: yes. It never ceases to amaze me how much Yalies stick together. Some institutions are heavily supplied with New Haven alumni. Neither have I seen much shyness or embarrassment about the Old Boy Network from Cambridge. (I myself had a grandfather and a father who carried the crimson. Of course, I was enrolled there as soon as I could walk. However, my advisors at Phillips Exeter Academy diverted me to MIT, which I've always been happy about.)

Without doubt, Harvard, Yale, Princeton, and Dartmouth do produce high-quality graduates. In addition, their strong alumni organizations provide valuable connections for the corporate climber. So boil it down: Don't aim your harpoons at an Ivy League school for *program* quality alone. There are many high-grade institutions that will teach you as much. But when all other comparisons are equal, the continuing relationships offered by the Ivy League schools might well tip the scale in their favor. Maybe it *shouldn't* be that way, but it is.

But all generalizations are sometimes false. The important thing is: Go to college somewhere. If you're a high school graduate and the best opportunity emerges at the state university near you, go there by all means. Costs are often the deciding factor. Whatever you do, don't say: "It's too expensive. I'll go later. I'll go to work now." Draw up a definite work-study plan whereby you're attending class in the evenings while working on the job during the day.

Visit to a Non-Name Campus

The University of Utah is certainly not a particularly famous school— and the way my firm hired a graduate from UU helps put education in perspective.

The University of Utah has experienced remarkable growth in the business school and other parts. It offers one of the nation's lowest tuition rates and that applies to out-of-state students too. UU encourages applicants from outside the United States and from Hawaii and Alaska.

I went to UU to speak on opportunities in management consulting. When I arrived on Sunday night, a delegation met me—three faculty members and eight students. They took me to dinner and grilled me on business practices. Then at 7 a.m. a new delegation of 12 took me to breakfast. The platoon system.

I talked for 15 minutes in each class starting at 8 a.m. I was in the hot seat all the way. I corrected a lot of misconceptions. Many saw consulting as very glamorous! "You're your own boss, you listen to people's problems and you come up with great solutions."

Some saw it as synonymous with psychiatry.

They were intrigued by the money ($47,000 a year to start). But against the money and the independence, I brought them back to earth. I discussed the breaking up of families because of consultants' heavy travel. I told about a percentage of trainees getting dropped. And the odds: Only 1 in 40 of the trainees we interview is accepted.

After class, student Stephen Smith came up and said he wanted to apply to Booz Allen when he graduated. I encouraged him. But I reminded him about the severity of our selection process.

Smith followed up in the spring: He sent in a résumé and letter. I gave it to our personnel people and they said: "Well, maybe."

So I told Smith if he had occasion to get to the East Coast, he should stop in. In three weeks, he replied, he'd be in New York. (I don't know how he made the trip, but he found a way.) We interviewed him and he's working for us today.

There's an example of a go-getter who saw his opportunity and acted on it. Not because his school record was good, which it was. Not because he attended the University of Utah, although I think highly of the school. But because he saw a niche and went after it. He wasn't going to be in New York—he made it his *business* to be there. He moved quickly. Maybe he hitch-hiked. But he presented the body at the right place at the right time.

Study Communications

Whatever your program in college, be sure to include courses in writing and speaking (you may think you learned *both* years ago, but for the fast track, you didn't).

Managers must constantly write instructions, reports and memos, letters, and survey conclusions. If this comes hard to you, it will hold you back.

Speaking to groups—effectively and persuasively—is a basic requirement of executive life. You'll probably need to continue with business speaking courses later as well. But get on the right foot by studying speech in school.

Some of the world's otherwise-sophisticates quake at facing an audience. Giants of industry become pygmies on a podium. Board chairmen self-destruct at stockholder meetings. Today, more than ever the ability to speak well in public is critical.

"On the list of executive skills," reports *The New York Times,* "public speaking has become virtually a must. With the visibility of business leadership in the media increasing, executives often have to appear at public forums, before Congressional hearings, and at conventions."

According to *The Book of Lists,* speaking before a group heads the list of the 14 worst human fears (beating out heights, war, and Christmas shopping). Make sure this doesn't happen to you. Good speech can be the cutting edge in outpointing a competitor who's almost as good but suffers from hoof-in-mouth disease.

College Sports as Manager Training

If you're a scrapper and a theorist on the playing field, the experience will be helpful in management. As a baseball infielder, you learn to evaluate the alternatives with each batter, decide what action you'll take to counter each alternative.

On each pitch, you plan ahead: What to do if the ball is hit to you or hit to third base or hit to first base. How can you make a double play? One man's on first. The ball is hit between second and third. Who's going to field it? And to throw to whom? When must you throw to first and not try for the double play? You go through this thinking from the first to the ninth inning. The spectator is primarily concerned with who gets a hit or doesn't. Or whether the runner gets tagged out at second. They see the color. But when you're playing you get the fundamentals. That's why *playing* is instructive to managers and *watching* isn't.

On each pitch in management, you constantly evaluate the alternatives of possible actions. If you increase advertising. If you cut production. If you add to salesforce.

Advanced Education: Yes or No?

When it comes to education, there's probably more MBA discussion per square inch in the business community than about any other issue, bar none. I'll come clean with you: I took an MBA from University of Chicago—evenings, while working—long before MBA was fashionable.

Think that puts me foursquare in favor of MBA? Not necessarily.

I favor continuing education for the corporate alpinist, as I've said many times. I also believe in added knowledge: It's powerful. So any way you can get education (and the know-how that goes with it) is good.

The MBA works best, seems to me, when taken along with work—*while* you're working rather than in *advance* of working. Or maybe after having put in some years on a job.

I agree with Richard Hillsman, a 23-year-old bachelor of business administration from the University of Notre Dame. He graduated in the top quarter of his class and is now an accountant manager at First National Bank of Chicago. To land that job, Hillsman completed a one-year training program with 20 MBAs and three other BBAs.

Nevertheless, he's planning to go to Northwestern evenings for his MBA, which First Chicago will finance if he makes passing grades. Hillsman wants the degree for defensive reasons.

"A couple of years down the road, if a choice is made between me and an MBA holder, I don't want to lose because I have one less feather in my cap," he says.

Start your work experience after you get an undergraduate degree and phase-in the MBA *when you're ready for it.* At my firm, we encourage our trainees to get settled in the job and then think about advanced education.

And I do think the MBA or its equivalent (and there *are* many equivalents) is a leg-up for the serious climber.

One advisor said recently that a masters degree in a non-business field is almost as impressive in corporate circles as an MBA. All right. Let's emphasize *almost.*

In any situation, once you're doing well on a job, it doesn't make the slightest difference whether you went to East Podunk or got a Ph.D. in animal husbandry. On the job, 95% of your chances for advancement within the company depends on how you perform—not on your academic credentials. (When you change companies, your education usually comes back up.)

But at the beginning, MBAs *do* have a leg-up. Also useful: a masters in sociology, psychology, or economics. Some fast risers come in with a masters in economics or banking and then go to school at night to double up with an MBA. That's the real express lane. It provides you added know-how. It's visible credentials. But I've known many rousing successes without it.

The MBA Profiled

What is this near-mythical entity known as MBA?

The MBA's reputation has followed the curve of a traditional business cycle: from boom times to bust. In the late 1970s, the MBA was the golden passport to the executive washroom and corporate boardroom—the open-sesame to power. One of every five CEOs and corporate board directors had an MBA, and that figure jumped to 50 percent for top executives under 40.

"It was the spirit of the times," says Elaine F. Weiss, Cambridge,

Massachusetts-based business writer. "MBA was tailor-made for the me-first generation. In the 1950s, bright young graduate students wanted to make life better through automation, so they became engineers; in the 1960s, students believed they could save the world and took up teaching and social work to prove it; in the early 1970s and early 1980s, they'd learned their lesson and wanted to become rich and powerful in business.

"For career-minded women, it guaranteed safe passage to a hitherto forbidden land. Undergraduates saw it as the quickest route to a six-figure income short of medical school. And companies assumed they could solve their most pressing problems by snapping up any available MBA in sight. As a result, the number of degrees conferred swelled from 19,000 in 1968 to 47,600 in 1978 to just under 60,000 in 1982."

More spectacular was the rise in women MBAs: Male recipients increased 50 percent between 1973 and 1983, from 30,000 to 45,000, but female graduates multiplied tenfold, from 1,500 a decade ago to 15,000 in 1983.

In 1982, *The MBAs,* a quartet of B-school grads from Harvard and Stanford, composed a hit song entitled *Born to Run Things.* Its refrain:

Sing hey, hey, the MBAs
Can't you see we're the latest craze?
Hey, hey, the MBAs
Having fun earning twice our age.

The hierarchial ranking of business schools resembles a pyramid, with 10 or 15 revered schools at the apex, another 30 or so one status-level down, several dozen respectable names below them, and then hundreds more spreading out to form the base.

A school's position on the pyramid translates directly into cash: Graduates from Harvard, Stanford, Columbia, and Wharton can command virtually double the starting salary of a candidate from Emporia State University in Kansas. With Harvard MBAs occupying 20 percent of those corner offices the Fortune 500 reserve for their top three executives, it's no wonder the Cambridge campus is a favorite corporate incubator.

The benefits of attending an uppercrust institution are established. But don't rule out other schools. Good regional colleges serve neighboring business communities. Students who want to work near home can often tap the local job market with a local MBA.

Specialty schools are strong in certain fields. The Sloan School at MIT and Rensselaer Polytechnic's business school in Troy, New York, offer programs in managing high-tech businesses that are quite appropriate to the overall mission of their parent universities. Michigan State is known for its excellent materials-management program. The University of Nebraska is strong in accounting.

"Business schools are like bottling plants," says Richard West, former dean of Dartmouth's Amos Tuck School. "The product is about 90 percent complete before we ever get it. We put it in a bottle and label it. The price is merely a function of what the market will pay."

Obviously the MBA has become a fad. And fads, by definition, wax and wane. MBA began to fade first with companies that had to fork out the higher prices for MBA-carrying trainees. One sign of the times is a rash of MBA jokes. Sample: If Thomas Edison had been working with MBAs, he wouldn't have invented the light bulb. He'd have made a bigger candle.

In a *Fortune* article headlined "Tough Times for MBAs," author Susan Fraker said:

> Many businesses now see a lot less shimmer on the sheepskin and question whether they should pay so many MBAs such high salaries. As the MBA falls from favor, graduates with B.S. and B.A. have returned to grace.

Thus getting a job after school with only an undergraduate degree is easier right now.

What Two Managers Think

"Our experience was that MBAs had all the answers but few of the tools," says James W. Motter, director of marketing at DeVilbiss, a manufacturing division of Champion Spark Plug. "Often we found them unwilling to consider the culture of our business. We parted company with three a few years ago."

DeVilbiss doesn't hire from the business schools at all.

"We grow our own," says Motter, citing DeVilbiss's in-house training programs. Another such company is CPT Corp., a Minneapolis manufacturer of word processors where chairman Dean Scheff believes successful managers don't need to be intellectuals but must have the common sense MBAs lack.

"I believe in scar tissue, not in 90-day wonders," says Scheff, who eased out six newly minted MBAs several years ago. MBAs who've been beaten up in the workplace make excellent employees."

Humbling experiences await the new MBAs: Their hard-earned degree soon loses its luster in day-to-day scuffles at the office. Many graduates do not realize that the degree only gets them in the door.

"The MBA is just a calling card," says Mary McKee, a strategic business analyst with Mostek, a semiconductor company in Dallas. "Then you have to learn the business from the ground up; you have to prove yourself."

Value of Second-Tier Schools

Corporations today need fewer would-be stars and more solid supporting actors. The fast track hasn't been torn up, but access has been limited. The new need for a solid supporting cast is music to the ears of graduates of second-tier business schools—Midwestern and Southern types who see red when Harvard is mentioned. Recruiters have learned that the best students in the second tier are outstanding.

R. William Holland, director of employee relations at PepsiCo, recruits about 35 percent of his management candidates from the second tier, not so much because salaries are lower but because he wants "people with a variety of ambitions." He finds "great people who know what they want and are willing to work very hard at it."

Similarly, a recruiter for Procter & Gamble said "second-tier students have the right kind of attitude for what we want them to do, which is to start in the trenches and work their way up."

The value of the degree depends on many factors, including the school you attend, the field you enter, where you live, and how you put the MBA to work on the job.

The mystique of the MBA took a long time to build. Demystification will take time, too. As the economy improves, some companies may start shopping for MBAs again the way George Steinbrenner buys ballplayers. Other companies have learned that MBAs aren't always the team stars—and that is is possible to compete with fewer of them.

If you do go for an MBA, do it for the long-range knowledge, *not* the short-range money.

Perfection Not Required

Throughout this talk of education, you may get the impression we're looking for perfection. Not so.

A prominent researcher once said that the perfect executive should be an accountant/economist, marketer, psychologist, salesman, and researcher/planner to understand and implement all of the problems confronting us. And he pointed out that no one possessing all these attributes was in the work force: If he existed, he'd be on a beach somewhere issuing orders and reinvesting his stock market winnings and dividends.

Perfection isn't possible or even desired. As we've pointed out, the solid B student with a campus leadership and productive part-time work record is far more likely to climb the corporate slope. Further, education—initial and continuing—is an enormous help. Remember what Mark Twain said about reading: "The man who *won't* read has no advantage over the man who *can't* read."

It works that way with education, too. The corporate alpinist who sees learning as a lifelong challenge and takes positive delight in satisfying his insatiable curiosity is a good bet to reach the upper slopes.

PART ____ 2

Acceptance by the Expedition— Getting on the Team

CHAPTER ——— 4

GETTING THE RIGHT JOB

All right. You've done your basic education—degree in hand. You may want to get advanced education later (such as an MBA). But right now you're eager to start work in the real world. The first job is an important step. Where do you want to work?

Wall Street offers the astronomical financial rewards. General Motors has the most organized management structure (outside of the Catholic church). Apple and Atari are credited with having the fastest-growing high-tech organizations. What do *you* want? Now is the time to set your sights on the Matterhorn you'd like to climb. There's a long trek ahead. But the first requirement is to decide where you want to go, then get on the team and get underway.

Someone once asked Senator Alben W. Barkley: "What does it take to make a great senator?"

"First," said Barkley, "You've got to get elected."

Same with career advancement. First, you must get elected—to the first job at the bottom of the slope. Obviously, the first step up is formative.

As Florida citrus growers pointed out to me many years ago, there's no point in pouring $2,000 worth of cultivation, fertilizer, and citrus seedlings (plus nameless amounts of personal energy and concern) into land that is too wet or too dry to grow oranges. Variance in the price of base land (where you intend to plant and work) somewhere between $200 and $600 an acre is not significant when a completed working citrus grove is valued at $4,000 or $8,000 an acre.

And so it is with career cultivation. Candidates put tremendous amounts of work into organizations that don't recognize or appreciate it, or aren't going anywhere.

So for starters, identify the organization in the industry that you'd like to be a part of. This is not a blind draw out of a hat. On the contrary, pick an industry you're interested in and know something about. (In fact, you'd *better* know something about it—come interview time.)

Your Ignorance May Help Your Competitor

American Sugar, after many years of plodding via ingrown management, decided to spruce up its production team. The company wanted to hire two hotshot youngsters fresh out of college and train them to be plant managers in three years. As a soon-to-graduate student at MIT, I heard about this recruiting. It was a great opportunity.

MIT nominated 15 students. Initial screening interviews narrowed it down to two—Will Marcey and me.

Then, much to our surprise, we heard that American Sugar's CEO was coming in person to make the final selection. We didn't sleep much that night. And since I drew the shortest straw, I went in first.

The CEO and I were getting along splendidly until he asked: "Newman, how do you think we go about making sugar?"

Here I felt on safe ground.

"Sugar is grown in cane fields of Cuba, Puerto Rico, and the

Hawaiian Islands, is cut in the fields, brought into a sugar mill, crushed, dried to a raw state. The crystalized raw sugar is subsequently shipped to New Orleans where it is redissolved, purified with carbon, and re-crystalized to make either white table or brown baking sugar."

I leaned back, proud of my memory. But something had gone wrong.

"Newman, I'm amazed," he said. "A candidate interested in this great opportunity should know the exact process we follow. We never ship a pound of raw sugar from the cane fields to New Orleans. We refine it in the sugar mills. I thought you would have understood this process!"

He excused me, and I went out to the reception room where Will Marcey was sitting.

"How did it go?" Will asked.

"You'd better know the complete process of making sugar," I said. He turned white.

"I don't know it," he said. "Can you get me that textbook on industrial chemistry?"

I popped around the corner, picked up my copy, and brought it back. He had a few minutes to study. As he was ushered in, the first question was:

"Can you tell me how we make sugar?"

Marcy told him, step by step, right out of the book. He got the job.

I've seen him many times since as he rose up the ranks at American Sugar. Each time, I've threatened to reveal the source of his information—unless he sends me a lifetime supply of sugar. He never has. I may tell on him yet. In fact, I just did.

Your First Selling Job: Selling Yourself

Sit down and carefully prepare a complete game plan of how you're going to get into the industry—and concentrate on companies you've already identified. What areas of each company might be needing people—and why?

Search out the names of key people in each company. Put down all the possible ways and connections you might utilize to reach those people. Thought-starters: Your classmates, your banker, trade association or country club, clergymen you know personally.

The introduction you seek may or may not be with the president or the marketing vice president. But get in contact with someone in the company that you're interested in. That person can refer you to someone else and you're on the inside.

Remember, you have your eye on the peak of the Matterhorn. You're not going to work as a clerk or a truck driver unless knowledge of that function is critical to your game plan.

On the other hand, don't shy away from entry-level gut-wrenching jobs if they are important to understanding the marketing or manufacturing part of the company you want to grow in.

What do you think of a distinguished MIT graduate in chemical engineering going to work sweeping out dirty scaly tunnels between the hot mills and the cold mills in a steel plant? Dirty and demeaning work?

I agree. I did it after graduation when I joined American Rolling Mill in Middletown, Ohio. But I can tell you this much: It was essential to my understanding and advancement in a steel mill.

I'll never forget vomiting over the hot zinc fumes in a galvanizing pit, while the foreman laughed and told me to work faster in pulling sheets out of the galvanizing bath. I endured these little unpleasantries and dozens more to gain advancement in manufacturing in American Rolling Mill.

Lack of willingness to do ground-up work is something MBAs are under fire about these days. You're not seeking the top executive job on opening day. Far from it. Heed the first-job advice of Earl D. Brodie, San Francisco business consultant!

Don't hesitate to go to work at the lowest possible level of production or sales in the company. Recognize you need to learn the nuts and bolts, the nitty-gritty, or how the company produces, sells, makes

*money. If you have a choice, head for the sales department first. Get
out on the firing line.*

THE RÉSUMÉ

So now you have a list of target companies. You're reading want ads
and seeing employment agencies. You're following leads from the job
placement department at school. And, by all means, follow personal
contacts—the most important of all.

Prepare an outstanding résumé. (Get a book on this subject.) This
is your selling piece. Don't scrimp on time or money here.

There's a fine line between a distinctive résumé and a résumé that
elicits a "not our kind" response.

"If your qualifications are strong and if you're suited for the job for
which you're applying, your best bet may be to play it safe," advises
William Marsteller, chairman of Marsteller, Inc., a large advertising
agency. "That goes for the form of your résumé as well as the style,
using a standard chronological recital of your employment rather than
the less common format in which you list your skills."

Remember: Your résumé has one function: to get you an interview.
It cannot get you a job. Only you can do that. The résumé is designed
to place you across the desk from a prospective employer. Write it in
such a way as to make the product—you—intriguing enough for
someone to say: "We'd better take a look at this one."

In writing it, forget about what *you* want. Concentrate on what the
employer wants. At this stage of your development, the employer
cannot buy experience. So he's buying promise. He's dealing in the
futures market and you are the commodity. He's betting you'll develop
into a profitable investment for his company.

The résumé gets the employer's attention and makes him say:

"Here's a possibility." The job interview confirms or denies that as-sumption. So if you flunk the interview and deny the assumption, you're back out on the street ("Don't call us. We'll call you.").

How To Control the Job Interview

Prepare for a job interview with all the care of getting ready for any important meeting. Be ready with good questions that (a) show you've done your homework and (b) provide you with decision-making data about the prospective company or post (perhaps you're talking about a promotion where you are).

To prepare, put yourself in the interviewer's shoes. What questions would *you* ask from *that* side of the desk? Also make up a list of questions of your own.

One over-confident type once told me:

"*I* never worry about interviews. I can always think of something to say."

Sure, you can. But chances of that something being right are not good. A person who wings interviews will wing a job. And wingers don't rise very far.

And, for pity's sake, don't get knocked out of the box by doing something silly like being late.

Early Bird Gets the Worm

A colleague said to me recently: "Jim, you're a great believer in punctuality. When you have a meeting at 8 a.m., you bisect the dot. You don't get there early, you don't get there late."

It's true. I believe in punctuality. You'd better, too. Nothing will give you poorer marks quicker than tardiness. The worst thing you can do in a job interview is to arrive five minutes late. At least 60 percent of interviewers will log you in as a problem.

Besides, being late makes you flustered and full of apologies—not a good way to start—rather than calm and confident.

I know what you're thinking: "On the face of it, five minutes is a fairly minor sin." Yet it indicates something bigger.

The rising executive is expected to be punctual. Get there early. You may have to wait 15 minutes but better early than late.

Oh, there *are* reasons for being late. But they'd better be damned good ones. Not the heavy traffic on the way over. Not the shortage of cabs or a place to park. Those are things you plan for. Or at least the real upward mover does.

Managing the Job Interview

Like the hunter that invested time selecting the terrain and getting his equipment in order, you're now on your way to meet your quarry—the prospective employer.

Check with the receptionist on the pronunciation of the inteviewer's name if you're unsure. While you wait, keep an opening remark on the tip of your tongue.

Make an entrance! Walk into the room animated, energetic, head up, chest high. Being pleasant to be with is written by implication into every job description. You never get a second chance to make a first impression.

Look the interviewer in the eye and shake hands firmly. A wet-fish grip makes a negative impression. Go for an upright chair. If you have no choice, at least resist lounging in an overstuffed chair or sofa. Sit up straight, only the lower part of your spine against the back of the seat.

Fidgeting, ear pulling, and leg swinging are distracting. Be eye-to-eye 90 percent of the time.

You're probably savvy enough not to smoke or chew gum—but for the record, don't.

Run-on talkers cost a company too much time and money. At the same time, monosyllabic replies present you as inarticulate. Avoid hard-luck stories, apologies, and recitals of past illnesses—don't leave negatives for the interviewer to remember you by. Listen thoughtfully. Ask pertinent questions in a nonprovacative manner.

Talking about your weakneses is an opportunity to show your strengths. "I have a tendency toward perfectionism," is something most employers welcome. "I tend to be a bit of a workaholic" is another. Employers love workaholics.

Here's how to react to questions about these subjects—and why they're asked:

Education. Talk about your best and worst subjects, how you financed your education, and your extracurricular activities. This will reveal your feelings regarding authority, your ability to acquire knowledge, your versatility, and qualities of leadership.

Early Years. Questions about family are designed to explore how much responsibility you're shouldering and how well you're managing it. Interviewers who ask casually about your childhood—the town where you grew up, your family structure—are not making small talk. They are probing your self-image, degree of motivation, and emotional social adjustment.

Leisure and Interests. Questions about recreation, hobbies, and goals give interviewers added insight into your judgment, breadth of curiosity, and social skills. Employers look favorably on staffers involved in some (but not too many) outside professional, political, and volunteer activities—particularly if they dovetail with your field.

When you feel the questioning is drawing to a close, end the interview—demonstrating that you value time. Shake hands smiling. Thank the interviewer, and depart with dispatch—don't ooze out.

Understanding the Boss-Oriented Interview

The best way to handle your own job interviews is to think like the boss.

In helping an electronics CEO cast for an important job, I read résumés and saw people. About his front-runner, I said:

"I know this fellow has done it, but I'm not overly impressed with his basic intelligence."

"Yes," the CEO said, "but he worked for Honeywell and produced $15 million worth of business."

So he hired him.

Later when I saw the CEO, I asked how X was doing. He said: "I fired the son-of-a-bitch. Dumbest bastard I ever saw. I sent him to Pittsburgh to obtain a repeat order on a product. He neglected to check on competition, and the competitors beat our prices 25 percent. Now we can't make any money on the job."

When your inteviewer uses résumés properly, he won't look at surface titles or what you say you've done. He'll use résumés as a source of questions: "How did you do this and why did you do this other thing."

The résumé as tip sheet is valuable. At face value, a résumé can be worthless.

Psychological Tests

You may be asked to take psychological tests. Such tests have become discredited of late because they were used too often as a bible instead of an indicator. Yet when properly used, tests make a real contribution.

Johnson's Wax was looking for a new chief engineer. After they gave Peter Walker, the prime candidate, a battery of tests, I sat down with the chief psychologist:

Me: "How did Peter do?"

He: "Well, he didn't score well in emotional stability."

Me: "What the hell does that mean, emotional stability?"

He: "Supplied the wrong answers on sex questions."

Me: "What do you think that means?"

He: "I don't know. But it bothers me."

So we checked with Larry Smithers, in Peter's former community in Pennsylvania.

"Gee, Larry, could you tell us about Peter? Did he ever have any trouble with women or was he a good solid citizen?"

"Well," Larry said, "you know, of course, that he ran off to Mexico with this girl in town and left his wife and four children. They had a terrible time getting him back."

So we re-called Peter's former boss and said: ▪

"You gave us a rundown on this fellow. But what about taking the girl to Mexico and all your problems getting him back?"

"I didn't want to prejudice his case," his ex-boss said.

That did it. If Peter Walker had been looking for a job in Chicago or New York, it wouldn't have bothered us too much. But sending him up to a small town! That story would be all over the place. He just wouldn't fit in.

An interviewer doesn't get these stories in either a résumé or a test. But he might get *clues.* Then he gets at the truth by talking to people the candidate worked with.

Any interviewer who doesn't ask probing questions about things indicated on the résumé and who doesn't talk to former colleagues isn't doing a professional screening job. (Remember this later when *you're* on the interviewer side of the desk.)

SELLING YOURSELF WITHOUT EXAGGERATION

In an interview, learn how you can sell yourself—and what the limits are. One day in my Chicago office, George Calhoun, a job applicant for a sales VP spot, reported experience as sales VP for A.O. Smith's water-heater division. He looked restless and ill-at-ease during the interview. I asked him if he felt sick. He said no, as he departed for another appointment.

On paper, he looked good. But I wondered. I called Tony, a friend at A.O. Smith.

"Tell me about George Calhoun, this great sales VP you had."

"What do you mean, sales VP?" Tony said. "We turned over a new product for him to sell. He was the market developer, sales manager, and entire salesforce for that product all by himself. But he had nothing to do with managing our salesforce."

"Well," I said, "then how come you paid him $47,000 a year?"

"We didn't," he countered. "Let me look it up. Last year George Calhoun made $13,500."

I thanked him and waited until George came back.

"I asked if you were sick last time," I told him. "Now I really mean it. You can't go around making up stories in business. When you get back home, I think you should see your doctor. Get a little counseling about what might be wrong with you."

His face dropped like a falling mask.

"Well, it was worth a try," he said.

Remember George when you're tempted to lay it on thick in a job interview. Your interviewer is interconnected within the business community. Chances are he knows people who know you. If he's doing his job, he'll talk to them—just as you must when you're the interviewer. viewer.

College credits are a popular exaggeration. Or the degree that you didn't quite get. Or the four years you claimed when you actually spent two. But these educational claims are easily checked. When they come up gray, that's two strikes against you before the game has started. Lying doesn't pay.

A colleague thinks that's too tough a stance in modern society.

"After all," he says, "even the FTC allows what it calls 'permissible puffery' in selling. Why can't the applicant pull the long bow a bit in selling himself? It's a competitive world."

Yes, that's true, but there's a difference between selling and outright lying. I've heard personnel experts say they'd hate to lose a good applicant just because of one white lie. Maybe. I still think the unvarnished truth is the best policy.

Now just like the witness in court, you don't have to volunteer negative matters. And, yes, by all means present your story in the best possible light—if you don't, who will? Nor do I believe in knocking a former employee whose sins were inadequacy—there are plodding jobs and someone needs to do them. When I got a call about Caesar Rodrigo one day, I said:

"Well, he always came to work on time and applied himself to his job."

I *didn't* say he was a star. He wasn't. But for some jobs, he's good and may be what they need. Keep in mind, though, a seasoned interviewer knows what I'm really saying. But since an organization needs support as well as stars—in fact, too many stars are sometimes a problem—who am I to prejudge?

The song *Accentuate the Positive and Eliminate the Negative* is a good rule for personnel interviews. But don't stretch it too far like George Calhoun did or you'll get in trouble.

First Job Is Not Drift Time

Never in your climb up the Matterhorn is there time to drift and let the winds carry you. This is particularly true on your first job.

One young climber told me recently:

"I'm going to have fun until I get some age and experience. Nobody's going to give me a top job for many years."

Well, they *may* not give you a top job at *any* age. But age won't hold back the exceptional digger.

Eugene Jennings, a Michigan State University professor, says candidates for top corporate jobs are too young these days. A company has a three or four times better chance of executive washout, he says, when a "too young" candidate gets the top job. He calls this the *Mobycentric Executive.* He says Mobycentrics move from one job to another so fast you never get a chance to evaluate how good they are.

Professors must publish or perish, and Mobycentrics *is* a catchy description. But don't bank on it.

Jennings deplores the young hotshot who's bigger on upward mobility than on smarts. He cites William Agee, the controversial CEO at Bendix Corporation in the early 1980s, as an example.

First, to me Jennings' theory doesn't hold water. Further I contend that Agee is an able CEO, he just got caught up or seduced into the acquisition mania.

Second, once you reach age 35, you are constitutionally able to go to the White House. I'd say that also applies to any corporate office—*if* you're qualified otherwise.

Now that's a big *if,* of course. A candidate could be completely *un*qualified in many ways. But once you get past 35, age just isn't a disqualifier or a qualifier. Sure, a young person can be thrust into something he or she is not equipped to deal with. This could happen at any age—and often does.

In fact, if there's any age weight in recruiting, it tilts the other way. Recruiters want that youthful drive and get-up-and-go.

CEO search specifications often call for age 50 or less. The directors want creativity and energy. Among chief executives of Fortune 500 companies, I'll bet one-third are under 50. Many assume office at 45.

Can a youthful job-hopper fool everyone by never staying in one spot long enough to be tested? No. In a company of any size, someone will catch the four-flusher—sooner rather than later.

Sorry, friends, there's no easy way. In the final analysis, you have to make it on merit. At least you can't say age held you back—because it doesn't.

You are the only thing that can hold *you* back. Think about it.

The Perpetual Job-Hunter

Once you get a job, concentrate mainly on your work. I disagree with the commentator who says most executives today keep a résumé updated to include their current job responsibilities—just to be ready.

Some executives do move from one spot to another. But a great many more do not.

Besides, I wonder about the motivations of a fellow or gal with an up-to-date résumé. It suggests that the person doesn't know how long he or she can play the game.

Unless you're getting off the corporate climb at a midway camp, devote your energy to your work. A University of Michigan management succession study found the best way to get to the top of the corporate ladder is to stay *on the same ladder.* I agree.

The Michigan figures show that 80 percent of executives promoted to chairperson, president, or vice president came from within—following an average of 11 years with the company.

Eighty percent seems pretty high. After all, hundreds of head hunters move thousands of people around each year. But you're still better off rising internally.

Management is better able to judge people they've seen in action. They will promote an enterprising mailboy from within. In looking outside, they seek a glowing record cast in marble. So consider your existing opportunities first.

At the same time, don't stay forever if you're not advancing. Anyone not making progress with his game plan after 10 years had better try his tools someplace else.

PErfORMiNG vs. AppEARANCE of PErfORMiNG

Of course, you must not only *do* the job—you must *appear* to be doing it. Back in the 1920s, itinerant American newspapermen drifted from town to town in a manner that would give modern personnel experts the willies. At that time, a hard-boiled city editor made a yes-or-no hiring decision based on a few minutes of observation.

"You can tell by the way he hangs up his hat whether he can do the job or not," one editor said.

What he was saying (although he would have scoffed at this phrasing) was that his decision was based on surface *perception* of the man's ability—not his real ability, since he had no way to know that.

Hiring practices are much more scientific today and probably much better, but one common characteristic remains: You still not only must do the job—you must *appear* to be doing the job.

This means in your field, with your superiors, you'd better not only appear to have the answers, you'd better have them. Not on all things, just your assignment. If production control is your bag, don't feel the need to sound off on marketing or finance. Leave that to others. When questions come up on cost structure or market customs, don't hesitate to say: "Let's consult with Jack—that's more in his line."

But if the question *is* in your area and you don't know, don't bluff. Admit it—but add: "I'll find out and give you the answer tomorrow at 10 a.m." Then do just that.

An attorney once said: "Lawyers don't know anything, really. They just know where to look it up."

If you don't know but can find out, you're giving the *appearance* of doing the job. You are communicating an impression of quiet competence and confidence. And if you keep your commitment, you really *will* be doing the job. And you'll be on your way up the slope.

CHAPTER 5

GETTING A BETTER JOB

Okay. Let's see. You've gone to school, you've grabbed the brass ring and started up the slope. They didn't fire you the first week (despite your flagrant mistake) and you're getting to know the job. In fact, your boss has said so, too.

Time to relax and enjoy yourself? Enjoy, yes, but don't get lethargic. Now's the time to start working for a better job. This means you should always look first to your own company for that better job for one simple reason—the odds are better.

This means you must develop leadership, prove yourself, and provide your own replacement. Let's look into each requirement.

Learning by Doing

In education, the Montessori system calls for learning by doing. The road to management works the same way. The most valuable lessons are learned on the job, no matter how much classroom seasoning you've had.

Like football, the best learning comes on the field.

When I entered college, MIT didn't have a football team per se. But we had a freshman team and a sophomore team that played one another. I coached in my freshman and sophomore years—where I learned the principle of understanding your people resources.

Our sophomore team beat the hell out of Harvard's Junior Varsity. We also beat Northeastern University. Both were furious. They couldn't understand how we did it. What they didn't know was my left guard and my left tackle played for the Newburyport Rams on weekends. All's fair in love and war. That was war.

There's great similarity between coaching and running a salesforce or production force. I recommend coaching to all corporate climbers.

In fact, playing football is great training for business. Right before the opening kickoff, you're tight as a drum. You wonder if you're going to be a total failure. But as soon as you get the ball and start to run, people start bouncing off you, and you forget your concerns.

Same in business. You're scared about taking on a new job. You lay awake at night and wonder. But once you get in the rough and tumble, you do fine.

So in your work, get as prepared as you can. But tell yourself as soon as you get going, things are going to be all right.

At MIT, we had a freshman named Craemer who only weighed about 145 pounds. He said:

"Gee, there's probably not much point in my going out for football, I don't have enough weight. But I'd like to try it anyhow."

I worked with him. He had a good mind and turned into our first-string quarterback. He called the shots the day we climbed all over Harvard's JVs. By that time, we were calling him The Bullet.

I'd lost track of The Bullet. Years later, a colleague came back from a consulting job with a major-money-center bank and said:

"A general manager named Craemer sends his regards—to see if you remembered him."

How could I forget? He wasn't floored by not fitting the specifications. He was too light. But he was quick and fast and he made up for it. The Bullet is a good example of positive thinking.

Football's valuable. It teaches teamwork—*the* key to business. Try your tools in managing a Little League team, or volunteer to coach your own leisure group. You'll learn to motivate your peers. You'll discourage backbiting and criticism. You'll concentrate on getting the team going. That's leadership.

THE GE PRINCIPLE—AT WORK

Getting handpicked at an early stage in your career as a promising management trainee is good. But once top management gets a better way to gauge you—by performance—early promise doesn't count.

When General Electric came out of World War II, chairman Ralph Cordiner had quite a job getting his company back on a profitable consumer basis. GE had been making everything from aircraft engines to radar bombing devices. He said: "Let's set up 50 divisions and make each responsible for profit. We'll have a lamp division, a clock division, a heater division, and so on."

"But," one of his advisors queried, "how the hell do you pick 50 vice-presidents to become general managers when all their experience has been limited to specific functions—sales, manufacturing, finance?"

Good question. Cordiner looked for answers.

A decade earlier, GE had started a Promising Young Men's group. Maybe this was a clue. Cordiner decided to study the PYM records. His query: How many PYMs had become managers in the years between? His findings: Just as many *non*-PYMs had made manager as the PYM group. So Cordiner concluded that early promise was far from conclusive.

"Since the PYM label doesn't tell us anything," Cordiner said, "pick 50 good executives, put them in charge, let them learn to be general managers. If some don't work, we'll replace them."

And that's what he did.

So what does the corporate climber conclude? Anytime you can prove yourself on the job, do so, even if the assignment is 10 percent over your head. If you feel confident, try it. Do the best possible job with whatever task you're assigned. Sure, if you see a loose ball rolling down the street, pick it up. But not at the expense of your main job.

"Yes," a young woman answered, "but how do I make sure they *know* I'm doing a good job? If the tree falls in the forest and nobody's there, does it make noise? Is self-promotion part of the game? Must I blow my own horn? If so, how much?"

This problem bothers many. But it shouldn't. Just remember nine times out of ten, your boss understands what you've done far better than you think. Pointing out how good you are is often perilous.

Sure, some real comers are adroit at getting a business publication to do a story about their division or their new product introduction. Others have no talent for that at all. But if it smacks of opportunism, it won't go down well in the corner office.

At one large automaker, the truck division head prepared a four-color annual report on his division—just as if he were a separate company. He distributed it to board members without clearing with the president or chairman.

The passenger car division people were incensed. They felt the truck division was taking credit under their own systems of costs along with certain corporate-wide achievements.

So that annual report didn't do the truck manager any good. A little later, top management maneuvered him out of the business into a trade association. The chairman didn't trust him. He didn't like the pressure the truck manager was generating. So this ambitious self-promoter lost out.

While we're on associations, let's analyze them as job opportunities. An association job, usually a career sidetrack, is basically a hand-holding operation.

When I heard a friend was planning to take a job with a New England manufacturing association, I said:

"All right, if you're bound and determined, fine. At least set yourself a timetable and plan, say, at the end of three years, to move out into something else."

But he didn't. After 10 years, he was still at the association. When he finally did get out, he had no place to go. Once head of a successful company, he ended up in a very secondary post up in Vermont. No, I don't endorse associations to corporate climbers.

Your Own Career Planning

So, associations aside, how do you plan your corporate career—long range? Mary Cunningham, in her first months at Bendix, prepared a 200-page career plan. In her 20s, she was going to develop her "instrument"; in her 30s, maximize her financial independence and credentials; in her 40s, position herself for real power. Now this sounds pretentious. But a career plan, the laying out of goals, will potentially go a long way toward improving your chances as you climb the rocky crags.

The essence of good career planning is casting a clinical eye over careers in general, and, finally and hardest of all, over yourself.

Know thyself, or more specifically, thy wants, skills, and style. *Wants* often prove to be the toughest. This seems especially true if you're a structured person who did well in secondary school so you could get into a good college, did well in college to get into a good professional school, go there immediately upon leaving college and do well so that you can get the job all your peers want. Suddenly you find yourself an investment banker with nary a clue to your *true* inclinations.

On the matter of skills, you might think that after 10 years in the work force, you have a pretty good idea of just what your aptitudes are. You just might be wrong, though.

Stephen Morris of Drake Beam & Morin specializes in outplacement, that is, ministering to the fallen executive. Morris counseled an accountant of 20-years' standing who had recently been fired. He administered a standard battery of aptitude tests and was surprised to find the accountant scored the lowest in quantitative abilities.

Confronted with this somewhat incongruous finding, the test-taker said: "Gee, maybe this explains why I've been unhappy for 20 years." A counselor at school had told him accounting was a good field to get into. Today he's a salesman.

A career plan also enables you to make strategic conversation when opportunity knocks. There you are, strapping yourself in for a trans-continental airplane ride when the vice-chairman of your company sits down beside you. Somewhere over the Rockies, after the second mar-tini, he idly asks you: "Bob, where do you see yourself in 5 or 10 years?" A career plan gives you an answer. A good presentation-type entertaining answer.

But in the meantime, examine the nuts and bolts of getting a better job.

Line vs. Staff

Career advisors often say: "Get a line job, not staff." A line job super-vising actual operations is valuable. But you really need staff experi-ence too. Staff might be an excellent place to start—maybe in long-range planning, or production management, or perhaps in finance. Then if you can jump into a line job, so much the better.

It worked that way for Bill May at American Can Company. In an endeavor to introduce better strategic planning, chairman Stolk set up a staff planning department and placed Bill May in charge. But trouble developed. May couldn't convince line division managers to accept and implement his plans.

Stolk, however, was convinced May was right. So he gave May line authority to implement his programs (not the best organizational ap-proach, normally). But Bill May soon became president and then had

many years as the successful chairman of American Can Company—
thus, he went from staff post to CEO.

On the other hand, I don't go to the other extreme, either. "Pure line
experience leaves you with a lack of perspective in dealing with the
larger picture," someone said recently. To that, I say: "Not necessarily."

The line can give it all to you. A staff person is the thinker and
munitions-maker for the line. When General Lucius D. Clay first took
over at another can company—Continental Can—he was asked:

"What's the purpose of staff?"

"To serve the line," he replied.

A line manager may not have the benefit of good staff help, but
running all activities, with or without staff assistance, is valuable.

So get experience with both. But if you *must* choose one or the
other, choose line.

WHEN YOU TAKE TOO LARGE A BITE

Walter Kiechel III of *Fortune* says:

> If you get a new job and find after three months you're miscast, go
> to your boss and say: "Let's talk about this job. Maybe it's a bad fit.
> I'd like to see about another assignment."

A very enlightened company just might believe you. Your boss
might work out a job that suits you better, Kiechel says—rather than
having you go for months without doing well.

Might is the point. But I don't think it happens often enough to
worry about. And if it did happen often, you'd have another problem—
admission of weakness. Some bosses will say:

"All right, Henry, we'll make you a shipping clerk and see if *that's* a
better fit."

Trying for the Boss's Job

More common is the aspirant who doesn't take a big enough bite. Every corporate climber worth his credit-card dues should be after his boss's job—all the time. What's more, your boss—who didn't get where he is not knowing the facts—will welcome it. After all, how can your boss get promoted (there's always another higher rung, remember) unless he has a qualified replacement to take *his* job?

"Sure like to give Jesse a promotion," one foreman told me. "But there's nobody to move into Jesse's job. And that function is critical right now. So we'll have to hold things the way they are."

What he was really saying: "Jesse didn't make sure Jesse's assistant was ready to move up."

Provide your own replacement. This alone will put you miles ahead of most of your competitors.

Consultant Allen Cox reports only one out of three executives is eyeing his superior's job. Well, that means two-thirds are *not* serious contenders for higher office—which I suspect is accurate enough. The question is: Which group are you in—climbers or sitters?

What about the person who thinks he can remain indefinitely in a cozy middle-management position, putting in perfunctory eight-hour days and counting the years to retirement? With hordes of highly educated people bucking for his job, the standpatter risks being unceremoniously dumped.

You've got to *want* to get ahead. If there are good reasons why you aren't qualified for your boss's job, look for a different job to aspire to.

Don't think getting promoted is automatic. It's not. You must work at it.

"Honesty, judgment, and loyalty will get you in the door," says Richard Considine, president of Lincoln Logs Ltd. "But after that, I'm interested in performance, action orientation, and continuing positive attitude."

At the same time, don't be too discouraged by peers who give you "the inside story that you're not being considered for promotion." Worry about your own situation—let the other fellow worry about his.

Value of Rising Inside

In the Army, when a platoon sergeant gets a combat promotion to second lieutenant, he's transferred to another company. That way he's not an officer supervising the enlisted men he served with.

In business, the exact opposite is true. Eight times out of ten, a company's better off promoting from inside—and keeping the new manager right there. He's a known quantity. You know his relationship to the other players. You know his shortcomings.

But if you take over a new job supervising former comrades, be careful. You're not only their boss—you must *act* like their boss. This means, obviously, that you cannot go out and get sloshed with the boys and girls like you once did. Remember the old army rule: "Familiarity breeds contempt."

When recruiters go outside, they often use a complex evaluation sheet to spotlight presence (or absence) of desired characteristics. (Sometimes this sheet is handy in blocking advancement of an inadequate candidate with a sponsor on the board.) The outside candidate may be an expert on machine shop practice, but only scores 45 in human relations. Being very strong in one area may be OK for a middle-management functional job. But a CEO must be a generalist. So get as much varied experience as you can—if you have your eyes on the corner office.

As the insider you hold the good cards. A nominating committee can live with a 60 or 65 percent rating in the case of an insider. But they'd expect an outside candidate to score 80 or 85 at least.

Judging a Stranger

Most managers probing potential employees feel totally inadequate judging a stranger sitting across the desk—even after a three-hour talk. There are too many unknowns. So they insist on documented performance in exactly the same areas. They judge the candidate by the success of his present company—which may or may not have anything to do with it. But that's the way they call it.

A young man called Johnny said recently:

"I'm marketing research head and I want to be a product manager. I'm looking for a job elsewhere."

"You'll never be able to make that jump outside the company," I said. "Yet inside someone will say: 'Have you seen Johnny's long-range memos? Let's give him a shot at being product manager. He's an able guy.' Stay where you are. You've got a much better chance to climb—inside."

Besides, the record shows that sometimes the best way to climb the ladder is to stay on the *same* ladder. Getting typecast as a company hopper can hurt you. Change jobs in less than four years and you'll be called a drifter. Then sophisticated management takes you with a ton of salt.

Changing jobs within your company can be a smart career move. Internal transfers expose you to new areas of operations, add to your expertise and so hasten your upward climb. They get you out of such sticky situations such as working for a boss you can't stand. They save you from launching an exhausting job search and starting over at a new company.

You may even get a *better* job inside your current company than you could outside. Diane Felmlee, a sociologist at Indiana University in Bloomington, studied 3500 women and their job changes. Felmlee found that women got better and more prestigious jobs by making internal transfers than by switching companies.

When you and your work are known quantities, your lack of traditional credentials may be overlooked. On-the-job performance count more. When you're applying on the outside, education or experience requirements can be barriers.

Develop Informal Channels

When Laurie Hutton was a staff analyst in the installation-and-repair department of Southwestern Bell in St. Louis, she cultivated contacts at company meetings and indicated she'd be open to a change.

The payoff? Hutton is now corporate communications manager at AT&T in Piscataway, New Jersey. Adding contacts in other divisions to your network may bring opportunities your way.

In engineering internal transfers, learn whether to involve your boss. Ask an experienced co-worker about the etiquette of bypassing your boss. Hutton proceeded on her own until she needed her boss's signature on the official forms releasing her from one department to another. Another woman, by contrast, knew her boss wanted her to grow, so she involved her supervisor from the start.

When to Worry

On the other hand, if you've been with a company 15 years without advancement, you have a different kind of problem. An outside evaluator will say: "He faced these frustrating situations, he didn't do anything about it—he just hung in there. Good old Henry."

That's not good, either. You can see the signs.

The job is almost rote, and the raises—sometimes annual but increasingly not—are paltry. The last promotion came long ago, the next is nearly indiscernible, and you're decades from retirement. Peaks of success seem distant and unattainable, and your future looks flat. Face it: You're stuck on a career plateau.

To prevent this scenario, fortify yourself early on with knowledge. To get a new skill—for example, computer literacy—take courses at a community college or specialized school. Tell your supervisor what you're doing to make yourself more valuable. Get the word around to other managers as well. They probably will be impressed, and it's quite possible that the company will subsidize your tuition. Look for professional seminars to attend; your employer may help pay that too. Read business publications thoroughly to keep up with changes in your field. All this helps you stand out from the pack.

Look for new duties. Identify a corporate problem and find a remedy. Propose the plan to your immediate boss. With his approval, you can present it more formally to his or her superiors. If they let you try it and it works well, you're in a position to bargain for a new title, a raise, or more authority.

Whatever you do, don't send an unsolicited memo to your boss's boss. Both probably will take offense. Try casually mentioning your proposal to the right person in the cafeteria or at the watercooler. If he or she is intrigued, he may well ask you to write a memo. Give a copy of your memo to your boss with a note explaining that his or her superior solicited your ideas.

Get involved in community or business projects. Holding office in a professional organization, writing a business publication article, or organizing a conference can broaden your experience and increase your visibility. If you're, say, a loan officer at a bank, you won't be asked to join the board of directors. But you could win a seat on a local charity board and learn to draft the organization's annual budget. During fund drives, you show your leadership abilities to prominent citizens and reflect credit on the bank. The publicity won't hurt your career either.

How To Get Promoted

Andrew Kershaw, former vice-chairman of Ogilvy & Mather and trusted colleague of my friend David Ogilvy, was a great believer in working actively to get promoted internally. Here is Kershaw's common-sense advice:

Many people have *talked* themselves out of a promotion. Nobody ever *listened* himself out of promotion. Don't talk unless you have something to say. Chatter annoys your bosses, who prefer to listen to their own voices.

It should not take more than a sentence or two to explain things. If it requires more, the idea is bad or you are making a hash of it. Great ideas are simple. They are easy to communicate.

Good questions can be memorable. Be sure they are good, not ho-hum. A good question elicits this response: "Hm, I haven't thought of that before."

Read everything. Almost indiscriminately. Learn to read fast, and to skip. Digest trade papers and professional journals. The things your bosses read.

Write. Short, clear, crisp sentences. No spelling mistakes. Good grammar. Read all the books on good writing and practice. Always edit or rewrite. If, after many attempts, you cannot shorten it, it *may* be okay.

Learn to speak properly. Watch for all the little things. Above all: practice. Presenting is theater. Act it out, persuade. Do not try to be dry, impartial, solemn. Rehearsal is the key to learning to be a good presenter.

Half the time, when people present things to me, they do not know all the facts. Don't let this happen to you.

Speak out. You are the most junior person in a meeting. Something worthwhile has occurred to you. Don't hold back. Speak out. Opinions and suggestions do not recognize age, experience, or seniority. Let them discover their level and worth.

Make sure you are noticed. Or heard. The squeaky wheel and all that. But let it be a musical squeak.

A Hungarian proverb says: "Not even a Mother can hear the words of her mute child."

When you get instructions to do a job, first consider how the assignment can be widened. Ask yourself: Is it possible to be useful by doing *more?* Outstanding performers always go beyond the narrow assignment.

Being good at a job is okay, but it tends to make you deadly dull if that's *all* you know. Most people have *one* hobby or special interest. Outstanding people converse intelligently about dozens of subjects.

The more you know, the more valuable and interesting you are. Let your interests be known. Don't hide your light under a bushel.

Exercise. Take time out. Nobody can maintain intellectual equilibrium without physical exercise and relaxation. (After many years, I'm still out jogging at 6 a.m. three days a week.)

Your cheerfulness, your concentration, and your optimism—which should be infectious—are adversely affected by keeping your nose to the grindstone too long.

Kershaw's sage advice, I believe, points up the most important issue of all: How *important* is your career progress in relation to family, home life, your hobby, adequate leisure, among other things? Don't be surprised—ever—if the person who puts career ahead of all else gets promoted faster. I could cite dozens of examples.

The Hidden Job Mart

All right. You've seen the advantages of internal transfer. You still want to explore elsewhere. Fine.

The best executive jobs are found in the *hidden* job market. Say you are referred by a friend. You haven't made the decision to look for a job—but you are willing to talk. Welcome to the hidden job market. Most employers fear the unwashed. They want job candidates recommended by friends, business associates, drinking buddies—almost anyone except someone off the street.

It's much better to look for a job when you're working. Always be alert to your current job situation. If things are not going well, be quick to see the handwriting on the wall—and make plans.

Above all, give yourself adequate job-change time—it usually takes three to six months. If you wait until you're out, then you're forced to deal with employment agencies or to read want ads.

Hobnobbing with Headhunters

Most ambitious climbers at some point ask: Do I consort with head-hunters? The answer is yes, within moderation, but keep this clearly in mind: headhunters work for—and are paid by—management. Every ounce of their efforts (evaluating questions, searching out hidden faults, sorting out dozens of people) is aimed at producing the best possible people solution for the company. Whether you get a job doesn't concern them.

As inspirer and instructor of a number of the foremost search firms (Heidrick & Struggles, Spencer Stewart, Elmer Davis, and other firms) I can explain the headhunter's philosophy: 75 percent of American executives can be moved—and *not necessarily* for *money.* An able executive can be seduced by greater opportunity, a position higher up the mountain, an escape from a young boss who will hold down advancement, getting wife and children moved into a better community, or other reasons.

The headhunter endeavors to identify the factors that most apply to the executive he wants to move.

Leading search firms control jobs ranging from a minimum of $40,000 a year to upwards of a million dollars in total compensation. They keep track of candidates, cross-evaluate them, conduct reference checks.

The headhunter exerts major influence. So, as a climber, you're likely to work with them, either voluntarily or because they come to you.

The best way to attract a recruiter is: Do an outstanding job where you are. At the same time, maintain a circle of relationships among managers in other companies—each is a potential recommender of you when *he* or *she* gets a headhunter call. Get involved in leadership at industry groups or trade associations. In short, do those things a rising manager does in performing outstandingly. Then you won't need to call headhunters. They'll call you.

THE QUEBEC CONNECTION

Once, on a headhunting assignment, I was seeking a general manager for a new paper mill in Canada. We contacted many pulp and paper executives, heads of companies, members of associations. We made frequent use of Lockwood, that peculiar industry bible which lists top pulp and paper executives.

Out of this search came the names of four people with the right background, the right training, the reputed personal characteristics—including a man in lower Quebec named Brian McBrae. We called to arrange a meeting with McBrae, explaining:

"We have a problem in the pulp and paper industry, a peculiar kind of problem. We think you can help us solve it—if you're willing to give us your time." He agreed.

In person, we told him that our problem involved locating the ablest person in Canada to head up a huge new paper mill. As we got into the discussion, we asked him his three greatest objectives in life.

"My first objective is to my family," he said. "I feel responsible for its growth and upbringing. I intend to do everything I can to see that they get every opportunity and are as happy as possible."

He really meant this. He didn't care about a higher job. He was already president and general manager at a paper company. But he was very much concerned about his family. (Later he took us home. He proudly lined up his eight children—as sharp as an army squad. He introduced each and spoke about achievements. Each dressed neatly. The house was immaculate. We believed his family dedication.)

"My second objective," he continued, "is to discharge a debt I owe to my employer, the Smith–Howard Paper Company. This Scottish company advanced me from the lower levels of a paper mill, selected me to come overseas, gave me a chance in this current mill, helped me rise to general manager. For that opportunity, I'm grateful. On the other hand, I've pretty well discharged that debt. We've made this company quadruple in size. Profitability has more than doubled. I have a great cadre of young managers. Any one of them could take my place. So I do think that my employer has been well rewarded. (As headhunters, we already knew about the success of his business. This was one reason he emerged as one of four possible candidates.)

"My third and perhaps my greatest objective," he continued, "is to try to break down the strife between the Anglican Church and the United Church of Canada. These are both excellent well-meaning organizations. I just can't understand the backbiting and bitterness that exist between them. Here in this Quebec town, I've made a lot of progress through the country club where I'm president and the community house where I'm on the board. But I travel a great deal across Canada. I know this bitterness exists in many other towns."

You guessed it. We had uncovered the candidate's hot button. We jumped on it instantly.

"In the town where we want you to move as president," I stated, "some of the toughest religious strife in Canada exists. The United Church launched meetings trying to dramatize faults of the Anglicans. The Anglicans are reacting in the same way."

Boy, did Brian McBrae react! Not because of a huge increase in money (we did offer a modest increase), not because he was jumping up the slope (he already was there), but because the new post offered him an unsatisfied personal objective. He took the new job and was abundantly successful in reducing the religious strife. He also made an outstanding CEO at the company.

So you can learn several lessons from the Brian McBrae story and other headhunter lore: (1) A good executive recruiter will try to serve the top candidate in noncompensation ways—that's a benefit, if you're one of the front-runners. (2) If you're not equipped to solve the searcher's client's problem, you will not be pursued beyond the preliminaries. (3) Since job specs are often quite demanding, you can be doing an excellent job and still not be the final choice of a search firm. Fine. Keep on doing a good job. There'll be other opportunities to grab the brass ring—perhaps internally even more than externally.

WHEN THE HEADHUNTER CALLS

So you're doing an effective and visible job. When that call comes, be cautious. If the headhunter asks if you want a job, the answer is: "No.

I'm happy where I am. Management treats me fine. I have no interest in moving." Why? You don't know who the headhunter represents— he may be hired by your own boss. Displaying any interest on the telephone inquiry is never good.

Usually, however, the telephone inquiry will request a meeting—as we did: "We have a basic question in the industry we're trying to solve. We've been told you have a good knowledge of this question and might be able to help us."

Or: "We've been told, Mr. Manager, that you are one of the most knowledgeable people in your industry. We'd like to explore your knowledge of candidates who might fill a given position."

That approach also allows you to say to your boss: "XYZ Headhunters have contacted me as a source. But as I sat down and talked to them it evolved they were really interested in talking to me, which I had not suspected."

Headhunters do represent a rope that helps you climb from crag to crag—if you don't use them too often. Contrarily, remember these professionals are smart. They know what they want. So your chances of getting one job from one headhunter are not high.

On every significant search ($40,000 a year and up), the headhunting firm will review files on people already documented. The firm's ads in the business press or in *The New York Times* or *Wall Street Journal* will bring in 200 to 300 candidates. Recruiters will also talk to people in the industry or with associations. Each contact will be used to identify more contacts. All in all, 300 to 400 prospects may be considered. Out of that list, the searchers will interview 10 to 20. If you're in that group the telephone will ring.

On the telephone, the headhunter will probably not tell you the name of his client or the exact nature of the job. You'll be expected to ask intelligent questions to identify (a) the genuineness of the inquiry and (b) its opportunity. You will probably be expected to prepare a summary of your background, education, and work history.

When you meet with a searcher one-on-one, be direct, straightforward, and forthright. Evasiveness or cuteness will score against you. Don't oversell yourself. Underpromise and overperform is the best policy.

Be prepared to answer all sorts of *why* questions: why you left previous jobs, why you did certain things in school, why were your greatest successes and failures such as they were—as well as dozens of other questions. When it comes to references, be careful.

Say: "I'll supply references but only when my candidacy has become more established."

The headhunter is a screen. Your primary objective: Meet with the client—if the situation seems interesting to you.

When you finally achieve that opportunity, do not—repeat do not—start talking about money. Assume the compensation is something close to what you're now getting. Your first need: to understand all about the company, the position, the responsibilities, the expectations, and the peers at your level.

Try to meet peers and some seniors—to see what kind of people they are. Specifications may appear a perfect match to your own background and experience. But if personal chemistry doesn't fit, forget it. However, only after you've concluded that the job is right for you and when the client believes you are right for the job can you negotiate the compensation.

Before the interview, do your homework about the prospective employer. If you know more about the employer than he knows about you, you're in an excellent position to guide the discussion toward the points you want to discuss.

If you are referred by an executive recruiter, those counselors can tell you about personality of the company and interviewer in advance. This insight gives you a devastating advantage. Many applicants lose out because of interview mistakes. To convey the self-confidence that stimulates job offers, be *ready* to answer questions and *eager* to ask questions of your own.

The business of getting hired is ruthlessly competitive. The race begins the moment you enter the interviewer's office. If you are prepared and know how to get hold of an interview, you are already ahead of many competitors.

HANdLiNG ThE OffER

Once you get a job offer, never make your decision in the interviewer's office. Give yourself time to think. Talk it over with friends and associates. Weigh information on the job and the company. Use a worksheet to evaluate the new job vs. your current job.

Never assume things that were not discussed. Ask.

Don't take on an employer you hope to reform.

Once you do accept, express your enthusiasm. Ask for a letter of confirmation that ties down details and eliminates possible misunderstandings.

So now, valiant climber, you've seen the headhunter. But working with searchers is a delicate task. It can backfire unless you move forward intelligently and with caution. Proceed carefully. Headhunters *can* become a conduit to your next important job.

PART 3

Moving Ahead of the Pack— The Long Trek Upward

CHAPTER 6

Adapting to Slope-Side Environment

So you've held your first job, you've moved on to better jobs (internally or externally), and you're now ready to settle in and move ahead of the pack as you work up the slope.

Good. First you must learn the importance of carrying your share of the load, learning how to be helpful, how to play the game, and what to do and not to do in business etiquette.

Carrying Your Share of the Load

In climbing the corporate Matterhorn, you must carry your share of the load to stay with the expedition. This is team effort. If you do your part, your colleagues will know it. Furthermore, at various points, the backpacks must be redistributed to compensate for varying strengths and abilities—all in the interest of getting the group to the next plateau. So keep an eye out for ways to help fellow climbers.

Do your own job first. That's primary. But after that, lend a hand to a fellow climber having troubles. Maybe you can analyze how his department is failing. Or help her with some people decisions.

You're growing, too, in the process. Ambitious climbers know they must work up to being a generalist—if they are to occupy the CEO's chair. But I often make this point: "You've got to be a specialist *before* you can be a generalist."

First you've got to learn one thing well—your own job. After you master that, take on contiguous jobs. You start, say, with market research or market analysis and in the process come up against what the product manager does. That may get you into price psychology and product structure. So, you learn that.

Then you find that product management depends on how much product is available. So you're into production planning. Then you hop back into what the selling force can do with a given type of product under certain conditions. Soon you get enough experience and somebody says: "Gee, George is the logical successor to the marketing vice-president."

So start by helping others. It's a valuable rehearsal for higher management. Helping others is what a manager does increasingly as he moves up. If you help, the bosses will find out in due course. They recognize who's really putting out and who isn't. Don't go around telling other people what you're doing, just do it. (*Worse:* Don't be telling stories about others—that's no way to build credit for yourself. It invariably backfires.) Anytime you can help somebody, jump at the chance—provided your own job is in order, but not just for the credit! Anytime you try to impress other people on what a helpful guy you are, you'll be called a "horse's ass" by the important people.

"Well, wait a minute," one trainee said. "If I'm going to spend my time and effort helping, why shouldn't I get credit for it?"

"Your mind is not working right," I told him. "The name of the corporate game is *Return on Investment*. Keep your eye on that. Do it for the overall good of the company's investment."

The best way to push yourself forward *strategically* is by selflessly helping other people *tactically*. You're working for the long climb.

"Suppose it's the other fellow that's not carrying the load and it affects *my* job," the trainee asked.

"Well, you can't allow that, either," I said. "You can talk to the boss, which is not the best way to go. *Better:* talk to the erring teammate and come to an agreement—then summarize your understanding in writing (with no copies to anyone) but as a guide to yourself. Tell him orally that you haven't copied anybody. The fact that you have a written agreement *dos-à-dos* will often motivate a lagging performance."

Peril of Short-Term Gain

Many times you'll get a chance to cut a corner for short-term gain. Something just a little shady. Resist these temptations. Your long-range interests lie in playing the game square. Sharpshooting was the central issue in the celebrated John DeLorean case.

John DeLorean was a successful climber up to a point. A very creative fellow. One of the best stylists and merchandisers the automobile industry ever had.

He did some fantastic things at Packard when he began pushing hydraulic transmissions. And then he brought out the GTO car for Pontiac and created a sensation. He lengthened the wheel base. Everybody said he couldn't do it. But he did.

DeLorean was a short-term winner, a manager of competence. At the same time on the minus side, he was considered devious and ruthless. He constantly sold people down the river.

Being hard-nosed and sometimes ruthless is necessary. But, if you're *that* ruthless you must keep moving unnaturally fast—so your enemies don't catch up with you.

When DeLorean got into the rarefied air at General Motors, his methods started to catch up with him. He was reported to be an investor in two or three GM suppliers. When a company does that, it's backward integration. But when an executive does it, it's considered "having your hand in the till." Top brass finally decided DeLorean wasn't the kind of cat they wanted at General Motors. Yet he was on a real roll for a long time. Many people bet he'd make it because of his track record. When he was let out at GM, DeLorean had a great compulsion to prove how good *he* was and how *wrong* GM had been.

But he kept getting further and further afield. Earlier, he had raised $80 million by convincing the British he had a great idea for a car. His DeLorean automobile had gull wings—just like the General Motors test car.

He convinced the British. He got the plant in Ireland. He romanced American dealers. They were excited. But they couldn't move the cars. DeLorean raised more money to prove it was a great car—which he still maintains. He put his other businesses up for sale. His finance fellow told me privately: "He's absolutely crazy to sell his Logan Manufacturing business. It's the best thing he's got."

But DeLorean has an obsession. Even after his narcotics indictment, he is still trying to prove everyone else wrong. If he is cleared of the narcotics charges, he'll go back and try to build the automobile again. He won't give up.

Nor will he stop (if his past record is any indication) trying to find a quick fix. He's an example of good executive drive and creativity run amuck because of need to feed an obsession with short-term gains.

An entire industry can be obsessed with short-term gain and cry for protectionism from Washington. This, too, is a moral issue. The steel industry took the short route and hid behind tariff walls. This allowed them to relax and now they're really suffering.

I agree with the MIT professor who suggested that the United States is no longer a manufacturing nation. Probably never will be again. We're gradually drifting off into a service economy—with more and more sophisticated kinds of service.

I'm very anti-protectionism. It's wrong, wrong, wrong. If we can't figure out how to do things better than the Japanese, we'd better buy their cars and let the consumer get the low price. And we'll do something else. There is no excuse for building these protective walls. In the 1930s everybody was screaming about protection after our depression. The Smoot-Hawley tariff set the whole world back about 10 years. It just stopped all trade between countries and everything stagnated.

Government bailout of top companies in trouble is another dangerous shortcut. If companies can't survive in this global scramble, better they should step aside and let more successful ones pass. I say this but quickly add that the few celebrated bailouts have turned out rather well. I'd hate to see it become a regular solution. Obviously, on an extended basis it would be a disaster.

In a related area, we are told that our annual support of farmers for financing, nonplanting incentives, subsidies, and other expenses approaches $20,000,000,000.

Most of this giveaway program is a disaster. Uncle Sam is never going to get that money back. That's just the very reason we don't want to get involved in government bailouts.

So seeking short-term gain happens to industries, to companies, and to individuals—always to their long-term sorrow. Don't let short-term-itis hamper your climb. Don't step off into the gray side because it helps you take one step up the ladder. Don't be wooed by situations slightly immoral in purpose or immoral in their accomplishment. Let's fight restrictive and regulatory legislation as hard as we can but let's do it according to the Marquess of Queensbury Rules.

Dick Magnum fell into this kind of slew. He was partner in a large engineering firm. And had been there for 10 years. But he couldn't resist using the firm's name to dabble into personal investments on the side (strictly against the rules). His senior partner discovered a prospectus.

The prospectus identified Magnum as a member of the engineering firm and featured the firm's name prominently to gain respectability for the venture.

Magnum and two friends were selling limited partnerships in citrus groves in Florida—10,000 acres. The senior partner minced no words: "Get out of this or leave the firm." Magnum was very bitter about that. But he withdrew and pulled his name out of the prospectus. He never forgave the senior partner.

Later he set up his own business and continued taking shortcuts.

He still wants to be accepted by his former firm. Whenever he sees the senior partner, he comes over and says: "Hi, Bill, how are you?" The senior partner refuses to give him the time of day.

Like DeLorean, Magnum wasn't content with things being good. He wanted to have his cake and eat it too. Yet he lost much more than he gained.

In your corporate climb, remember the steady, ethical route is often fastest—on balance.

Corporate Etiquette

A bright Harvard Law School graduate, in the Army briefly during the Korean war, barged into his sergeant's cadre room during basic training and sat casually on the bed.

"Get your _____ _____ off the _____ bed and get the _____ out of here, you _____," the sergeant said.

The proper New Englander left. Later his friend, hearing the disturbance, asked what the sergeant had said.

"He said it just wasn't *done*," the proper trainee said calmly.

What the temporary soldier knew—and what a trainee from a less structured society wouldn't have understood as readily—is that each society exists by certain rules. To get ahead, you walk within the framework of acceptability. At the very least, learn the rules first so you'll know *when* you can deviate.

"This general principle of etiquette certainly applies to the corporate climber—often for your own protection." says Tish Baldridge, former White House social secretary and corporate manners expert.

Suppose you arrive early for lunch with a business colleague. He's invited you as a guest. Do you take a table? If you take a table, should you order a drink? And if your host arrives, what do you do?

Take the table, but not the drink, "because it looks sloppy," says Baldridge. Nor should you eat the breadsticks: "It gets the table all crumbed up." If the host fails to arrive after 40 minutes, tip the waiter $5 or $10—and let the host know, so you can be reimbursed. "A host is a host," Baldridge says. (Now I'm not simple enough to say this bit of knowledge is critical. And personally I'd not try to collect the tip money—too petty. But the fact that a noted manners expert turns her attention to business tells you there's a need for attention to such. And, incidentially, never be the cause—by late arrival—of the need for this note in the first place.)

Learning To Play the Game

Mountain trekking and Matterhorn climbing also demand a good understanding of the unwritten rules of the road or *how you play the game*. You, as the CEO aspirant, must embrace a set of conventions on male–female relationships, working habits, internal gossip, and pride of accomplishment, which govern all the players on the expedition.

In managing some of my own divisions, several times have I encountered the office sex problem. In fact, on three different occasions I received impassioned pleas from wives asking for their husbands to be transferred to faraway cities so they would be separated from their secretaries.

Sex within the office is no good. It's distracting from quality work and it suggests shabby standards. What a person does at night is his or her own business—as long as it has no adverse reflection on the firm.

George Mazzei, the office etiquette authority, says the idea of restricting all romance just because both work at the same place is probably too severe for modern times—but adds: "Be discreet in approaching them. And one-night stands are to be avoided."

Harold Ross, the legendary editor of *The New Yorker* and a fanatic on the subject, said: "I'll keep sex out of this office if it's the last thing I ever do." John Barrymore, on the other hand, thought sex with co-workers was a natural law. When a theatrical reporter asked him if Shakespeare had intended a sexual relationship between Hamlet and

Ophelia, Barrymore said: "I don't know what Shakespeare intended. But when I'm playing Hamlet, I *always* do."

Business Party Manners

Then, of course, there are group manners—what to do when hordes of *Genus Commercialis* mingle.

Standing in the midst of his company Christmas party, the tipsy salesman scanned the hotel lobby, fascinated by the enormous, red-bowed wreaths hanging just above his colleagues' heads.

"Whatta ya wanna bet that I can put a chair through the center of that wreath?" Before anyone could stop him, the salesman hurled a lobby chair right through the evergreen bull's-eye and through the massive plate-glass window behind it.

For him, the company party ended with a pink slip.

"As many people ruin their careers at parties as at the office," says John Molloy, the business consultant and author. "Only dummies party at corporate parties."

Don't confuse an office party with fun and games.

"It's not a party, it's a political event," says Marilyn Moats Kennedy, managing partner of Career Strategies of Evanston, Illinois, and author of *Office Politics*. "The office party is the equivalent of the May Day parade in Russia, where who is standing next to whom, who is seen with whom, is tremendously important.

"You need to circulate, speaking to everyone, even your enemies. Thank the janitorial staff, the switchboard operators. Give everyone a lot of strokes. It will leave your colleagues impressed, and even through a hangover they will remember you as one of the nicest people at this company."

As for the social conduct expected, "people should think of office parties as part of the office day, only with drinks," says Judith Martin, author of the Miss Manners syndicated newspaper column and books.

This makes the office party sound like a morality play, "like the boss is passing moral judgment on everyone," Molloy acknowledges. "But it's really a practicality play. The boss is looking for people who aren't going to blow under pressure, and he's got to wonder how he can trust a guy in the field when he gets crocked at the company party."

It's accommodating of etiquette mavens to counsel us on office socializing, and you'd have to be pretty thick to disagree with most of the rules—*assuming you must go* in the first place. I've certainly logged-in time at such soirees. But when I hear someone say: "It's an office thing, I must stay to the end," I say: "Sounds like rationalization to me."

Sure, you are obligated to put in an appearance—but this can be mercifully brief if you're courteous and inventive (and if you're not, you're going to have other problems).

There's no obligation, ever, to overstay and do foolish things. I've know many charmers who can attend, get credit for speaking to the right people, order a glass of club soda, tour the room, and be gone—having done all the right things, none of the wrong. You can do likewise when that's the proper strategy.

Nonsocial Business Etiquette

Probably the most serious faux pas occur in so-called normal business hours when a slow-footed climber zigs when zagging would have worked oh so much better.

Janet Greene decided, *Savvy Magazine* reported, after her branch had been visited by Mr. Big from HQ, to write Mr. Big this letter:

> Dear (Mr. CEO),
> The nature of today's large corporations usually precludes one-on-one contact with top management. Such interaction is a rarity, even (sadly) within corporations that specialize in communicating.
> That is why I was particularly pleased to meet you during your visit here. I'm not sure if you appreciate the whole value of seeing you chatting comfortably with employees. The fact that you made the effort is important to me and, I'm sure, to many others.
> I enjoyed your talk about the principles that guide our company, and

was glad to have the chance to ask questions. I asked you about our training program. I'm interested in learning more about the intensive training program you discussed, and I trust that management can tell me more about it. Perhaps I'm not ready for that step yet; however, a clearer picture of the program will help me establish it in my mind as a career objective.

Again, thank you for taking the time to visit us. I hope we have a chance to meet you again.

She didn't go through channels. Her boss knew nothing about the letter. The CEO, rather than reply, forwarded her letter to her branch manager—suggesting that she be filled in on the training program. Conclusions:

- ☐ She was naive. It was poor judgment. You don't write your boss's boss without your boss knowing and approving.
- ☐ If you do write, you don't patronize ("I'm not sure you appreciate the value of your trip here.").

This brand of behavior is corporate downhilling—on a bobsled.

Your Slope-Side Plan

So where are you? You're adapting to your environment by managing your work, covering your rear, getting along with your colleagues, avoiding social and personal gaffes. Good work habits alone go a long way toward insuring your place on the climb team.

Remember, lacking prosperous parents or a rich spouse, you will be forced to work quite hard even if you are blessed with uncommon talent. (Otherwise it's better to get a couple of graduate degrees and take up teaching or else get a job in a political bureaucracy.)

Smile a lot. Never forget that promotions come from the kind of press you get from the people alongside of and below you. Toadying to bosses is self-destructive.

Choose hobbies or outside activities that involve meeting new people and keep it up all your business life.

Always spell people's names right. Neatness counts.

Read a lot. Don't skip the society section, the sports section, business section, or book reviews.

Don't get a reputation for last-minute work. Living dangerously destroys the confidence of customers, clients, management, and anyone who takes Gelusil.

Remember what your mother taught you to say—please, thank you, you're welcome.

Make your boss close the door, sit down with you, and talk over your progress, or lack thereof, once a year even if it embarrasses him, or, increasingly, her.

Worry a little, but not too much.

All in all, you're embarked on a mission that has been establishing roles of proper behavior for the last century. Learn what the rules are and pay your dues before you start breaking them. After all, the system works pretty well. And you're the new kid on the block—for now.

CHAPTER 7

GETTING ALONG WITH Fellow Climbers

TWO Alpinists are climbing the Matterhorn, linked together by special ropes. During the ascent, each saves the other dozens of times. One cannot make it without the other. Cooperation and communication are vital. One may go on, at some future climb, to greater fame and world acclaim. But right now, as Ben Franklin said: "We must all hang together or, most assuredly, we will each hang separately."

The similarity to corporate climbing is astounding.

Two department heads are level on the organization chart but must work together. Neither can tell the other what to do. They must cooperate for the good of the company *and* for their own advantage.

Many an aspirant en route to CEO status neglects the peer problem and falls by the wayside. Your ability to get things done makes you a star in the boss's eyes. Fine. But to be a *rising* star, you must get peer cooperation.

Jack Hopper, one of the smartest guys I ever knew, was a star. As lone product manager, he did everything right—but he paid no attention to his peer group. He wasn't sympathetic. He wouldn't mold his department actions to solve problems in advertising and promotion. He'd raise hell with others and build a case as to why he was the strongest.

This came back to haunt him.

When it came time for promotion, the CEO said:

"Jack is too devious. He's always shooting people down. He's not a constructive team player. He's not bringing the rest of the guys along. Yes, he's a superstar. He's doing all kinds of things by himself. But he's not a person I'd advance to a higher job."

Top people can usually see through grandstanding. After all, they've experienced it for years. They know it for what it is. A real thruster may think he's outsmarting the boss—but he's not. He forgets the immortal words of John Donne: "No man is an island."

There's another aspect of this peer thing. In a big organization, if you ignore peers, you can be boobytrapped. Your peers get disgusted, and consciously or unconsciously (consciously more often) let you get in trouble.

So doing the job alone is not the only answer. you must perform "with advice and consent" of your peers, as they say in Washington.

Suppose a fellow is strictly an SOB. (It happens all too often.) So his colleagues just leave obstacles in the path. Rocks can come rolling down the street. He trips all over them. Nobody tells him they're there. There's nothing so sabotaged as a self-sabotaged SOB. He's pressed his own self-destruct button.

In your climb, you must also use sensitivity toward people in dealing with competitors—your colleagues also climbing the ladder. Say you're one of six vice-presidents. But only one of you is going to ascend to executive VP. Believe me, you need the support of the other five to get appointed to the executive VP slot. And if you are named, you're sure going to need their support afterward. Either way, you're all on the same climbing team.

In contrast, if you're buddy-buddy and sympathetic, you can collectively solve problems. Ignore your peers at your peril!

Can a Leopard Change His Spots?

The chairman of a large midwest paper company was looking for an operating vice-president. One day on the golf course, he met Charlie Simpkins. He liked Charlie and, on impulse, offered him the job— good money and stock options.

In a few days, the chairman told me proudly he'd made this decision. I did a little research and came back to report:

Me: "You know, Charlie has real difficulty relating to his peers and he doesn't communicate very well. That's probably why you got him. His current management isn't too happy with him."

The Chairman: "That's all right. I can take care of that."

Me: "Well, can a leopard change his spots?"

The Chairman: "Don't worry about it."

Six months later, back in the city again, I stopped to see a banker on the paper company's board.

"What happened with Charlie?" I asked. "How's he doing?"

"What do you mean how's he doing?" he said, "I was in the Caribbean and I got a frantic call. The chairman told me to get the hell back here. Charlie was getting in all kinds of trouble. He couldn't communicate with the marketing head or anybody else. And besides, the chairman said that Jim Newman asked: 'Can a leopard change his spots?' So the chairman fired him."

So learn two lessons from this experience: (1) Snap judgments are often wrong. (2) The person who doesn't relate to peers is an accident looking for a place to happen.

CYA in High Places

Directors of a large company in New England were considering which of three top people to promote to CEO. The board wanted a strong leader. The frontrunner was George Hopkins, the financial manager. As a descendant of the founder (and you know what that means in New England!) he had several board members pulling for him.

This board asked its management consultants to interview Hopkins. We asked Hopkins leading questions about the *other* candidates—always a good indicator.

"This manufacturing fellow is pretty able, don't you think?" we said.

"No," he said, "he doesn't follow through."

Hopkins reached in his drawer and pulled out a whole file of memos. Damnedest file we ever saw. Documentation of dozens of discussions with other department heads. In fact, so many we challenged him:

"George, why did you write all these memos? Did you talk with the people about these problems?"

"Oh, no," he said, "I just think it's important to record my position in all situations."

This game, called *Cover Your Assets,* is sometimes necessary in corporate infighting—although not near so often as some people think. But CYA must never replace management. A manager is charged with achievement through others—including peers—not in building a position record. You can't show a file of memos to stockholders to explain a down year—or any year for that matter.

To make doubly sure, we talked with two of his peers. Said one:

"Oh, George always writes memos. They're his fantasy. He puts down things we never discussed. At the beginning, we wrote memos back—but we gave that up as a waste of time. After that, we just ignored them."

So we concluded that George couldn't be the next CEO. His zeal in CYA proved he couldn't handle the top job.

With the leading candidate disqualified, we recommended that the board go outside. The fight became bitter.

One director felt a responsibility to the former CEO. He tried a muscle play to force his candidate in. The other directors put their backs up and said no.

While they were thrashing around, a huge consumer goods company bought the whole business. They put their own people in. That took care of that.

So, memos that started out as evidence about one man backfired on their author. Tip to the corporate climber: Memos can pull you down more often than push you upward—as this extreme case shows.

When Peers Frustrate You

Sometimes you're on the receiving end of an uncooperative peer.

Say you and Esmeralda, another department head, are co-equal. She's a political animal—more interested in appearance than in doing. Do you assume she'll hang herself if she gets enough rope? Or do you actively combat her?

She's getting a lot of credit because of politics. You resent standing by idly.

Good questions, classmates.

For starters, talk about Esmeralda's problem with your cooperative peer group. Someone may suggest an active program to put her down. But that probably won't pay.

Another immediate impulse: Tell your boss that Esmeralda isn't cooperating. But that's the hard way.

Again, your co-op group can solve the problem by not helping when she gets in trouble. And you won't have long to wait—if you stick together.

The more you can avoid criticizing other people, the better off you are. Being critical of peers, subordinates, and bosses is almost always counterproductive.

When I ran the London office, Jerry Peterson came in to complain about Harry Tudor.

"Whoops, wait a minute. Wait until I get Harry in here. Let's go over this situation together."

Jerry balked.

"Gee, you can't do that," he said. "He'll just tell me I'm wrong and he'll disagree and say I don't have the facts."

But I insisted on both—or none. English common law gives you the right to face your accusor—before an objective judge who weighs one testimony against the other.

This also defuses the problem. Once you get both together, the accusations are not near so violent.

It also scotches future complaints. The guy who cannot face his adversary won't come back next time. He knows he's going to either defend himself or end up embarrassed. You've proved the point: Criticizing peers is a waste of time and effort.

"Yes," Nan Robertson said, "But suppose you've got a peer who really is doing a *lousy* job! I'm talking about a real nemesis to the company! You could follow your doctrine of no-criticism out the window!"

Well, let's see about that.

If your colleague's lousy job doesn't affect your work, keep your mouth shut. If you're in a good company with discerning management, they'll find it out in due course.

On the other hand, if this lousy job *is* affecting your work, you must holler.

But even then, don't go to your mutual boss. Go to the offending person—privately. Go on record with what needs to be done. See if you can understand why he or she isn't doing it. In many cases, you can work it out one-to-one.

But if the peace talks fail, then lay down what you're going to do and what he or she is expected to do. Write out a schedule without copies to anyone else. But keep the schedule—something to go back to three months down the road.

When the job falls apart and your boss says "What the hell happened?" you say:

"The Screw Machine Department didn't come through with its commitment. I sat down with the guy three months ago. Here's the schedule we laid out. This is what he agreed to."

A schedule is better than a memo. Every time somebody writes me a memo, I wonder who's getting copies. Memos are generally written more for copies than for originals. Stay out of memo wars if you can.

Top business managers are a pretty able bunch of cats—even though they're individualists and demanding nuts in some ways. But they're generally competent.

If you keep your nose to the grindstone, your merits will be recognized. The more energy you spend on work and the less you spend on memo wars, the better off you'll be.

Office Politics

Be very wary of office politics; you're playing with fire.

"But at my office, the politics is rife," one climber told me. "You gotta fight fire with fire to survive."

Maybe so, maybe not. But if you do jump into an office who-shot-John, size-up the playing field first.

Office politics is always played within the organization context. In one company, it might be wise strategy to purchase a house in the CEO's neighborhood. In another company, that might be pushy and offensive.

Apply your political ploy with sensitivity and tact. Suppose you discover your boss is receptive to feedback about attitudes. Providing him with a five-page document won't do. Offhand verbal comments are much better.

Andrew J. DuBrin, professor of behavioral sciences at Rochester Institute of Technology, suggests you check into these areas:

What practices irritate the boss? If your boss prefers telephone conversations, keep memos to the absolute minimum. If your boss does not smoke, get your nicotine fix elsewhere.

Does your boss accept compliments graciously? Many supervisors are turned off by compliments.

An astute office politician doesn't comment favorably about the boss's enemies. Ask friendly secretaries who the boss likes the least. Or ask your boss "Which departments cooperate least?"

What is your boss's most vexing problem? If you find a solution, you'll get points. If you find no solution, you may get credit for trying.

Make notes on important personal facts such as the names of the boss's family members (including household pets), favorite sports, hobbies, personal gifts, and colors. But capitalize on this adroitly. Don't be a servile flatterer.

What are your boss's mood cycles? Ask his secretary. Most executives are best approached after sorting through major problems. During a down cycle, stay away—except for emergencies.

Other political considerations:

Identify the power through innocent questions to an older person, unlikely to be threatened: "I'm new here and I'm trying to understand the company. Could you please tell me what that kindly gentleman does?"

"Believe me, Beth," said Jack Portland, "the president will not go ahead with any new plan unless it is approved by Mr. Lawson, the controller. Mr. Lawson brought the president into the business. He's the wisdom behind the throne."

Ask indirect questions. Charlie asked his boss: "Who at the top of the main office really cares about Operations Research?" His boss answered: "Ed Boswell." Charlie wrote Boswell a handwritten note accompanying a report. Charlie is now assistant to the general manager.

Analyze political ploys to effectively guard against being a victim. A subordinate may say:

"We're all rooting for Jasper. He's made great strides in overcoming his marital and financial problems."

Does Jasper really have a problem? Or is the informant merely trying to remove Jasper as a contender?

Determine what activities have high status. In some organizations, playing squash and/or tennis is definitely in. Golf is on the wane. Keeping *World Tennis* on your office coffee table impresses people.

Boats are definitely in, particularly when physical activity is associated. A photo of yourself fixing your sailboat would be helpful.

Carrying *The Wall Street Journal* is not an automatic status symbol. One politician carries the *National Enquirer* ("I'm trying to understand the mental make-up of little people. After all, they're the real consumers of our products.")

Plants are status symbols. One company gives the tallest and rarest plants to the highest achievers. To give the impression of being powerful, a middle manager brought in a five-foot fig plant. It was impressive, all right—the CEO ordered it removed!

WHEN PEERS ARE SUDDENLY NOT

At a large chemical company, John Smithers worked for Judson Pease, a competent man not slated to go higher. John kept making suggestions to the department head. In two years, John was promoted to a new post supervising three people—including his former boss, Judson Pease.

That's unusual enough. But they remained friends, which is even rarer.

More typically, one or the other would have been transferred to another department—a better bet, when you have the option with people who work for you.

Congratulations. *You've* just been promoted. What do you do about your relations with your peers—or former peers?

Begin by assessing precisely why you were promoted. First get rid of the illusion, surprisingly widespread, that it's because the company loves you. Corporations don't love people, at least not the way parents do. On the other hand, neither should you assume that the blindly bureaucratic moguls promoted you because you've served time and paid your dues.

The big boys apparently see in you the qualities they seek for getting results. It could be your masochistic tendency to work inhuman hours. Or your Mack-the-Knife ability to fire people, which promises eventually to send your spouse to divorce court and your kids to reform school.

It's possible you're the right-body-in-the-right-place-at-the-right-time. Moreover, the big guys may be wrong.

To bore through the confusion, go to the brass and ask. If you're replacing someone, and he's leaving the job amicably, tap into his database thoroughly and diplomatically. Stress reporting relationships, hidden agendas, and the political lay of the land. If the company believes in written job descriptions, examine yours. If you want to negotiate changes, it's better to do so early on.

Talk seriously to your new boss. Take notes if that doesn't freeze him up. Listen, and I mean listen! Get his version of what the person in your job is *supposed* to do. Be alert to what he thinks of your subordinates, how the last incumbent screwed up, and what he likes and dislikes in his *own* work. Most important of all: Get very straight on what he expects of you.

The higher you rise, the more you find business wheels are turned by an elaborate Old Boy and Old Girl network. To play this game in a new place, you must adopt the folkways of the natives—quick.

If your new peers are a bunch of tony Ivy Leaguers, do think twice about mentioning your bowling scores. If they're all burr-headed ex-Marine commandos, go easy on the big words and the Nuit du Wimp cologne.

Promotions can chill relations both with your *former* peers and your *new* peers, who used to be your superiors. You're still the Parvenu to managers with more time in grade.

"It was rough," a 28-year-old newly promoted manager in a biomedical company says. "Rather than go out with me for a beer after work, they'd find something else to do."

Others arrivistes noted testing questions from former peers, in the guise of joshing—"Well, how's the air up there?"

When former peers are now working for you, steer into serious conversations. Open with banter like the luck of the draw and the mysterious ways of corporations. Then discuss what each of you hopes to get out of your work together.

If you've got a boss's job, play the boss. "It's a big challenge when you move from running yourself to running other people," one junior executive said. "I had to throw out a lot of personal habits"—in managing time and delegating work.

But while you're learning the ropes, everyone will be watching. *Appear* to know what you're doing.

Don't become too dependent on subordinates for advice—a natural enough response, but you may regret it when you get your feet on the ground. Making a plan is a good idea. Make it a step-by-step program to acquire necessary technical skills or a systematic scheme to meet your new staff. A plan serves two functions: It steadies you and provides a sense of accomplishment.

Working with Peers Outside Office Hours

As you climb to higher levels, you must inevitably become more and more exposed to outside people through trade associations or professional societies, business or country clubs, and charitable boards and committees. Conduct yourself well with these people: they're your colleagues on the climb.

In your out-of-company relationships, you're often working with a potential employer. Or a grapevine recommender to a new post. Or a college friend of your current boss who'll put in a word—good or bad—depending on you.

Be selective about the organizations you join. Don't just be a joiner. Unless you're willing to take an active role, save the time and dues money.

But once you've decided to participate, go all out. If the organization has a problem, volunteer to fix it. Contribute time. Concentrate on *giving* more than you get. Get on a committee. Work your way up in the structure.

Current and potential CEOs grab these volunteer responsibilities and run like marathoners with them. The founder of Burger King retired to Miami then took on United Way and all the problems connected with it. United Way in any community is headed up by a rising or already arrived executive.

"If you want a job done, ask a busy person," they say. Get known as a busy person. Join to participate.

NOT A **Climb** FOR **INTROVERTS**

"If you're introverted by nature and you'd rather go home and read escapist mystery novels at night, you must change your mode," I once advised.

A careerist took issue with me, saying: "I need time to decompress. The most therapeutic thing I can do is something solitary. I need time alone."

"Maybe you do," I told her. "But you're not really going to work up to the corner office that way. And maybe you're happy with a different goal. Now's the time to determine where your priorities lie."

Sure, you need to recharge your batteries once in a while. I go out in the backyard in my country place and talk to a hive of bees. You may want to lie on a beach and stare at the sky—occasionally. But not most of the time.

More and more, you've got to be in the thick of things. Seek out the excitement and challenge. Associate with others who get things done. They stimulate you and you them. It's synergistic.

Drop by to see an acquaintance. He introduces you to a colleague who's a prospect for your service or product. If you don't go, you never meet the man. It's just that simple. You can't stay in your cubbyhole. "Get out," as H. L. Mencken advised "and stir up the animals."

The successful climber makes maximum use of time. Utilize your social time in a productive way that relates to career advancement. Reading paperback novels at night is not the answer. (*Remember:* We never said this climb was *easy*. It's a rigorous trip with great rewards to the few who make it!)

Be organized about your outgoing activities. My firm wanted our people to associate with others at a certain level in business. We took theater seats in groups of four, passed them out to our guys, and told them to take their wives and another couple to the show. This is one way to make it systematic. If you commit to theater tickets, something's got to happen.

KEEP YOUR EARS TO THE GROUND

Imagine yourself as a giant set of mammoth ears—always attuned to business opportunities for your company. Do this diligently and you'll learn of job opportunities, too.

"Don't," as a Senator once accused a colleague, "keep your ears so close to the ground that grasshoppers get in them."

Remember your main assignment: pushing your company and your career forward.

Your peers are also often your competitors—and naturally, you want to be updated on what they're doing. Don't spend too much time, however, trying to psyche-out your peer–competitor—like the two competitive salesmen who met at the Atlanta airport.

"Where are you going?" one asked.

"To New York."

"Aha, I know you," the first salesman cried. "You say that you're going to New York because you want me to think that you're going to Chicago. But I happen to know that you're really going to New York. So why did you lie to me?"

THE OUTGOING VALUE

The outgoing person will discover 16 opportunities a week. Visible people attract attention. A recruiter typically goes to his industry association and says: "Gee, who do you know that's been making a name as a sales promotion manager?"

The association staffer says: "Well, I saw this guy at our meeting down in Bimini who was pretty exciting."

The ball's rolling.

The corporate climber must function in the outside world as well as on the job. Building acquaintances with the idea of *giving*—not just *taking*—is what makes it work.

A lobbyist for Bethlehem Steel worked actively on committees for coal industry associations. Amax learned about him and hired him away for a better job. It happens to the activists. Your boss will support activism. The company also benefits by having you out and about. CEOs and potential CEOs are doers. They thrive on challenge.

"But," a colleague asks, "can't even an energetic talented person spread himself *too* thin? There are only 24 hours in each day."

No. The really able person decides when he or she is devoting enough time to the job and backs away from outside responsibilities that jeopardize the main assignment—like Bill Hartman, head of Interpace, declined continuing on a bank board.

"I just can't do it," he said. "We've got too many problems. I've got to give up three board posts for the next two years." The Bill Hartmans in the corporate world don't participate unless they can be effective.

Be chary of the person that attends every business seminar plus The Aspen Institute and AMA's management sessions. Such people bounce from one thing to another while their company job suffers. Balance is the key.

Geoffrey Gregarious, the sales manager—my god, he knows everybody in the industry. He spends all his time at lunches and dinners. Sometimes he forgets he's got a job to run. Yet his job description includes many things besides fraternizing. Sure, a sales manager's going to get out more than a researcher. But a researcher who fails to get out to industry meetings will miss a lot of valuable interchange, too.

Everyone needs to get out some. The long-haul climber determines how much.

Meetings: Boondoggle or Benefit?

"I can't believe this," a friend said. "You're not recommending *more* meetings! We're trying to stay out of *useless* meetings."

Sure, we all want fewer boondoggles. But a good convention—if organized properly and with programming that solicits participation from people in other kinds of business—serves a valuable purpose. You meet new people. You find out what others are thinking. You participate.

On the other hand, attending to hear celebrity speakers is a waste of time. ("Find out what Barbara Walters is really like!" crows the promotion). But the informal interchange in the corridor during coffee break might well pay out. Again, participation is the key.

Don't be passive. Get involved. Volunteer to report on a topic. Work with people from other companies. If you're just there for fun and games a la American Legion conventions, all you'll get is a king-size hangover.

Working on Committees

A committee has been described as "an agglomeration of the incompetent assigned to do the unneeded." The group tries to make a horse and ends up making a camel.

Yet committees are not *all* bad. If you're heading up a hospital or school fund-raiser, you want as many people involved as possible. The more people, the more success. In that case, you encourage committees. Delegate tasks to them. This is the route to participation.

It's true of associations, too. The more people you get involved, the more persuasive your findings and the more support you get. Using task-groups is a valuable tool for a manager. By encouraging participation, you get support as well as input.

Working with peers inside and outside is a vital and often-ignored requirement of corporate climbing. You must get continuous favorable word-of-mouth ratings from your peers. As Victor Hugo said: "Be it true or false, what is *said* about a man often has more influence on his life, and his destiny, than what he *does.*"

Right on, Vic. Only today you'd probably say *person*—or you'd draw low ratings from 50 percent of *your* peer group.

CHAPTER 8

MANAGING YOURSELF
AND YOUR WORK

BEFORE you can manage others, you must manage yourself—to many, the thorniest task of all. The Scottish poet Robert Burns prayed: *"Wad that God the giftie gie us/To see our sels as others see us."*

In modern group therapy, the knowledgeable counselor says: "George is much improved over a year ago. Now he has a good idea *who he is.*"

Well, I agree with all these savants—within reason—but I say the best way to get yourself in hand is also the simplest: positive thinking. This theory's been with us so long because it's basically true. New medical experiments indicate cancer patients can actually *think* themselves well in some cases.

My football coach used to say:

If you think you're beaten, you are.
If you think you dare not, you don't.
If you'd like to win, but you think you can't,
It's almost a cinch that you won't.

If you think you'll lose, you're lost.
If it seems too tough you'll find
Success begins with a fellow's will.
It's all in the state of mind.

I believed this then, and I see no reason to disbelieve it now.

Marvin Bower of McKinsey and Company describes positive-ism differently—but compellingly—in his book *The Will To Manage.*

Is Charisma Necessary?

"It's all well and good for Ethel to preach positive thinking," a disgruntled manager said. "If I had her charisma, I'd be a positive thinker, too."

That reminds me of a story. A fellow who was worried about his inferiority went to an analyst. After six months of therapy, the doctor said: "We've found the trouble. You really *are* inferior."

But getting back to charisma: *how needed an ingredient?* At one time, this fad word was called *personality* or *personal magnetism,* and even *charm.* Sure, if you have *it* (by whatever name), it helps.

Tom O'Ryan has it. O'Ryan is a legendary figure in transit advertising. As founder of Tom O'Ryan Advertising Company in Memphis, he's probably the best known name in his industry. It wasn't always that way. Back when O'Ryan first started selling transit advertising, he was assigned a territory in Georgia and the Carolinas. O'Ryan's first prospect was a bakery—Craig's Honey Bread. On Monday, O'Ryan called on the president.

"Young man, we've never used your advertising, and we never will," he said.

Tuesday O'Ryan was back with a smile—and a new advertising idea. No sale.

He came back Wednesday, Thursday, and Friday.

On Saturday, he arrived at noon. The proprietor was getting ready to close for half holiday.

At this point, O'Ryan didn't even know all the advantages of his service.

"I've been taught to answer all sorts of objections to transit advertising," he said, spreading his sales literature on the table. "It's all in here somewhere. Anything you ask I'm sure we can find—even if I don't know the answer."

It was a naive statement. No experienced salesman would have said it. And yet the baker looked at the literature, back at the appealing O'Ryan, then sighed:

"Well, this looks like something I'm going to have to have. Reckon you'd better sign me up."

O'Ryan wrote up his first customer.

O'Ryan soon turned his Irish brogue into a plus. People remembered him. He became a distinctive personality. Soon O'Ryan ranked number one in the nation. He didn't know novices aren't likely to lead the pack.

"Nobody explained the averages to me," O'Ryan recalls. "I tried to sell one contract a day. I thought that was expected."

Ace salesman or not, O'Ryan always retained some of that early innocence. It is his key to charisma. But you can certainly build a successful career without an extraordinary ration of magnetism. I've known hundreds of able executives who *learned* how to become effective managers even though they were *acquired tastes* rather than *instant* charmers.

They get there by performing, which is why you're reading this—to learn how to be a better business performer. If you lucked out with more than your share of charm, add boldness and even *chutzpah* to it—when the time is right.

Stuart Browne did that when we walked into the *Encyclopaedia Britannica* executive office. It was plush. The manager had a long oak-paneled room with pile carpet four inches deep. Original paintings on the walls. We had to walk the length of the room to get to his desk. Our high priest was on a throne on a dais under a ceiling spotlight.

Stuart was not intimidated. He walked that long walk holding a long cigar with a long ash. Halfway he stopped and aimed that cigar at a standup ashtray—six feet away. He missed and got ashes all over the floor. He stopped and looked around and said: "Jesus, what a dump!"

His actions were saying: These trappings don't impress me. They're all meretricious.

It worked. The encyclopedia executive thought: Anyone this outlandish *must* be good. But remember: Stuart *was* good. If you're going to be outrageous, better be good enough to back it up.

If everywhere you go, people want to do something for you and if you get letters from 50 people signed "your best friend," consider yourself blessed. But don't make the mistake of many charismatics and rely *solely* on charm (going light on work). If you do, you'll be typecast as a matinee idol—not a heavy hitter. Matinee idols don't end up in the CEO's chair.

And if you don't have charisma, don't try to create it artificially. Concentrate on performance. It's more important in the long run.

PERSISTENCE: A GOLD MINE

Nowhere in schools do they talk about the value of keeping everlastingly at it. They should.

A young reporter once asked Thomas Edison how it felt to have failed ten thousand times with a new invention. Edison said, "Young man, since you are just starting out in life, I will tell you something of benefit. I have not failed ten thousand times. I have successfully found ten thousand ways that will not work." Edison estimated that he performed more than fourteen thousand experiments in perfecting the incandescent lamp.

Ray A. Kroc, founder of McDonald's Corporation, agreed—and posted this maxim on his wall:

Nothing in the world can take the place
of persistence.

Talent will not; nothing is more common
   than unsuccessful men with talent.
Genius will not; unrewarded genius is
   almost a proverb.
Education will not; the world is full of
   educated derelicts.
Persistence and determination alone are
   omnipotent.

Value of Sponsor

In the New York Police Department, old-timers say: "The only way to get promoted around here is to have a rabbi down at Centre Street headquarters." In business, we call it a *mentor* or *sponsor.* Same idea—a supporter in high places.

A mentor will help you up the slopes. (It's also dangerous. Your peers may resent it.) But the higher you go up the slope, the less a mentor matters. More and more, as you ascend, you're judged on a performance and—even more important—the way others *perceive* your performance.

Charles Percy was an enterprising student at the University of Chicago. He formed a campus co-op purchasing agency and doubled its business. That, plus his academic brilliance, attracted the attention of Joseph H. McNabb, CEO at Bell & Howell. McNabb gave young Percy a summer job at Bell & Howell and kept pushing him up the mountain.

Charles Percy became president of Bell & Howell at age 29—an unusual accomplishment. Later he changed course and became U.S. Senator from Illinois. Thus a man with great native ability was helped up the ladder.

Advancement and exposure are two critical benefits a mentor provides. Says Clare Keller, vice-president for human resources at the Automobile Club of Michigan, who has had mentors since her early career days, "You could do your job wonderfully well and nobody will know it. But a mentor will mention your name."

For men and women, a mentor relationship almost never begins with, "Will you be my mentor?" A more common and acceptable method is to ask for advice on a tricky matter, then later discuss what action you've taken. Gradually, the relationship builds—if you play your cards right.

MENTORS VS. NEPOTISM

Nancy W. Collins, author of *Professional Women and Their Mentors,* suggests you look for a mentor who is:

- ☐ A senior executive or manager able to advance your career.
- ☐ A recognized authority in the field who has more experience and knowledge (but is not necessarily older).
- ☐ Influential and close to the lines of power and authority in an organization.
- ☐ Genuinely interested in your growth and development.

Finding a mentor doesn't make you golden. Experts say it carries risks and consequences:

Be wary of personal relationships. Romance can be disastrous for your professional collaboration and your position at work.

Expect a certain amount of jealousy from co-workers or spouses who feel left out.

Stay on top of office politics. Your mentor's fall from grace with top management can sour your fortunes.

Be aware that supervisors who serve as mentors can become un-mentors when you get an outside job offer. It would be the rare person with that much objectivity.

Of course, it helps if your sponsor is really a key person—but *not* your father. Sure, the younger family member gets special treatment. But he or she becomes very unpopular. This works against you.

One family company head made his inexperienced daughter vice-president at age 22. This tended to downgrade the office in the eyes of the older, more experienced, key people.

There are always exceptions, of course.

From S. C. Johnson and Sons, the consumer wax company, young Sam Johnson came to me for advice—while he was still in business school. What should he do about a business career? He couldn't see going to work for other companies. He knew what he wanted. He could get it better at the family company than anywhere else. He didn't want to waste time in a foreign environment.

He went to work directly at Johnson's Wax and has proved to be one of the country's brightest business managers! But that is distinctly the exception. In most cases, nepotism is bad for the company and bad for the careerist.

Unless you belong to a family company with fine management (and how do you have the objectivity to tell?), think several times before staying there. Sooner or later, you'll get caught up against a fence.

It's much better to go out and get an outside epaulet or two on your shoulder and then come back. Then you can say: "Here's the way we did it over in such-and-such a place" not "Dad thinks we ought to do thus and so." Even if you start out in a family company and do well, you won't get credit. People will say: "It's a thanks-Dad-type job."

In fact, you may go somewhere to avoid nepotism, find out you like it, and never come back. If that happens, you've found a home. That's good, too.

Plan Before You Jump

But sponsor or not, certain basic self-management needs remain. You must become an effective communicator. At each level, someone is always going to want you—the corporate climber—to produce a report on this or that. Report writing, if well done, is a key to advancement.

So if you cannot write effective reports, learn—fast. Your competitor will.

When you get ready to do a report, organize your thoughts carefully. Make sure you know where you're going *before* you start. It's a disaster to bring in the finished product only to have the boss say: "You aren't going in the right direction."

Very frustrating. Yet it happens all the time.

How many times people have come to me and said:

"Gee, I've got a dictating machine, Jim, and I can just sit down and this stuff will flow all out. I've been working on it for a week. Let me go ahead for just three more days."

Then they give me a pile of 100 pages. As I read, I make my own outline, sit back and look at it, and restructure the whole thing. Then I call the person in and say: "This is what you *should* have done to begin with. Now go expand this outline and bring it back. Don't write a word until you know where you're going. Great outpouring of raw data is not a report."

A Northwestern University political science professor once gave only one piece of advice on essay exam questions:

"Take 15 minutes to make an outline *before* you start. It'll be the best 15 minutes you've ever spent."

For the smart money, it worked. But he couldn't get most students to do it. Most wanted to start writing right away.

As a chemical engineering major at MIT, I chose this task for a thesis: *A cheaper way to extract beryllium*—a metal one-third lighter than aluminum. I plunged in to set up chlorine reduction retorts and reflux condensers in the laboratory. Then old Professor McAdam, the chemical engineering head, came in and said:

"Newman, what in hell are you doing?"

"I'm working on ways to try to extract beryllium," I said.

"Put all that stuff away," he snorted. "Go get the six best books that deal with the reduction process on basic ores. Read them all. As you read them, ask yourself 'Have they got support or are they just taking positions?' Decide what conclusions they've reached that could be challenged. After you've done that for a month, come back here and do your lab work. And you ought to be able to do it *in one week*."

Well, I went home for a month and studied and came back. The lab work took only 10 days. It worked like a charm. I've never forgotten the principle: *Know where you're going before you try to go there.* Go *before* you know where you're going and you get in trouble.

This principle is important in report writing. But reports are just the microcosm. In all self-management, know where you're going before you try to go there.

Making Decisions

In managing yourself, welcome decision-making—it's the basic stuff, the protoplasm of management.

You *must* be a decision-maker. That's what you're paid to do. Don't shirk it. Try to get as many facts as possible first; of course, you'll never get them all. When you get all you can, make the decision. Once you make it, assume it's right—even though occasionally you may be wrong.

Don't play it safe. IBM founder Thomas J. Watson said it best: "Each of us must be alert to the dangers of playing it safe. Act courageously on what you believe is right."

Don't try to hide behind a committee. Eight people get together to rebuild the building. When it doesn't work, you can't put the finger on who decided it. Weak executives skulk behind committee skirts.

Coming up the line you're far better going out of your way to record as many clear-cut decisions in your name as possible. Ask for responsibility *and* authority. And give your people the same. Tell your staff what you expect. Give them the authority to do it.

Don't be a phony delegater—giving work to subordinates just to keep them busy when you intend to make the decision, all along. That's a waste of time and effort.

Once you give a person a job, step back. Sure, he or she won't do it exactly the way you would—perhaps not as well. But judge by the result, not the way they get there.

Keep Your Eye on the Main Task

Probably the most important single principle in managing your career climb is a variation of the classic: Keep your eye on the main chance.

Bart Lytton, the savings and loan tycoon, once told a crew of business filmmakers:

"You've made a wonderful movie. For that you get A. Since it wasn't the movie we wanted, on that you get F. Your final grade is F."

Donald P. Horton, executive vice-president of Sales and Marketing Executives International, said it differently:

"If John would do John's job, not be an expert on Susie's job, we'll all be better off. But to make it worse, Susie's worried about how to do Simon's job. I have an old-fashioned idea, tested in the crucible: Each person should attend to his own job."

It's true. A recent study showed that many executives excel in side issues—but fail the fundamentals. Why? They don't keep their eyes on the main chance.

In your career, concentrate on doing the basic job. Do not get distracted. A Federal Reserve Board chairman once told me his formula:

I tell my people to know clearly what their job is, to work at it 24 hours a day, and never do anything else. If there are any extraneous balls rolling down the street, don't pay any attention to them. The few people that stick with their jobs'll get to be the president just like me.

At the time, I decided that was just about the best advice on self-management I'd ever heard. I still feel that way.

Putting Yourself to Work

In writing as Poor Richard, Ben Franklin said: "Keep thy shop and thy shop will keep thee." It's still true. You must take yourself in hand and put yourself to work each day. The successful climber is a self-winding, self-propelled mechanism. No one can do this for you.

Dr. Whitt N. Schultz, a self-management consultant in Kenilworth, Illinois, offers good counsel:

- ☐ Effective managers are solution finders. They go after facts; find them, then use their imaginations to come up with positive answers.
- ☐ The best managers are hard on themselves and easy on others.
- ☐ Go that extra mile—it's never crowded!
- ☐ Always determine the objectives before tackling any significant jobs. Write them down. Study them.
- ☐ Organize. Deputize. Supervise.
- ☐ Never do anything that someone else can do for you—and probably better.
- ☐ A good manager is also a good follower. Know when to command and when to consult.
- ☐ Effective managers are paid to produce—not to be comfortable.
- ☐ Run your job. Don't let it run you.
- ☐ Ideas, like babies, don't pick their parents.
- ☐ Welcome ideas from everyone.
- ☐ The tongue weighs practically nothing, yet few of us are able to hold it.

☐ A brain is like a wagon—the lighter the load, the noisier it becomes.

☐ A good manager has a sense of urgency, a demand for excellence, a healthy discontent with the way things are.

☐ Beware of creating conformity in your organization. Free enterprise demands boldness, high risk, innovations.

☐ The professional manager meets conflict head on. He or she resolves conflicts in a solid and creative manner—without delay.

☐ In thinking, look at the forest first, then see and study the trees and their relationships to the forest. This conceptual thinking leads to greatness.

MANAGING YOUR TIME

When business publications run special issues on time management, reprint requests flood the editors. Why? Time is the basic stuff of the universe. Each person has only 24 hours a day. And most people have the deep-etched feeling they are wasting a lot of this irreplaceable commodity. They're right.

Correct management of time is probably the single most important factor in managing yourself, your work, and indeed, the work of others.

One popular way to squander time is called acquiring information. Sure there's an ocean of material you must go through. You just can't read it all. Yet I have no patience with the manager who reads *Business Week* or *Fortune* or *The Wall Street Journal* page by page. Scan. Suck all the nourishment out. Then throw the rest out.

In a magazine, go to the table of contents first and pick out the things important to you—and read those. In a newspaper, scan the headlines. You do not have time to read it all. Extract the essence and let the rest go.

Business is a world of changing priorities. The successful climber adjusts those priorities every day, every month, every minute. As you get higher, you must know more and more about what's going on. Priorities prevent you from casually reading a magazine. Yet at each step up, you've got to be better informed. Figure out a way to get this information and not go crazy in the process. (If that sounds like a tall order, it helps explain why the apex is so narrow at the top.)

I'm aware of the flurry of speed-reading courses. Probably speed-skimming would be more useful. Not long ago, I saw a well-organized manager go through a copy of *Nation's Business.* He tore out two articles to read. He routed one to somebody else. He ignored a topic he was interested in last week, but not interested in today. He resisted the temptation to read an amusing article (he didn't need entertainment at that point). Then he threw the magazine in the wastebasket—not to be bothered with wastepaper.

I do that with *The New York Times* and *The Wall Street Journal* every day. Every three days on the average, I'll pull something out and direct it to somebody else.

Read and clip and *get rid of paper.* The advertising manager for a large business machines division felt he should read *The Wall Street Journal*—every word. But he never did have time. So his office suffered from three months of journals stacked up. He said: "I'm going to read them." Of course he never did. Silly.

Clear the decks every day.

At day-end on a daily newspaper, the editors throw everything away. They know they're going to get a lot more the next morning. They just can't cope with residue. Everything unused goes in the wastebasket. This causes some problems. But it also sustains life.

Keep your paper under control. The wastebasket is your friend.

COMMON SENSE IN TIME MANAGEMENT

Sometimes it's the common sense that's difficult—and that applies to time management, too. People still make a note about memoing

George—when they could have written the memo in the same amount of time. Remember the advice of Admiral Horatio Nelson: "Do it now. Do it *right* now."

Many memos or letters can be handled by writing your answer on the incoming paper, marking it for photocopy (if you *really* need a copy), and moving on.

Richard Considine, president of Lincoln Logs Ltd., Chestertown, New York, the do-it-yourself housing firm, is a great believer in "The Little List."

"Each evening I make a list of the ten most important projects to be done," Considine says. "Then next day I make a new list—incorporating what wasn't resolved from the day before. I find the priorities change. What was most important today isn't the most important tomorrow. When I find one of our managers getting off the track, I frequently discover he or she isn't working that little list."

The Little List—as basic as block, tackle, and run in football. Yet how often coaches go back to basics to get the team to start functioning again! Fundamental rules exist because they've proved out over the years. When you're erring, you're probably ignoring the classic rules of time-and-work management.

As paper flows to you, handle most of it immediately. All bills for approval must either go forward for payment or back to the supplier for adjustment. Don't hold bills, ever. And horror of horrors, don't file bills before they're paid (gross mismanagement in action!).

Think of paperwork as fluid (some see a sewer analogy). Handle the flow quickly (sometimes this indicates straight into the deep six). Never send someone paper just to get it off your desk. Have the courage to X it.

In the old sailing ship days, a captain's nightmare was sailing east to west around The Horn (the southern tip of South America). The prevailing westerly winds blew through the Straits of Magellan like a giant wind tunnel. With no room to tack, the ship was forced to sail directly into the howling gale. Some days, making a few yards west was an achievement. One old salt, discussing the round-the-horn formula, said simply: "Make Westing each day. Make Westing."

Paperwork is like that. Make Westing each day or you'll never get around The Horn.

LEARN TO KEEP YOUR MOUTH SHUT

My climbing years at Ingersoll Steel taught me many important lessons like: Don't talk too much, buddy-buddy, with people. I learned this when Roy Ingersoll fired me.

Roy, as head of the Ingersoll division, reported to Howard Blood, the chairman of Borg-Warner. Howard's son Charles was in the Norge division in Detroit. At this time, Ingersoll was making Sears Roebuck's warm air furnaces, hundreds of them, all different sizes. Norge had a private line—much smaller volume. I conceived the idea of manufacturing under private label for Norge.

Charlie Blood and I became friendly. He invited me out onto his father's yacht, tied up on the river north of Detroit. We had a few drinks.

"Jim," he said, "in Borg-Warner, we're having a terrible internal political battle. Awful fights between Roy Ingersoll, your boss, and my father. Yet I think each division is trying to achieve its own objectives. Don't you think that's right, Jim?"

"Well, I suppose to a degree that's true," I said. "We see evidence of these kinds of things."

The next morning, I got to the office. Bzzzzz: my intercom—direct to the CEO's office (status!).

"Jim, come in here," the voice said. Feeling something amiss, I went in.

"I understand you think we have terrible wars in Borg-Warner and I'm battling with Howard Blood all the time and we have great strife," Ingersoll said. "You're fired. We do not need this kind of stuff around here."

Apparently young Blood had talked to his father and attributed to me what *he* had stated. All I'd said was a grudging "I suppose so." But obviously I shouldn't have gone that far.

I was mortified. I'd never been fired before. Dazed, I went back to my office. What to do? I decided to ask advice of Ray Sullivan. (Earlier Ray had recommended me, at 27, to Roy Ingersoll who said: "My God, he's so young." Ray, who later became manufacturing head of Ford Motor Company, was a tough-as-nails executive.)

I told Ray: "Jesus, Roy's fired me. What do I do?"

"Just ignore it," Ray said. "Go right about your sales calls. Do everything you're supposed to do. Don't say anything."

So I went ahead and did my work. But I had trouble sleeping at night. After Roy Ingersoll had been out of town for 10 days, bzzzzz went the intercom: "Jim, come in here."

"Oh, God," I said. "Here it comes."

When I got to Roy's office, he said, "What the hell's the matter with Kalamazoo Furnaces! Look at the cost those bastards are reporting. They're doing a terrible job up there. Jim, you've got to get on top of those guys."

"Mr. Ingersoll, I'm fired."

"Oh, for heaven's sake, get up to Kalamazoo and get them straightened out."

That was the last I ever heard about being fired. But I learned a good lesson. You never gain by tearing somebody else down. Let somebody else assassinate character. Don't you do it. If you don't like the way someone's performing, talk to him or her directly. Don't tell A about B. If someone wants to talk personalities, listen and keep your mouth shut. Knowing when *not* to talk is valuable intelligence.

Roy Ingersoll, a successful and dynamic manager, did play A off against B. But you can encourage competition without setting one off against another.

Sure, everybody is in competition. That's healthy and part of life as well as business. But don't say. "Joe says this and what do you say?" That causes nonproductive trouble.

Meeting Deadlines

As you rise in management, you'll be setting deadlines for your people. And meeting deadlines in your own work as well. Word soon gets around whether a person meets due-dates or not. If you don't, you're putting big rocks in your backpack as you try to get up the slope.

If you've ever worked on a newspaper (campus or otherwise) you probably came away with a healthy respect for deadlines. Deadlines occur constantly, and everyone works by the same clock. Produce or perish.

People who live by tough deadlines get a lot more done. Some of the best work comes from moving quickly from the heat of ideation to the immediacy of execution.

Delay is stultifying. The meeting harvests dozens of great ideas. Everyone goes away excited. But follow-through is postponed for a few days. Other problems intervene. Then, when people get down to implementation, enthusiasm has wilted, memories have blurred, the thrust dulled.

When time is merciless, and people go from the warmth of inspiration right into execution, the excitement shines through the finished product.

Nothing much is accomplished by delay. Remember the adage: "On the plains of hesitation bleach the bones of countless thousands who, on the threshold of victory, hesitated and, while hesitating, died."

Time in the Office

There's no way you can get your work done without spending some time in the office, but don't become anchored there. You need to get out and see what's happening. Out-of-the-office time ranges from minor (research or laboratory work) to major (selling or sales management). Strike the right balance in your area.

Too much out-time marks you as a Meetings Junky—not a serious contender for top office. MJs spend half their time going to association meetings, conferences, briefings, conventions, and miscellaneous gatherings of the clan. Between times, they drop names, relay misinterpretations of what a speaker said, and handle trivia that keeps them away from everyday problem solving. MJs are often pleasant, well-mannered, and moderately interesting people. They are experts on the Waldorf, Drake, Fairmont, Century Plaza, and Shamrock-Hilton. They know the best menu choices at the Greenbrier, Homestead, Breakers, and Broadmoor.

The trouble is, MJs toil not, neither do they spin. Neither do they climb.

WHO'S GOT THE MONKEY?

A powerful way to save the time you probably now waste with subordinates—thus freeing you to do your own work, without sacrificing your supervisory role—is to avoid being the subordinate's *subordinate.* Or as William Oncken, Jr. and Donald L. Wass, chairman and president of a consulting firm, put it: Don't let your subordinate put the monkey on your back. In fact, make sure you put it on his or hers.

In a discussion in *Harvard Business Review,** Oncken and Wass say:

Imagine a manager is walking down the hall and he notices one of his subordinates, Mr. A, coming up the hallway. When they are abreast of one another, Mr. A greets the manager with, "Good morning. By the way, we've got a problem. You see . . ."

As Mr. A continues, the manager recognizes in this problem the same two characteristics common to all the problems his subordinates gratuitously bring to his attention. Namely, Mr. A knows (a) enough to get involved, but (b) not enough to make the on-the-spot decision expected of him. Eventually, the manager says, "So glad you brought this up. I'm in a rush right now. Meanwhile, let me think about it and I'll let you know." Then he and Mr. A part company.

*"Management Time: Who's Got the Monkey?", *Harvard Business Review,* November-December 1974. Copyright by the President and Fellows of Harvard College. Used with permission.

Before the two of them met, the monkey was on the subordinate's back. After they parted, it was on the manager's. Subordinate-imposed time begins the moment a monkey successfully executes a leap from the back of a subordinate to the back of his superior and does not end until the monkey is returned to its proper owner for care and feeding.

In accepting the monkey, the manager has voluntarily assumed a position subordinate to his subordinate. That is, he has allowed Mr. A. to make him his subordinate by doing two things a subordinate is generally expected to do for his boss—the manager has accepted a responsibility from his subordinate, and the manager has promised him a progress report. The subordinate, to make sure the manager does not miss this point, will later stick his head in the manager's office and cheerily query, "How's it coming?" (This is called "supervision.")

Or let us imagine again, in concluding a working conference with another subordinate, Mr. B, the manager's parting words are, "Fine. Send me a memo on that."

How does it all happen? Because in each instance the manager and the subordinate assume at the outset, wittingly or unwittingly, that the matter under consideration is a *joint problem*.

The monkey begins its career astride both their backs. All it has to do now is move the wrong leg, and—presto—the subordinate deftly disappears. To solve this problem, Oncken and Wass say, you should:

☐ Call your subordinates in, one by one, aware that each has a monkey he'd like to leave on your back. Place the monkey on the desk between you and decided jointly what move the *subordinate* might make next. Once this is decided, the subordinate takes the monkey and leaves.

☐ Even if you cannot decide today, the subordinate takes the monkey with him. ("Monkeys can sleep just as well on subordinate desks.")

☐ As each subordinate leaves with his monkey, he is no longer waiting for the *boss* to do something. The boss is waiting for the *subordinate* to do something.

☐ When the subordinate (with the monkey on his back) and the manager meet at the appointed hour, the manager explains the ground rules in words to this effect:

At no time while I am helping you with this or any other problem will your problem become my problem. The instant your problem becomes mine, you will no longer have a problem. I cannot help a man who hasn't got a problem.

When this meeting is over, the problem will leave this office exactly the way it came in—on your back. You may ask my help at any appointed time, and we will make a joint determination of what the next move will be and which of us will make it.

In those rare instances where the next move turns out to be mine, you and I will determine it together. I will not make any move alone.

The manager follows this same line of thought with each subordinate until at about 11:00 a.m. he realizes that he has no need to shut his door. His monkeys are gone. They will return but by appointment only. His appointment calendar will assure this.

Thus make sure you keep the initiative where it belongs—with the subordinate. (This will not only preserve your time. It's also good management.)

Namely, before a manager can develop initiative in his subordinates, he must see to it that they have the initiative. Once he takes it back, they will no longer have it and he can kiss his discretionary time good-bye. It will all revert to subordinate-imposed time.

Oncken and Wass's final advice:

Monkeys should be fed by appointment only. The manager should not have to be hunting down starving monkeys and feeding them on a catch-as-catch-can basis.

Monkeys should be fed face-to-face or by telephone, but never by memo. (If by memo, the next move will be the manager's.) Documentation may add to the feeding process, but it cannot take the place of feeding.

Every monkey should have an assigned "next feeding time" and "degree of initiative." These may be revised at any time by mutual consent, but never allowed to become vague or indefinite. Otherwise, the monkey will either starve to death or wind up on the manager's back.

So it's simple enough: Keep the monkey off your back and you'll have time to do your own work *and* give better supervision.

CHAPTER 9

Managing Your Boss

WHEN Ralph Ginsberg, the publisher of *Eros,* went off to jail for sending obscene promotion through the mail (a miscarriage of justice, but that's another story), one friend asked a Ginsberg intimate: "Don't you think Ralph will get a parole for good behavior?"

"Depends if he meets the warden or not," the Ginsberg insider said. "If he doesn't, he'll probably get time off and out early. If he meets the warden, he'll serve *every day* of his sentence."

Portrait of an otherwise accomplished man who never learned how to manage his boss.

Put it down as gospel—people skills are your greatest aid in climbing the corporate ladder. Then as topic A under that, note this: Nowhere is this truer than in communicating with your boss.

If your boss doesn't believe you're doing a good job, it doesn't matter too much what anyone else thinks—you're in the soup.

Begin by understanding bosses—they have an ego all their own. Think about the boss and his characteristics. In the United States (more than in other countries—Japan, for example) the boss can say:

- ☐ "No, you can't do it."
- ☐ "That's enough of that discussion."
- ☐ "Go do it."

Some bosses solicit your opinions, but they don't really want them. If the boss says "what do you think about so and so" and really doesn't want to know, better not spend half an hour telling him.

Be particularly careful about nay-saying the boss with other people around. Counter the boss's idea when you're alone. Telling the boss his idea is no damned good with others sitting around may be suicidal. You may as well play Russian Roulette with all cylinders full.

In making suggestions to the chairman of a Midwest gear company, we always sat with him alone first. If we presented anything with other board members around, we got absolutely nowhere fast. He felt the need to defend his position.

This is particularly true when a younger woman presents contrary ideas to an older man—he of unreconstructed male chauvinist persuasion. Do it in public at your peril. Alone and you'll find it works.

From painful experience I learned to introduce ideas to a banker carefully—not when other people were around. Whenever this principle was violated he would invariably and promptly say no. Later, he'd review his thoughts and agree. But his mind-change occurred in *private*.

Working Boss vs. Ideal Boss

Is there ever really an ideal boss? Rarely. A workable boss? Often. Not an ideal person, but one that works. To progress up the mountain, better understand the elements of an ideal boss–subordinate relationship. Then you can get as close to it as possible.

Begin by analyzing your boss. Reflect on what he expects from you. Then convert these needs into actions that suit his needs—no matter if he's a real gem or an S.O.B.

To outline what constitutes an ideal relationship, start with what it's not. The subordinate is not a yes-man. The boss doesn't want this—cannot afford it. It's amazing how often this principle is violated.

I recently sat in the back of a room to watch senior executives in a large service organization make a presentation on a new product package, the result of many months of effort. The company's chairman also sat in the back.

The lights came on. The presenter and interlocutor started around the table to get reactions.

"A very profound presentation."

"Well put together."

"Extremely interesting viewpoint."

"Should be a valuable management tool."

Every senior executive endorsed the product to a greater or lesser degree. Finally the chairman stood up quietly and said:

"That's one of the worst things I've seen. It doesn't make any sense. There's no logic from the facts presented at the beginning to the conclusions drawn at the end. There's a huge gap in the middle. I just don't understand what leads you people to think this is such a great package."

Suddenly the tide turned. The second endorser jumped up and said:

"I wondered all along why there wasn't a clearer theme of logic throughout the presentation. It simply doesn't hang together."

Executive Number 4 answered:

"And I don't think enough thought was given to the market and the customers we're trying to sell this to. I can see there are some real problems there."

And so on. What a revelation to that chairman! A clear insight to the strength and character (or lack of) of his people—regardless of the quality of the presentation.

From now on, when presented any recommendation, the chairman will say to himself: "Is that what he *thinks*? Or what he thinks I *want* to hear?" In the final analysis, yes-men are not valuable. And most good bosses know this. Bootlicking 101 doesn't deceive the astute boss. It merely lowers his opinion of such opportunistic ploys. As Hamlet said (when swapping jokes with courtiers seeking to manipulate him as if he were a fretted lute): "For though you can fret me, yet you cannot play me!"

On the other hand, in your zeal to display proper independence, don't go too far and become combatative about every issue that comes along. Your boss, with probably half again as much experience as you, can probably appreciate factors you haven't thought about. Your first departure from the pack gets greeted with hushed respect. Do it too often and you generate more and more skepticism. Finally when your boss starts to deprecate your against-the-tide ideas with sarcastic humor, you've pushed independence too far—you're now destroying the relationship.

At a board meeting, I watched one member's acrid, frequent, and overly inflated criticism. On each point, his nay-saying dominated. Finally the chairman was forced to hold him back and solicit opinions from the more thoughtful directors. When time came to renew appointments to the board, the chairman took our hero aside and explained he was not being renominated.

Honest dissention is often valuable. Constant nattering is disruptive. There is a good range in the middle.

Lone Wolves Belong on the Prairie

Career climbers who are lone wolves often get trapped. One howling indicator: not telling your boss about severe problems.

John Hickerson, head of retail fuel distribution for a medium-sized diesel oil company, should have seen the red flag when his boss, Gene Porter, told him to increase inventory to meet an expected jump-up in volume.

As it turned out, Hickerson was unable to get the deliveries he expected. He said nothing to Porter and kept on trying to get product.

Finally, came showdown day. His company got a big order from the Air Force base they couldn't deliver.

Porter was irate. No manager likes surprises. He fired Hickerson on the spot.

Keeping the boss in the dark doesn't pay. Hickerson had three weeks to let Porter know about the problem. He should have known at the end of the first week that trouble was brewing. He should have asked for help.

But Hickerson, an ambitious man, wanted to run his own show. He hoped to head up the whole oil section someday. Independent action would help him attain that job, he thought.

So learn from Hickerson. Don't try to wing it in a crisis. You can also learn a different lesson from Porter.

A few days after he fired Hickerson, Porter asked me: "What would *you* have done in that situation?"

"I wouldn't have fired him," I said. "I'd have made this an example to the man and to others. It would certainly have affected his year-end bonus. But we all make mistakes. And he was a good man in most ways."

Firing, as the CIA says, is "elimination with extreme prejudice." Sometimes it's the best solution. More often, it's not. Remember that bit of advice in managing your own people.

Building Confidence

When your boss feels confident in you—when he sees you are willing to assume total responsibility—you're on your way. Learn to listen, understand, ask searching questions, and think your own way through situations. These traits build confidence. Then the way you tackle problems, pick them apart, and carry them through to solution will reinforce his confidence. Gradually, you'll be assigned more and more responsibility. When he appoints you to act in his absence as he travels around the world, you've arrived.

The worst way to ingratiate yourself with your supervisor is to knock the work of a peer. In 1863, President Abraham Lincoln was beset with political problems in the Union Army. One political appointee, General John McClernand, had the hubris to suggest that Lincoln fire General Henry W. Halleck, McClernand's superior. Said Lincoln to McClernand, with far more patience than you'd expect from a modern corporate commander:

> *You are doing well—well for the country and well for yourself—much better than you could possibly do if you engaged in open war with General Halleck. Allow me to beg that, for your sake, for my sake, and for the country's sake, you give your whole attention to the better work.*

Do better work! That's the way to the boss's heart.

(P.S. McClernand did not do better work but continued to intrigue. He himself was fired and passed off the stage into obscurity. A lesson in boss relations here.)

UNdeRSTANd THE Boss HiMSELf

Anticipate your boss's intentions. In reconnaissance prior to Waterloo, Wellington dropped his glove on a little hill. One of his generals returned it. Later, Wellington said to him: "I want your battery where I dropped my glove."

Replied the general: "Yes, my lord, I've already done it."

Learn what the boss is trying to accomplish. List his objectives— for example: growth in size and profits. Breaking into a new market. Getting promoted to executive VP. When you go over budget plans or specific projects, you can enlarge your list. Ask questions about roadblocks and difficulties that need to be overcome.

Understand her frustrations. Is she striving to achieve impossible targets pressed on her by the gods above? Does she lack sympathetic understanding at the home office? Is she understaffed to achieve the goals set out for her?

The more you know what the boss wants, the better you can help him or her get there. And the more you boost your boss upward, the faster you rise.

If this requires night and weekend work, remember you're not a production worker punching the clock. You're a corporate climber. Do what you must do to make it work.

List the boss's strengths and, particularly, weaknesses. Not too quick a thinker? Sensitive about someone else coming up with a solution? Lazy—likes to leave early? Demanding family that takes up too much spare time?

Insight into these characteristics gives you a role to play in achieving your objectives. His goals are your goals. His problems are your problems.

(*Warning:* Understanding doesn't mean buddy-buddy.)

(Being the boss's favorite sounds like the ideal spot for the ambitious Alpinist. But it's fraught with peril—particularly if you become a confidant as well. It can get embarrassing. You become aware of inappropriate actions taken by peers. Restrictive confidences are advanced. Finally, if the boss proves inadequate, you may be carried down the slope with him.)

Equally important is understanding what the boss expects of you. Many companies supply written job descriptions. Unwritten responsibilities are often more important. Jot down your own expectations. Review them with the boss. Get his reaction as to accuracy and completeness.

Ask for Clarity Before Starting

Once your job is thoroughly defined, learn to cope effectively with each task assigned. In many a meeting, I've heard the boss say: "Let's color New York white" and his people say "OK, OK." They walk out without the remotest idea of what they're supposed to do. But they wanted to be agreeable! This is folly. And gets you into hot water PDQ—particularly when you're dealing with completion dates.

Ask questions at the *beginning*. Not two weeks later when you're theoretically underway. When you get an assignment, go back to your office and think about it—carefully from beginning to end. If you foresee problems before you get to the end, for heaven's sake, go back and tell the boss.

Say "I'd like to understand the priorities and how they fit with your goals." Or: "I have to be clear about which is more important, A or B?"

One veteran manager said: "The worst way is to wait until Friday the 13th in February—the deadline—and then go to the boss and tell him you're not going to deliver."

Going in Thursday the 12th and saying: "Geez, I don't think I'm going to make it by Friday the 13th" is almost as bad.

But at least, the day's grace gives the boss time to decide what apologies to make or what handsprings to turn. And brothers and sisters, if you're the cause of your boss's doing cartwheels, better make it as easy as possible—and better not do it at all again for years.

Be Sure of Adequate Resources

When you understand exactly what your responsibilities are, think about the resources you need. Funds for advertising or promotion? New computer programs required? Any unusual expenditures? Enough people in your department or will this mean extra hands? People of the right caliber?

Adequate resources may mean the difference between success and failure.

Know Boss's Standards

On any job, specifications invariably include what he expects of you as a person. I've seen many major disasters brought about by the boss's frustration with personal characteristics! The head of a large world banking empire said to me:

"John Worthheim will never be of any real value to us. On Friday afternoons, he's off playing customer golf. Friday evenings he's never available. I can never find him over the weekends. He'll never get very far in this organization until he dedicates himself to the company."

Now if John *knows* the chairman feels this way, he's suicidal. If he doesn't, then he's guilty of not knowing his boss. Either way, he's in deep trouble.

Is your boss a bug on promptness? Don't be misled by the boss's own behavior. I learned this years ago working for George Smathers. He chewed me out for being late. Since he was often tardy, I asked with a straight face:

"Do these promptness standards apply to *everyone* here in the office?"

He saw what I was doing and bounded back:

"If you're talking about me, Jim, remember this: Do as I say, not as I do, and you'll be a success in the world!"

Reporting Back

Some bosses, once they've assigned a project, are delighted if you carry the project through to completion without reporting interim steps. This is often an excellent mode—*if* The Big Guy likes to work that way.

Ask at the beginning: Does he want to be kept informed?

Or will he be happy if you just bring him back the completed package. (On some tasks, critical steps really ought to be checked out with the boss.)

One CEO, Bill Jordan, was explaining why revenues were running below budget on his defense contracts:

"My general manager, John Aruba, the dumb S.O.B., is running behind completion dates in his work schedule," Jordan said. "I gave him hell about this. I hope he's going to do better. Let's see what happens in the next quarter."

Then Jordan left on a four-week trip around the world. When he came back, work was on schedule but costs for materials and labor were skyhigh.

"It was John Aruba again," Jordan said. "While I was away, he took parts of the assembly line and jobbed them out to outside contractors. Costs ran way beyond what he should have paid. I don't know what to do with the man. He's probably fattening his own pockets, perhaps getting a kickback."

So he fired John.

A manager trying to get the work out faster got fired for runaway costs. Is this a case of damned-if-you-do, damned-if-you-don't? Not really. It's a case of a man who didn't understand his boss—or communicate with him. Sure, John had the mandate to speed up production—but not the authority to increase costs markedly. Once he investigated the method (that is, costs) of increasing production, he should have presented Bill Jordan with the package:

"Yes, we can increase production to save three days per month. But it will cost $X more. Are we interested? Or do we keep looking for other ways to do it?"

Then Jordan could compute the benefits vs. costs and make an evaluation. Rarely will a CEO allow a manager to increase costs dramatically without discussion. When in doubt, ask. Know your boss and your situation so well your handling is automatic.

Liaison with Your Boss

There is a fine line between too much liaison with your boss and not enough. You're hired as a manager. So manage. Don't wait for assignments like a clerk. Don't get in the habit of checking every detail. You can easily over-check and over-clear. Sure, some ego-involved bosses will be flattered and say: "He respects my opinion so much he comes in every day." But most good executives will not.

On the other hand, always clear your overall plan. Then carry out the details on your own. When direction changes, review it face-to-face again. If you err, err on the side of too much communication. But use good sense. You can't run in every 15 minutes. Again, be a manager—not a clerk.

Incidentally, while we're about it, don't ask for a raise. If you're worth a raise, your boss will feel guilty because he didn't get you one. If you're not worth a raise, he will feel guilty because he did not explain things to you.

The proper course is to ask for more work or more responsibility. What matters is not what you earn now, but what you will earn in the future. It's a long climb. Progress each day will work wonders.

DEALING with CORNER-Office MEDDLING

When your erratic genius boss interferes with your work and causes long-range problems, you've got to call his hand.

I worked for Roy Ingersoll, a popular speaker and bon vivant, who served as head of the National Chamber of Commerce. He loved to make deals with other wheels on his speaking trips.

One day in Bridgeport, he talked with the GE head about wash tubs and made an off-the-cuff offer to sell 50,000 tubs at $18.75 per unit. Back in Chicago, he called me in.

He: "That takes care of sales for the whole year."
Me: "Gee, that's wonderful, Mr. Ingersoll. What price?"
He: "$18.75."

Me: "For God's sake, I told them they couldn't have our product at anything like that price. I quoted $21.00 as an absolute bottom."

He: "Well, Jim, I had to do it."

Me: "All right. Just don't get out that book later and say I'm not making any money on tubs."

After that, he let me make the decisions in my area.

Incidentally, as you climb, be concerned about responsibility—not title. Recognize opportunity when it knocks—regardless of nomenclature.

When I was at Ingersoll, I first became sales head for Kalamazoo Furnaces along with sales for washing machines and tubs and other things. Then, since Roy Ingersoll lacked confidence in the general manager in Kalamazoo, I gradually, without title, started running that whole division.

I didn't care about the title. I was getting great experience. Besides, my most important audience—my boss—knew who was doing the work.

Be a Solver, Not Causer

On the wall behind Ben Helms' desk is this sign: *"Are you here with a solution? Or are you part of the problem?"* Helms, president of The MaLeck Group, Wingate, North Carolina, emphasizes this basic cornerstone of boss relations: Come in with solutions, not problems.

Chris Hegarty tells of a CEO who also endorses this principle:

"Dennis came to me only when he had a problem. I soon came to associate him with trouble. Whenever I saw a memo from him, I became upset. 'I'm willing to listen to any problems,' I said. 'But from now on, each problem must be accompanied by a solution.' Dennis was visibly disturbed by this. But after a short time, the procedure caused him to grow as a professional. Now he's doing quite well."

Be a subordinate who *solves* rather than creates problems. Spotting the smoke is only half the battle. Come in with axes and hoses, not just the alarm.

Don't run in shouting: "Our shipment never arrived in Youngstown." Say: "The shipment to Youngstown never made it. I've put a tracer on it. There's a flight that arrives in Youngstown at 10 a.m. tomorrow. If you can spare someone, we can drive a new package to the airport to make the plane."

When it comes time to promote someone, who do you think the boss will pick—the problem carrier or the solution carrier? You know the answer, boys and girls.

Delivering the Bad News

How far can a climber go in expressing unpopular ideas and recommendations?

"If you've done a good job for a year or two and the boss has confidence in you, put forth your ideas," says Earl D. Brodie, San Francisco publisher of business newsletters.

"It's a selling process and all the rules of salesmanship apply.

"But if he's strong-willed and you think he's making mistakes, don't tell him. Let him tell you. Use the Socratic method—everything comes from his own mouth. Go back and re-read your Plato."

All too often, if communications aren't effective, subordinates wait for the boss to make the first move. Worse yet, they may simply assume their priorities are their boss's priorities. This is downright dangerous. You'll be judged on the basis of how well you meet your boss's *actual* priorities. Don't be passive.

Culturally, Americans inherit passivity from parents and teachers (children should be seen and not heard). The successful climber must change this.

Don't wait for the freeze-out when you can't reach the boss, don't get invited to meetings, and hear about important issues on the grapevine. When this happens, your communications have reached the crisis stage.

Sit down regularly with your boss to air grievances—that's the best way to deal with the problem. Pick the right time and place, find the right words, and be prepared with specific examples. Don't play games or take too much time.

THE REAL GEM

Suppose you luck out with an excellent boss—it happens!—who:

☐ Recognizes that everyone approaches a job differently and respects that uniqueness.
☐ Doesn't try to herd every subordinate into thinking one way.
☐ Depends on his or her own instincts when there is a difference of opinion, but doesn't fault you for sticking to your guns.

If you ever have a choice that includes a boss with any of these characteristics, grab it. You've hit the jackpot.

THE REAL S.O.B.

What if, in spite of all your efforts to understand the boss and his requirements, you wind up with a real S.O.B.? Well, remember the expression: "He may not always be right, but he's always the boss."

The ogre who starts taking you apart in front of others needs to get a taste of what he's dishing out:

"Now, John, you object to my trip to Peoria. But remember you've given me the job as regional sales manager. And I'm exercising that function. Now the way to judge me is to look at the overall achievement, don't you agree? I may not do each thing the way you would. But it's overall results that are important, don't you think?"

Put your foot down. Otherwise public abuse gets out of hand—and degenerates into disaster. Know when to call the boss's hand. (Incidentally, poker and management and war all share astounding characteristics. If you don't play poker, learn. It's part of your liberal corporate climbing education.)

When you first go to work for a difficult person, establish what he or she expects and say:

"I've got the responsibility but I don't have the authority and I can't have one without the other."

Your first reaction to working for a real knee-cap buster might well be: "I'm going to put everything in memo form—for protection."

Yet a record of why you lost the war may make it worse—particularly if he's a bastard. He won't pay any attention to it. And then you're really on the griddle.

So document it, but don't let *his* boss or *his* peers see it. You're not trying a case in court. You're not adversaries (or you'd better not be).

A colleague once said: "Jim, you obviously believe in dealing privately with people and not involving others in problems."

Guilty as charged, Your Honor. Make this policy a reflex action. This is absolutely essential in climbing to the rarefied heights.

Volunteer for Work

Subordinates who remain on assignment are not climbers. The climber looks for work that needs doing and volunteers to do it.

Attend a meeting your boss finds difficult to make. Present a cogent summary of findings from the viewpoint of the company's interest.

One boss was great at motivating his salesforce but knew nothing about finance and cared less. On her own time and expense, his assistant—Adelle Platt—took accounting courses at a local college.

Later, Adelle was promoted to marketing vice-president.

When volunteering for work, you'll find that conferring with the boss's secretary/assistant provides valuable data—no one knows his idiosyncrasies, likes, dislikes, or habits near as well. Besides, your boss's opinions are influenced by impressions he gets from his assistant.

Managing the Boss from a Distance

Suppose your boss isn't down the hall at all, but resides in corporate headquarters. When you see your boss once every four or five weeks, each meeting becomes a presentation—sometimes feared the way General Electric field people describe CEO Jack Welch: "You've heard about the neutron bomb? Well, when Neutron Jack visits, he leaves the building standing, but the people are dead." When Maximum Tamale is about to descend on you, don't panic. Plan.

The meeting, if properly planned and implemented, can send the boss home invigorated, with a fresh sense of his own potency and a first-hand impression of the really solid job the people in the field are doing (so unlike the backbiting at headquarters). And the local manager establishes the same sense of closeness experienced by head office guys who rub shirtsleeves with His Corporate Eminence daily.

Plan the whole encounter, consulting and informing the boss (or more likely, his staff) at every stage. This includes advance information on the visitor's personal tastes in food, drink, lodging, and recreation.

A decent regard for small things makes everything else that happens more pleasant.

And so, corporate climber, as you learn to manage your boss, you'll be learning to avoid the dangerous crevasses.

You'll understand the sage advice of Jack McCarthy, former New York cop who now works in an executive suite:

Rule Number One: He's the boss.
Rule Number Two: Go back and re-read Rule Number One.

"I learned this by dealing with my father," McCarthy says.

PART
——————— 4

That Healthy Push from Below— Auditing the Climb Team

CHAPTER 10

Halfway Up the Slope: A Personal View

YOU'RE no longer one of the pack. You're clearly out in front with your own group following. You're in middle-management—at the treeline on the mountain.

The vegetation is scrubby. The trails are narrower (fewer climbers so you don't need such a wide path). You're out among the rocks, more dangerous to climb, more visible to your competitors. (As Fred Glass, former chairman of New York Port Authority, sees it: "The higher you climb, the more exposed your assets.") The trail isn't marked, you can get lost.

Now that you're halfway up, planning has become much more important. As a branch manager, division head, or chief of a subsidiary, you must know where you're going with your unit and how to get there. Further, make sure your subordinates plan and follow plans.

As a business colonel, you're out in front. What you do (and how you do it) will be instantly noted and long remembered by corporate generals above and captains and lieutenants below. Both upper and lower will be quick to note shoddy plans or indifferent leadership. Ambitious climbers below will be quick to see themselves as your successor. You must move *up* or *off* the slope.

To be a visible leader, you must also set the pace for other unit managers at your level. If the other colonels are aiming at six percent growth, try for eight percent. If they're aiming at eight percent, figure on ten. Be the pacesetter that others watch.

In middle management, you've got to watch your peers more. If they're doing something you're not, evaluate it. See how it works for you. Doing your own job alone is no longer enough.

Nor can plans exist in a vacuum. You must present your unit's plans to your boss at company headquarters. First gather facts. Ask key questions. Put it all on paper: (1) the objectives or problem, (2) the method of solving or reaching it, (3) the time it takes to get there. The reasons why your unit can do it. Be prepared to summarize this plan verbally before an executive committee—and be particularly sharp for the vital Q & A at the end.

Working with Superiors

As a middle manager, you have fewer superiors to worry about—but the brass you report to is powerful. In boss relations, remember the army advice about going on guard: "I will walk my post from flank to flank and salute all bastards of higher rank."

Think in larger terms. Don't get involved in petty matters, think concept: where you're going, competition in the marketplace.

Even if you didn't rise through marketing, you're a marketer now. If your unit's output doesn't sell, you're in deep trouble.

Delegate more, so you'll have time to plan and think. Be certain you have the right people in the right places to carry out your unit's objectives. (This means more work. Earlier in your climb, you became acquainted with the 12-hour day. Welcome to the middle-manager's 14- to 15-hour day. You've moved up to a more demanding job that's voraciously hungry for your time and attention.)

You'll face real demands as you climb to the higher reaches. Your time commitments will become severe. You'll be thrust into more social responsibilities at a juncture when you have less discretionary time—since you're taking on more responsibility for other people. This seesaw conflict will war within you.

Re-assess the Trail Ahead

That's the drill at mid-slope. Before you dig into the details, it's a good time to look at where you've been and where you're going—to answer this realistic question: "Do I want to continue straight up? Or do I really prefer a side plateau?"

Midpoint is also the time to pause and ask:
What's the future of your industry?
Your company?

Do comments about your company and industry in *Business Week, Forbes,* and *Fortune* sound like you're on a winning horse? Does your own industry press hold your business up as a leader? If not, why not?

By viewing your own strategy with as much objectivity as possible, you can better shape the years ahead. Some find this objectivity hard to conjure. Radison Wells, industrial engineering head of a metal fabricator, had worked hard for three years putting in measured time standards for hourly people and engineered standards for materials and waste. He was good at his job.

One day I talked with his firm's general manager, took away background material, and came to a horrible conclusion: This unit was in serious trouble. The company's two prime customers were shrinking.

When I next met Wells, I explained that while he had done the greatest job in setting standards, his company was going broke. He was dumbfounded. He had no idea. This is the sort of problem you better recognize in your company or industry.

Evaluate the Organization, too

Remember *organization,* oversimplified, is the process of matching people of varying talents in a structure that optimizes achievement of goals. Take a look at the two to four layers of management above you. Write out a short evaluation of people holding these posts. Are they turned on, motivated, educated people dedicated to moving up? How long have they stayed in their current jobs? Who at this level left recently to go to other companies?

Has top management encouraged the development of any of these people? Have they suggested transferring you to other functions to broaden your knowledge? Or do you each plod along taking the line of least resistance? What about the organization structure? Are there six levels between you and the CEO? If so, it'll be difficult for your accomplishments to be noted by Mr. Big.

Are your chances better in the spokes-of-the wheel structure where many people report to one person? On Sears' retail side, as many as 25 A-store managers report to one group manager. The operation of Sears' retail stores has become so standardized, the elements so well known, that the group head only spends time on the few stores having problems.

Is this structure better for your advancement? Or are you better with the traditional pyramid? You should know the answer. If you're miscast, midpoint is the time to consider a change.

Evaluate Age vs. Achievement

Look at your age vs. achievement vs. ambition. Somewhere between 35 and 45, your career passes through a psychic sound barrier. Before 35, you're prepared to conquer the world and become president of your company. After 45, objectives and ambitions become more modified. On the far side of 45, you may well become more philosophical: "Well, I might become the regional sales head but after all I do have a good job now. They're paying me well. It's a good group. They have a great retirement program."

Not only should you evaluate what the company has been doing for you at mid-slope, but be aware: The company is evaluating you, too.

At Procter & Gamble or Honeywell or GE, top management makes its evaluation of rising management: Which men and women can go all the way and which have no chance. Cards are sorted and coded—literally.

Be aware of this, too, as an employer interviewing applicants. If you get a 40-or-over candidate from a large up-or-out company, you can assume he or she has been sorted out as top management material. (This may make no difference in the job you're recruiting for—in fact, in some cases it might be an advantage. You may already have a full complement of stars and stand in need of a good worker—not another prima donna and the problems that go with it.)

Re-evaluate Your Homelife

When you started the climb, you acknowledged the rigorous course. You accepted the impact on your homelife. On mid-slope, it's time to evaluate it again. After all, personal happiness is your ultimate goal.

Do you really want to continue the battle to become the CEO? Or would you really rather spend more time working in the garden? Perhaps you're interested in teaching part-time in nearby schools? Or concentrating on weird antics and peregrinations of your teenagers? You know: those semi-strangers around the house.

I visited the home of a CEO of a Midwest steel company regularly and got to know his son Roger. Then later at Ravinia, the fascinating evening concert spot north of Chicago, I bumped into Roger, a freshman at Dartmouth.

"Roger, have you had a good summer?" I asked. "What are you doing for excitement? How is your dad?"

Roger gulped and paused, then said: "Well, I haven't really seen Dad all summer—he's been so busy. He did get home once or twice but with an awful lot of homework. So I've had a good summer, but I really didn't get a chance to see my father. I guess he's fine."

And as Katherine Graham, CEO at The Washington Post Company, points out, these hard decisions—work vs. homelife—must now be made by an increasing number of women as well.

"To get to the top, women—like men—will simply have to put their careers and companies first for some part of their working lives," Graham said.

"Their families and children may suffer to some degree, as may their friendships. I know mine have. But men in power have always been willing to pay this price. When women are equally committed, they will reach the top of the pyramid.

"Finally, power demands dedication, hard work, and, in most cases, long hours at the job. This presents enormous conflicts to women who want to combine high-power careers with husbands and families. The trade-offs are enormous. So are the accompanying guilt and even agony for those who leave children at home or in day-care centers, or unfinished work at their desks.

"Women will get to the top and gain power the same way men do, not with artificial aids or special deals, but by working harder, knowing more, taking risks, and being better than their competitors, male and female. Today's generation not only has the freedom to succeed, but the freedom to choose where success shall lie."

So, corporate climber, that's the problem. Is a variation on that satisfactory? Have you a better way to do both? Many successful corporate climbers do have good home lives as well. But you really must work at it. It won't just happen. That's one more task to be accomplished along with the other challenges ahead.

Hundreds of midpoint climbers re-assess their objectives at this stage. Do you want to stay on the express, or change to the local, or get off the track? It's time to know—really know—the answer.

ERRATIC GENIUS

All right. Now that you've elected to continue the climb, remember this: In middle management, you often must learn to work *with*— usually for—an erratic genius. This is a difficult (but usually rewarding) situation. So be prepared for it.

For example, Bill Paley at CBS is an emotional guy. He makes judgments on the spur of the moment and then the next day calls up and undoes them. But the record shows he was usually right. Glamor was often the overriding criterion for his decisions. He was always trying to prejudge how the public would react to a performer, a show, an idea. That's a terribly difficult thing—judging what the public will do. He was also a genius at persuading talent to come with his network. For all these reasons, working for Bill Paley has often been called difficult.

My own erratic genius experience was Roy Ingersoll. Ingersoll Steel and Disc Company in Galesburg, Illinois, made farm equipment components—the discs in harrows farmers use to cut up fields before planting. Long before I went to work there, Roy Ingersoll and his brother Steve sold their company to Borg-Warner, based in Chicago.

I worked for Roy Ingersoll, who continued to head up Borg-Warner's Ingersoll division. He built Ingersoll up bigger and bigger, and finally rose to the presidency of Borg-Warner.

(Later Roy's son Bob became CEO—not a "thanks, Dad" job either.

The versatile Bob Ingersoll later became Ambassador to Japan, then deputy Secretary of State, and was chairman of the University of Chicago. Quite a contrast to his uncle Steve, Roy's brother. Steve decided to cross western cowponies with Arabian stallions to get the best characteristics of each. He bought hundreds of Arabian horses at great expense, sent them to the Ingersoll's ranch in Montana, and waited for the miracle. What he got was disaster. The Arabian horses broke their legs on railroad crossings. They fell in gopher holes. He lost two-thirds of the herd before he gave up.)

Roy Ingersoll was tough, demanding, and often a bastard. Yet we loved old Roy—most of the time. A popular man, he became head of the State Republican Committee and of the prestigious Chicago Club. He played one middle-manager against another—mischievously. He enjoyed conflict.

He kept three sets of books on the operations. As sales VP, I'd go into his office. He'd wheel around and pull this book out and say:

"Jim, our sales are just miserable. Manufacturing costs on these furnaces (or tubs or washing machines or whatever) are very reasonable. But we're not getting enough money for the product. Besides, our volume is terrible. We ought to get twice as much volume."

"Jim, you're doing a miserable job. I just don't think you're functioning at all."

I'd go away. Then Ray Sullivan, the production VP, would come in. Ingersoll'd wheel around, get a *different* set of books, and say:

"My God, Ray, we're getting as high a price as anybody in the industry for these tubs (or stoves or furnaces). Look at our volume! But my God, we can't make them at this price. We're losing our shirts. Look at the cost of raw materials. Why don't you do something better, Ray? Maybe I ought to get somebody else on your job."

The first time this happened to me, I was shattered. The second time: I began to see the pattern. Then I conferred with Ray Sullivan (the value of staying on good terms with your peers!) and found out Ingersoll had three sets of books. So his performance lost some of its bite. But none of its emotion. He screamed and yelled regularly.

I don't recommend this behavior. But geniuses get away with it because they're good. Besides, even if an erratic genius isn't that good, he's the boss—for the moment. With an E.G., you must be constantly prepared for bizarre experiences.

One day, I noted applicants showing up for interviews with Ray Sullivan. He usually found a spot for them—shipping department, or somewhere. I asked Ray where they were coming from.

"Roy Ingersoll gets stopped speeding on the outer drive," Ray said. "So he asks if the cop has kids who need a job. Result! Roy doesn't get a ticket. We get another employee."

Ingersoll, often a disruptive presence in the office, came back from Camelback Inn in Arizona late one Monday to keep a golf date with the Sears CEO at 11 a.m. Tuesday. But he decided to come first to his downtown Michigan Avenue office to review the latest reports. He got caught up in rush traffic, came rushing in screaming "hold the elevators," and went through his papers, then vaulted into his car and went roaring down the outer drive.

On this frenzied day, he soon had a police car pulling him over. What could have been a routine traffic ticket soon escalated: He didn't have his driver's license. He told the cops: "This was a very critical day, I'm terribly sorry. I've lost everything. I wasn't thinking."

He made a convincing case with an empty wallet. The officer told him to be more careful.

Then Ingersoll got back in his car and pulled out around the squad car—but not far enough since he knocked the rear fender off the police car! This time they took him to the station house.

To those of us who knew Ingersoll, this was the funniest story of all time—to be retold when he *wasn't* there, of course.

Value of Military Experience

To learn to scourge a gigantic beast forward as a middle-manager, you can't beat military experience. In 1942, I got into Air Force production control as a stepping stone from Borg-Warner (where I'd worked my way up pretty fast as a young whippersnapper).

General K. B. Wolfe, in command at Wright Field, Ohio, bought airplane engine fuel pumps from Borg-Warner. General Wolfe often sat down with Roy Ingersoll to talk about ways to improve those pumps. One day the General said to me: "You know, Jim, there's a war on. How come you're not involved?"

"I am," I said. "I'm in the reserves—in chemical warfare."

Right away, he saw his chance. He painted a dire picture of chemical warfare compared to real contributions of the air force.

"Why don't you transfer to the Air Force at Wright Field?" he said. "We'll put you on active service as a first lieutenant." I agreed.

Getting in was easy—getting out was impossible. I spent the next four years trying to get over to Europe. But the B-29s held me back.

Early in the war, President Roosevelt said to Air Chief Hap Arnold: "We're getting plastered all over the place. The Japanese are beating the hell out of us. We must take the pressure off. Can't we get some distraction? When do we get those B-29s?"

General Wolfe was assigned to research and develop B-29s. We were frozen. We made arrangements to fly a wing of B-29s to India so they could go over The Hump and bomb Japanese points. I did my damnedest to get in that wing bound for India.

"Stay where you are to run production," Wolfe told me.

I soon became head of radar and worked with General Jake Harmon, Wolfe's executive officer, in supervising 300 officers, 300 enlisted men, and 3000 civilians. I also learned what not to do in consulting— from a consulting firm, MacDonald & Company, and its project manager, Jim Sutherland. Sutherland went into General Wolfe's office, put his feet on the desk, and said: "General, you don't know what the hell you're doing." (If we had Sutherland in our organization today, we'd fire the bastard—quick.)

Wolfe turned 16 colors. Sutherland *was* brilliant. He pointed out what was right and wrong in production or supply. ("The order you placed for oxygen masks will equip all the people of China and 16 other nations for 75 years.")

He made the General look like an ass—regularly.

Finally, the problem got severe and the generals got Sutherland inducted into the Air Force as a first lieutenant where he could be court-martialed. It did not affect him. He was never court-martialed. He went right on. Brilliant, but abrasive.

Sutherland did plant a significant ambition within me, though: To become a consultant and say what I believed. I did resolve to do it more tactfully.

Military Strategy in Management

You also learn how to transfer wartime experience to the business battlefield. Lesson number one: A frontal assault is seldom the best strategy in trying to dislodge a well-entrenched competitor.

Flanking. A combat army is strongest at points it expects to attack or be attacked—less secure on its flanks and rear. Its weak spots, therefore, are natural points to attack.

The aggressor may pretend to attack the strong side—then launch the real attack at the weak side or rear. This turning maneuver catches defenders offguard. Flanking attacks are particularly attractive to an aggressor with fewer resources. If he cannot overwhelm the defender with brute strength, he can out-maneuver him.

There are two types of flanking attacks: geographical and segmented.

Geographical. The aggressor spots areas where the opponent is not performing well. (IBM's rivals set up strong branches in medium- and small-sized cities relatively neglected by IBM.)

Segmented. The aggressor spots market needs not served by leaders. German and Japanese automakers did not compete with American automakers by producing large flashy automobiles (supposedly the preference of American buyers). Instead, they identified unserved customers who wanted small fuel-efficient cars. They filled the niche, and to Detroit's surprise, American taste for smaller cars grew to a substantial market.

By discovering the light beer market, Miller Brewing Company vigorously developed an unserved gap—propelling itself from seventh to second place in five years.

Instead of a bloody battle between two or more companies trying to serve the same market, flanking leads to a fuller coverage of the market's varied needs.

By discovering needs and serving them, flanking is more likely to succeed than a frontal attack—borne out in military history. Of the world's most important conflicts (including more than 280 campaigns), only six produced decisive results with a head-on assault.

Encirclement. Pure flanking capitalizes on a gap in the enemy's existing market coverage. Encirclement disperses this coverage so the enemy's differentiation (and therefore brand loyalty) is diluted.

For several years, Seiko has been acquiring distribution and overwhelming competitors and consumers with an enormous variety of models. In the United States, Seiko offers some 400 models. But its marketing clout is backed by the 2300 models it makes and sells worldwide.

Bypass Attack. This means avoiding the arch-enemy and attacking easier markets by diversifying (1) into related products or (2) into new geographical markets for your existing products.

Colgate has always struggled in the shadow of Procter & Gamble. In heavy-duty detergents, P & G's Tide outsold Colgate's Fab nearly 5 to 1. In dishwashing liquids, P & G had almost twice Colgate's share. In soaps, too, Colgate trailed far behind.

When David Foster took over as CEO, Colgate (despite its $1.3 billion in sales) still had reputation of a stodgy marketer. By 1979, Foster had transformed Colgate into a $4.3 billion conglomerate, perfectly capable of challenging P & G.

Foster recognized that the head-on battle with P & G was futile:

"They outgunned us 3 to 1 at the store level," he said, "and had three researchers to our one."

Foster's strategy: Maintain Colgate's lead abroad and bypass at home by diversifying into markets ignored by P & G. He arranged acquisitions in textiles and hospital products, cosmetics, sporting goods, and food products.

The outcome: Instead of being underdog to P & G in about half of its business, Colgate was either comfortably placed against P & G or didn't face it at all in three-fourths of its business.

Guerrilla Warfare.   This involves small intermittent attacks on the opponent's territories to harass and demoralize and eventually secure a limited victory.

The guerrilla uses both conventional and unconventional means: selective price cuts, supply interferences, executive raids, intense promotional bursts, and assorted legal actions (an effective way to harass).

A Seattle-based distributor, supplying beer in Alaska by ship, was upset when West Germany's Oetker Group got the state to grant it 75 percent tax credit for 10 years to establish beer production there.

The distributor slapped a lawsuit on Oetker, charging that the tax incentive was unconstitutional.

Oetker eventually won in the courts, but the four-year delay crippled its hope of capitalizing on the pipeline construction boom. After operating it for just 30 months, Oetker closed its Anchorage brewery.

Military principles demonstrate ways to attack another company or defend against an aggressor. All too often companies resort to foolish head-on attacks and fortification defenses when more subtle strategies are available.

Middle-management is a good time to deepen your understanding of military strategy. Find weaknesses, exploit them. But you must also out-maneuver competitors trying to do the same against you.

Entrepreneurs in Middle- Management

America, long the land of the entrepreneur, was born of an entrepreneur—Christopher Columbus.

Columbus approached his venture capitalist, Queen Isabella, with a strategic plan to exploit business opportunities in distant lands. Isabella's investment paid off handsomely—Spain gained a dominant hold on new world markets well ahead of its competitors.

For Columbus, the tale was less happy. A poor manager, old Chris was replaced in 1499 as administrator of the Indies and died several years later, frustrated, humiliated, and looking for work.

But the entrepreneur has returned full cycle.

"Entrepreneurship will be the major impetus of the decade immediately ahead of us—and what's ahead is terrifically exiciting," says Donald C. Burr, an entrepreneur who is founder and president of People Express Airlines. Burr, 42, is one of today's new entrepreneurial superheroes.

Management officials of larger companies are often quoted these days: "What we want to head this division is an entrepreneur."

Trying to separate the fad word from the principle, a colleague asks: "Aren't entrepreneurs those dedicated start-up operators with a bright idea who work in a basement 16 hours a day to launch a dream?"

Well, yes. What establishment companies are seeking (trying to have it both ways) is an organizational manager with the bright dedication and offbeat approaches of a true entrepreneur. They want a developmental person who cuts new trails—working within the established framework.

Is it possible to get an entrepreneurial mind in a corporate setting? It's difficult. The person grows up learning to conform with established practices and standards. Now you suddenly say: "You are on your own. Go." Sometimes it works.

The 3M Company, which makes some 84,000 products, is a corporate haven for entrepreneurs. The company goes along with wild offbeat ideas. Some hit it big. 3M awards corporate incentives to innovators—employees share in the profit of ventures they start, even long after they started another project.

Even giant IBM tore a page from the entrepreneur's book to get into the exploding home computer business. IBM freed a group of employees from corporate red tape, set them up in Boca Raton, Florida, and gave them the resources to design a personal computer in a year's time. They did, and the computer they created has dominated the personal computer market.

Entrepreneurship doesn't always succeed. But when it works, it works at the middle-management level. After all, you must learn the rules before you break them.

And I do endorse the idea of less constriction and less straitjacket thinking—coupled with encouragement for experimentation. It's good not only in getting results but in psychological development of the individual.

A fellow or gal that feels freedom and is encouraged to take pride in work gets excited and tries.

Today, incentive systems are becoming much more geared to the entrepreneur. Westinghouse managers hold a specific financial stake in improving product quality. Each division has a fund where product service costs are charged against profits.

The formula: The better the product, the lower its service costs, the higher the division's profitability, the greater the manager's incentive compensation.

It'll be interesting to see how far entrepreneurship goes with today's instant computers all over the place. The guy who moves out on his own isn't going to get too far before the numbers reflect results or lack thereof. So the emphasis will be on shorter and shorter payout for new ideas.

But I still say an entrepreneurial mind in middle-management can put you ahead of the pack. Just make sure you work for a CEO that gives you the latitude to try new things.

When you're encouraging entrepreneurs among *your* people, you'll view the problem differently. Don't build a compensation plan that rewards the entrepreneur so much he makes a bundle of money by screwing his buddies. That has happened. A few years back, Gillette threw out its whole compensation structure because it worked against the organization.

Don't create warring duchies. You still want to conduct a harmonious management orchestra.

THE MANAGEMENT ORCHESTRA

William V. McDonnell, sales/marketing VP at Honeywell's Residential Division, compares management's role to conducting an orchestra.

"The people you manage—the instrumentalists—are either entrepreneurs or objective managers," he says.

Understand the difference.

Entrepreneurs work on the future. They identify new opportunities
and inject new dynamics. They (1) create strategies and new product
opportunities to help you grow, (2) provide insight into our future, and
(3) search for new and different ways to run the business.

They visualize major changes and related gains that move us into a
whole new level of accomplishment—and take risks to achieve these
gains.

They often lack patience and persistency. They move around the
business rapidly—oftentimes leaving one area before the work is finished. They sometimes disrupt the organization.

Objective managers work to keep you profitable today. They do a
balanced job of efficiently carrying out well-developed and proved operations. They develop small gains, minor changes, and economies.
They dislike anything other than modest risks.

They marshal resources to accomplish well-established long-
accepted goals. They keep people functioning smoothly and working
well together. They maximize profitability today.

No successful individual is all entrepreneur or all objective manager.
We all lean one way or the other. The senior middle-manager must
bob and weave between the two extremes to maintain profitability.

To insure profitable growth, keep both types active and functioning,
but not as much as 50 percent entrepreneur, certainly. That would be
more development than the organization could handle.

But make certain there are entrepreneurs among your managers.
Maintain an atmosphere where each managerial type wins something.
This requires orchestration. Choreograph exhilarating wins and stress-
ful losses to keep all managers functioning close to their potential.

Each type has weaknesses and blind spots. Each also has valuable
input.

An objective manager's style may fail when business environment
is undergoing major change. The American business scene is littered
with many such cases—people too devoted to tried-and-true to function with change.

Adjustment to change requires vision and courage—ability to live
constantly with risk. The conductor must encourage visionary managers when they appear.

On the other hand, entrepreneurs can harm business, too, by spending recklessly, ignoring necessary details, and squandering assets on unproductive investments. '

Senior managers must allow each type to function up to the point where the good outweighs the harm. This requires effective blending. Entrepreneurs must dominate during times of rapid adjustment to significant environmental change. Objective management must dominate during consolidation periods.

Entrepreneurs initiate strategic adjustments required for successful growth—sometimes even for survival.

Then, starting immediately, new business strategies must be fully institutionalized as operating philosophies, This takes time. Objective management, rather than entrepreneurship, is critical to success during integration periods.

Successful companies undulate in long cyclical waves between entrepreneurship and objective management.

Senior management must be both entrepreneur and objective manager—and the more we lean one way, the more we must be able to work with our opposite number, Honeywell's McDonnell says.

We must sometimes act like the consummate entrepreneur and sometimes like the most dedicated apostle of management control. As the leader, remember to set a tempo the organization can follow. If you break the baton in frustration, the music stops, and a new conductor steps up to the podium.

Encourage Entrepreneurship

Encouragement of entrepreneurship stimulates change and inventiveness. But keep an eye on the *kind* of entrepreneurship you spawn.

At Marathon Paper, we studied productivity and found one plant manager exceeding industry standards by 30 percent in turning pulp into paper. We were mystified. He wasn't using that much more pulp.

So how could he turn out more paper? Finally, we asked him how he did it.

"I go down to the feed store," he said, "and collect brown paper sacks that feed-grain and chemicals come in. I take all those sacks and throw them in the pulp beater. As a result, I come out with more product."

So when you encourage entrepreneurship, sometimes it comes up in strange forms—like seeding the pulp beater or too much backward integration.

Mark Twain said when a man reaches 70 "he knows enough not to frolic with mince pie after midnight." Ditto when a manager reaches mid-slope, he or she must be savvy about backward integration.

Goddard Lieberson, a violinist who rose to head up CBS' records division, did well selling records. Then he decided it would be neat to sell instruments as well—so he bought a drum company. This was a disaster. He couldn't make the drums loud enough. In its 1983 annual report, CBS discussed "reducing operating losses" and failing to "meet profit objectives" in its musical instruments division.

Moral: Being your own supplier sounds neat—you make his profit *and* yours. But there is no reason to think you're gonna be an instant expert in your supplier's business and it often fails.

In the 1960s, Ford opened its own tire factory—but soon gave it up. Management finally determined that its main business was making automobiles. So backward integration is a mine field. As leasing CEO Bob Esseks said about an unsuccessful middle-management ploy: "You know there are two kinds of toilets. The kind that flush slowly down and out of sight. And the kind where it's a straight drop down to the sewer. *That's* the kind we were on."

Importance of Decision-Making

When you reach mid-slope, you should be a seasoned decision-maker—a quality you'll need more and more topside. Economic historians are quite critical of non-decision-makers. Wall Street Week emcee Louis Rukeyser made this pronouncement (with his self-satisfied smirk) about White House fence-sitting:

> *Richard Nixon and Jimmy Carter both were guilty of the same crime—terminal vacillation. They were all over the map on all these issues. Nixon's economic program consisted of the most spectacular reversals since Christine Jorgenson. Carter carried on a four-year sequence of non-stop debates with himself—in which, incidentally, both sides lost.*

Again, you as manager must decide something over nothing. Even if you're wrong, it's a lesser ill than endless agonizing. Often, a poor decision-maker is a manager without an action plan.

The CEO of a large plastics manufacturing company hired Jared Bakerson, a CPA from an accounting firm, as financial officer. Two years later, the CEO said Jared Bakerson "wasn't working out."

"In the long run, he is not what I want. He's done an adequate job but he's not facing up to decisions. He's a damned grandma. I don't care what you say, he says 'let's think about it.' He wants more information all the time. A manager has to make decisions with information that's available. Jared makes me crazy."

What the CEO was saying is this: Jared had not developed the management mind. He was promoted beyond his level of competence. He was a good accountant and he liked to keep all the numbers but he simply didn't have the capacity to think broadly and decide where things were going and make decisions.

You never have *all* the information. So you have to make a decision without it all. But, of course, over time you must make the right decisions in *most* cases. Management is a ruthless procedure, not a lightweight undertaking.

A financial fellow who moves into broader management must possess a duality. He must be specific when it comes to financial matters but must also take the broader view.

The common denominator in business is numbers. A person that can backtrack numbers and figure out what caused them to come down—that's a valuable contributor.

Typical accountants can't do that. They just say "this is what the numbers are" and they can't think beyond that. They do not have the management mind.

Negotiate from Strength

At lower levels, you arrange job interviews. In middle-management, you negotiate for position. There's a vast difference. When possible (and it often is), negotiate from strength. My air force colleague, Lieutenant Colonel Billy Billington, told me that right after World War II:

"Don't go back to Borg-Warner without other jobs lined up as well."

When I started following his advice, I found I'd racked up quite a reputation as a young hot-shot—plant manager at 27 and sales VP at 28. So before going back to my alma mater at Borg-Warner, I went to see three management consulting firms—including Booz Allen.

Then I went to Roy Ingersoll at Borg-Warner who said: "Jim, I'd love to have you back. Of course, you realize a lot of things have happened. I moved Anderson in as sales vice-president, reporting to me. But we're so glad to have you back. We brought in John Bigbee under Anderson to run the West Pullman plant. But there is a key role for you working for Bigbee."

"Wait a minute, Roy," I said, "I ran the Kalamazoo plant. I don't want to come back as a third-layer flunkie. If you make me manufacturing VP of all of the Ingersoll divisions, I'll come back."

"Jim, that's a tremendous job," he said. "A terribly important job. That job would require approval of Mr. Blood, the Borg-Warner chairman. Let me work on that and see what I can do."

In the meantime, I went back to see John Burns, managing partner at Booz Allen. He listened to my job history and said: "When you go back to see what Roy's got to offer—go back with the knowledge that I'll guarantee you a job here if you want it."

This made a tremendous difference. I was in a catbird seat. Three weeks and I didn't hear from Roy, I called him.

"Gee, Jim, I just haven't been able to get to Mr. Blood, he's been terribly busy."

"Sounds like you don't want me back very much. I tell you what. As much as I love Borg-Warner, I'm going to go with Booz Allen."

I did. A year later, we did a survey for Borg-Warner. Our fellow in charge of the work, John Adam, told me over dinner: "I've been commissioned to pose a question to you. Roy Ingersoll wants to know if you'd come back as a manufacturing VP."

In one of the greatest satisfactions of my life, I said: "Go back and tell Roy Ingersoll he can take that vice-presidency and stick it." And remember: I loved Roy Ingersoll personally.

Evaluating the Job Offer

When you're negotiating for a middle-management job, the more you know about your prospective employer, the better. Work out your deal *before* you get on the job rather than *after*. If you cannot work the right deal with an erratic genius, don't take the job. It'll be hard enough under the best circumstances.

Evaluating a new job is difficult, but mighty important. I've seen many intelligent people make absolutely asinine moves from one corporation to another. Remember what Ann Landers says: "Never take on an imperfect mate that you hope to reform!" Same with a company. You have two chances of reforming the E.G.: slim and none. Get your agreement in advance.

"But I don't have objectivity about myself!" a burned job-changer told me recently.

In that case, get yourself an objective consultant—attorney, friends, uninvolved executive, management advisor. Give your confidant the facts and listen. It works.

Gardner Barker came from Pepsodent to invigorate Simoniz. (You recall the famous slogan: *Motorists wise Simoniz.*) Barker built Simoniz back up to a roaring success. Then the Rich family, heavy stockholders in the company, put young (about 30) George Rich in charge of the business.

Barker told George Rich:

"Look, two of us can't run the business. If you want to run it, fine. I'll get out."

So Barker started evaluating an offer from Gillette. Gillette was anxious to have him. They offered him all kinds of inducements. Barker asked me to help decide.

Me: "What specific job did they offer you?"

He: "Well, I come in as vice-president and I'm going to be in charge of administrative development."

Me: "Come on, are they going to give you razor blades or another product line? Are you going to be head of marketing?"

He: "That will come. They told me not to worry about it. Within a year or two I'll be in a position like that."

Me: "Gardy, don't take it. You're heading for real trouble. Your role is not defined. Other key executives are going to resent you stepping on their toes. You have no clear-cut mandate. It's not promising."

He turned it down—even though the money and stock options were out of this world. Then he talked with Bob Smallwood head of Lipton.

"You come in and we'll make you tea division manager," Smallwood said. "Later you can take my place."

A specific job. Barker took it. Three years later, Smallwood retired and Barker took over Lipton. He built Lipton into the most successful company in the 100-unit Unilever structure. In Unilever's annual meeting in England, Barker was cited as the prize manager: biggest growth and biggest profits.

He then put Lipton into dried soup and drove Campbell's out of the product category. For years Lipton had the dominant position with its dehydrated onion soup.

Not getting a specific job offer is a clear and present danger. Another frequent error: seeing the money as the *sine qua non* of your job-change decision.

Don't get into discussions about money until you've been over all the details and you've decided you fit—or the candidate fits, depending on which side of the desk you're on. When you decide, it's just what you want, then talk about money.

Evaluate a job as a challenging and exciting task first. You get into all kinds of peculiar twists if you don't.

Don't Neglect People-Mingling

David Ogilvy, an old acquaintance and a most successful rascal, always advises going to the subordinate's office rather than having a subordinate in yours. ("When you summon them, they're tense. They don't know what they have done. Better to go to his or her office unannounced.")

I agree. Sit down with them and bring up your points. You get a lot more done that way. They're more at home. You sense little things going on or not. Watch how they react to their own subordinates.

When they come in the home office, they're polite. They watch their language. You are not getting the real person.

In *Industry Week,* Westinghouse chairman Douglas Danforth reported "no compunctions" about picking up the phone to talk to a divisional manager four levels down. And he pledges to spend 50 percent of his business hours away from the office, meeting with Westinghouse employees around the world.

Will his interest in operations inevitably turn to interference?

"I am very careful when I am visiting a plant or a division not to issue any mandates or to change the direction of the division," emphasizes Danforth. "The purpose of the visits is to get a feel of how they are doing and what their concerns are."

In that same spirit, Danforth solicits counsel from the company's customers. "I ask them: 'What can we do to improve our relationship with you?' "

The Westinghouse chairman is convinced that people like doing business—and perhaps will do *more* business—with people they *know.*

And production employees work better when they *know* the CEO. Says R. L. Radt, president of Wausau Paper Mills: "When I come into work, I go into the plant, walk around, and talk to people. And I've come to really enjoy those impromptu conversations. That the guy on the plant floor operating some machine knows more about that piece of equipment than anybody. If you want to find out how it works, you've got to ask him. And when the boss takes time to notice employees, they really appreciate it."

Yet this is an area CEOs feel is still lacking in middle-management, according to an *Industry Week* survey.

Asked if their middle-managers *deal effectively with subordinates,* 43 percent said "yes" and only 4.5 percent said "no." However, a majority—52.3 percent—said "sometimes, but not always."

Many executives confirmed: If they could improve a single characteristic in middle-managers, it would be the ability to communicate with, and relate to, subordinates. (Grades for *dealing with bosses* were slightly better; 54.5 percent said mid-level managers are usually effective in boss relations.)

Enough Control—But Not Too Much

A work-oriented middle-manager who expects mistakes is much better equipped than the politics-oriented manager who tries to cover up mishaps, says Richard White, general manager of Solar Additions, Inc., Cambridge, New York.

"But, unfortunately, most people get too involved in politics and not enough involved in doing their job," White says. "Then when the inevitable mistake occurs, they're much more vulnerable.

"Expect mistakes. Learn from them. But don't turn up the political knob to try to salvage them. I don't look over an employee's shoulder all the time. I can accept the fact that some of his actions will be wrong."

The effective employee works in a fear-free atmosphere. If you let people make mistakes, they'll go that extra mile, they will try harder, they'll be more venturesome. A company in that milieu will be more successful in the long run. The mistakes en route will be insignificant.

"Don't worry if the job's not done the way you'd do it," White says. "Look at the end product. Never go back and redraft letters your people write, if the message is there. If, on the other hand, the person cannot get the message across, he will have to learn or go."

View systems and policies as guidelines—every company needs a roadmap. But don't overcontrol. When you impose your thoughts and ideas on somebody else, enterprise is stifled.

Sure, you need control over your people. But if you over-control, you're never giving the people confidence to flex their muscles. You won't build as strong a team. If you've got to err one way or the other, under-control.

Some advisors say it's easier to remove people-controls than to install them. I disagree. Better not to have controls in the first place, unless you really need them. When it comes to financial controls that prevent loss and protect assets, don't stint yourself. But with people-controls, don't put something in place and then tear it down.

So what do we know about you as the middle-manager? You're a special person with achievement behind you and aspiration ahead. To make this a stepping stone rather than mid-career crisis, you must develop a different relationship with bosses and employees. Become a skilled motivator. Think in larger strategic terms about management. Learn when *not* to be one of the boys, particularly in after-hours grousing.

Above all, don't get complacent. You're CEO material. You're not there yet. But you're earmarked for greatness if your desire-to-do still matches your energy and ability.

CHAPTER 11

Developing the Team—Unhooking the Losers

On personnel development, Dr. Samuel Johnson—the sage of the coffee houses—delivered this classic opinion:

"Much can be made of a Scotsman—if caught young."

Good tip to the corporate climber assembling a team. You must select your people carefully, evaluate their performance regularly, and let them know how they're doing—good, bad, or so-so. Then you must surgically and systematically unhook the drones that are slowing up the mission.

(Never think you can eliminate the unhooking—no matter how expert your selection, no matter how diligent your training. There will inevitably be travelers who're miscast, or who became miscast via their own change of mission or who find they cannot keep up with shifting priorities of the expedition.)

First you need to start with good people.

Don't Be Afraid to Hire Good People

Hire people who specialize in areas you *don't* specialize in. Keep good people moving up—so you can move up.

A department head of an Iowa-based manufacturing company was afraid that if he hired somebody good, it'd show him up. So he hired the biggest non-entity he could find. This made him look bad, not good. It kept him from promotion. No one could take over *his* job.

It works at higher levels, too. One company president wouldn't let a plant manager become manufacturing head because he hadn't groomed anybody to take the plant job. He was afraid to risk production in this critical plant. I've seen that happen dozens of times.

So train your own replacement. In fact, train two. You'll get five times more productivity out of two in competition than one secure heir-apparent. Just as competition between companies is healthy, so is competition between individuals.

At General Electric, the chairman was ready to retire. His deputy chairman was a very able financial fellow. But the chairman didn't like this heir-apparentness. So he took three of his line heads and made them vice-chairmen also. Now he had four to choose from. He did that to create competition.

Citicorp has done it. Chase Manhattan did it. Complacency in the heir-apparent is only a minor part of the problem. Much worse: The rest of the people get discouraged. They don't have a shot at the top job. Productivity lags.

How Not to Hire an Assistant

One management study unearthed a common problem: The boss often hires a subordinate in his own image—rather than a subordinate that complements him. Avoid this mistake and you'll be ahead of 20 percent of your competitors.

Oscar Spandel is an engineer and he hires another engineer. He doesn't need another engineer. He needs a marketer to understand where the product should be sold. It happens an astounding number of times. (I even see it in marriages. People get divorced and remarry someone just like the mate they've put aside. I could name a dozen.)

Find out where your business weaknesses are. Bring in a counter ingredient. You've heard the advice: "Hire someone smarter than you are." To that I add: "Yes, smarter—in different areas."

A large bus line's go-go division head shot from the hip. When he got promoted to a higher post, he hired his spitting image as a replacement. This made other managers unhappy. In addition, he couldn't decide what to do with this hotshot assistant after he got him.

The net effect: He doubled his weaknesses. He created problems among his peers. What he needed was a planner who analyzed problems and mapped out solutions. He didn't need another cheerleader. He realized it later—and fired him. What a waste of time and effort for both!

One California consultant believes you should redesign the job specs for each new hiring situation—and his comments make sense:

> *Before hiring cat-sitter, carpenter or controller: redesign the job in practical terms as it should be done now. Don't be governed by the previous jobholder. Do not assume duties will remain the same. Instead of writing out one of those pompous-sounding job descriptions, simply list, precisely, what the person will do all day. You're looking at the situation now, not as it might have been.*

> *By using these methods, you'll hire the most profitable employees. And if you treat your present gang right, you'll have less hiring to do.*

Select Key Subordinates with Care

Your career depends on it. If you're working through a personnel department, beat into their heads at the outset: "I'm depending on you to do an outstanding job, sooner rather than later." Insist upon seeing two to four candidates. Ask how they're going to unearth these candidates (headhunters, ads, or conducting the search themselves).

Remember: It's difficult to judge those inner motivations and wheels within wheels in the candidate's brain when he's sitting across the desk from you. The road to hire is strewn with judgment land-mines. Sure, department heads *want* to pick the right person—wrong hiring choices can be costly and time-consuming.

Throughout the entire evaluation process (whether with résumés, tests, or references) structure the answers toward a given set of questions. Get each source to corroborate or deny what the others said. Look hard at any disagreement. Don't view a negative as sufficiently strong to axe the candidate. But note it for further exploration.

Finally, after all else is done, pick a candidate whose personal chemistry fits yours. This is often the biggest flaw in hiring decisions.

Use All Aids to Sharpen Your Selection

To minimize hiring mistakes, start by examining the résumé (see Chapter 4) from the boss's standpoint. Read between the lines. A résumé is a balance sheet without liabilities. The best résumé does not always come from the best candidate. Too often it comes from the candidate who had the most jobs or hired a résumé writer.

Don't neglect diagnostic tests if they're permitted in your state. As you've seen earlier, tests do not provide go or no-go gauges. But they are valuable indicators. They often do suggest clues to be pursued elsewhere.

But when you get nonprofessionals making up their own tests, you get lot further from reality. My client, Bert Paddell, produced compounds for use in steel fabricating. He'd built the business from scratch over the years and was looking for a successor.

After we started sending him candidates, we were shocked: He was giving them his own "psychological test"—11 questions, all conundrums. (Sample: "What was Harry Truman's middle name? Answer: Truman had no middle name, only the initial S.)

Paddell refused to consider a candidate who didn't "pass" his "test." Frustrated at trying to explain the silliness of this approach, we asked Paddell himself to take a series of intelligence and personality tests. He only got partway through the intelligence tests, threw in the towel, and said: "No more."

We pointed out how poorly he'd done and why his answers didn't necessarily reflect his ability. Only then did he agree to give up his conundrum test.

Moral: Don't ask a test to make your decision any more than expecting a computer to do the same. Both are clue-finders, *not* decision-makers.

An additional technique I've found effective: Ask the candidate to write a five-to-ten-page paper on what his program would be if he becomes marketing manager (or product manager or whatever). This exercise will reveal (a) how much research he's done on the company, (b) how well he listened during the interview, and (c) how creative and practical he is in designing programs.

Finally, two heads are better than one, they say, and if you have any doubts about a candidate, ask a trusted colleague to do an interview as well. Just be careful not to turn it into a committee decision. Another view is also helpful when the candidate appears too good to be true and you are still looking for that Achilles' heel.

Old Bosses Are the Best Judges

Reference checking is extremely important—far and away the best evaluator of a candidate's strengths and weaknesses. References are better than one-on-one Q & A, better than the candidate's history, and better than psychological tests.

After all, you're talking to people who have seen the person in action. This is potentially invaluable. The difficulty, of course, is getting an *objective* story. It must be done verbally. Written letters are worthless.

Also be chary about using the candidate's own list of references. Unless he's a damned fool, he's only going to give positive endorsers.

Make up your own list of the candidate's peers or bosses—one or two levels up. If possible, sit down with these people in person. Ask well-thought-out questions that reveal how he got along with colleagues, what evaluations they've given your candidate, some typical examples of how the man or woman excelled on the job, and examples of disasters.

Make sure you thoroughly understand why the person left that company and under what circumstances.

Pose all these questions with a preliminary announcement that all comments are totally confidential. Also say: "If you describe the candidate's individual strengths and weaknesses, it will help the candidate. It will help us to shape programs to improve his weaknesses and capitalize on his strengths."

When you offer confidentiality, be sure to keep your word. Not long ago I talked with the chairman of a large bank about Hilton Doane, who had headed up the corporate loan department before he left to go to bank number two. Bank number two got into serious trouble because of previous problems—which were not Doane's doing. So Doane wanted to leave again to become CEO of a third bank—our client.

I talked to the chairman of bank number one on a confidential basis about Doane. Said the chairman:

"He was a sharp loan officer, totally dependable, persuasive in bringing in new clients. He'd been head of corporate loan for a year. But that year had been most unfortunate. Doane couldn't get along with key climbers coming up under him. He was considered arrogant by the retail department and trust department."

As a net result, the chairman had suggested a change—the real reason why Doane had left. We reported this to bank number three. Three weeks later the chairman of bank one called, sputtering: "So everything I say about a reference is confidential, is it? Hilton Doane just called and challenged my statement about how he got along with his peers and his subordinates."

What happened? Bank number three, when interviewing the candidate, had read our written reference aloud—in violation of the agreement. So conduct reference checks. But respect confidentiality. Otherwise the whole system breaks down.

Building Team Spirit

Early on, as a person manager, you must concentrate on building team spirit. Conquering the peaks ahead requires powerful collective efforts. A chain of climbers is only as strong as its weakest link.

Build this esprit de corps by holding frequent team meetings at the same time each week or month. Genuinely solicit advice and counsel. Urge them to achieve tough goals or targets. Point out accomplishments as well as frustrations. Get each member to report individually on his or her progress. Build pride.

In one-on-one talks, don't play favorites by revealing secrets selectively. Noses get out of joint. People feel discriminated against. Somebody will leak a secret to somebody else. Keep secrets to yourself or share with all. Never criticize one team member to another—it doesn't pay. Praise in public. Criticize in private. This classic rule is still quite sound.

Establish departmental bonuses to encourage one team member to volunteer to help a lagging peer. Recreate the tradition of the Three Musketeers: One for all and all for one.

When the team *does* achieve significant goals, celebrate. Let other departments know you're a winner. Brag a little. Hold a dinner party in a fancy restaurant. Put yourself out to let your team and the world know about your pride in group accomplishment.

Systematic Evaluation and Communication

Once you get your team in place, plan a program of individual employee evaluation—written and oral—for your sake as well as theirs. This is a vital part of management.

Evaluation is pleasant when your findings are good. When the findings are bad, communicate them just the same (here's where many managers drop the ball).

Start an on-going *Management by Objectives* program. Get each subordinate to spell out exactly what he or she plans to accomplish during the next year. Ask for numbers, but also for quality evaluators. Make damned sure they understand the objectives and that you approve their plans. And make sure their objectives support *your* overall plan.

Sit down quarterly, or at least semiannually, and talk to each person on progress vs. objectives. This gives you a track to run on in judging each individual—much better than how you feel about the person that specific Monday morning (seldom objective).

More importantly, this routine insures that you and Elmer have a frequent and frank discussion of how he is doing. Many times I've seen Elmer as he approaches his annual review date—thinking he's doing fine. Then the boss says:

"Elmer, you're totally inadequate! I'm going to have to replace you with somebody else."

Why the surprise? They haven't communicated. And sometimes the boss doesn't feel he could *do* anything about the problems if he *did* communicate.

Hold your evaluation meetings regularly. Then they lead logically to the year-end review. But remember year-end reviews and salary recommendations are supposed to be consistent.

I researched a company once and found 25 people had been promoted in the past year—but only five of them were high-rated in annual reviews. And the people that had been fired had beautiful annual reviews!

The Soap Company Contradiction

I found the same thing at a large soap company. The chairman asked me to speak on Management by Objectives at his annual executive meeting in Florida.

To prepare, I drew upon efficiency ratings of their top 200 people. To go with that, I got the personnel department to give me salary changes among the top 100 people in recent years. And all the promotions, additions, or dismissals.

I presented this in Florida—to the great amusement of the managers. There was absolutely *no* correlation between these annual effectiveness reports and promotions or raises.

This illustrates once again the widespread practice of avoiding unpleasant chores. The managers criticized people in writing and gave them salary increases face-to-face. They'd rather say: "George, try to do better next year. We're giving you an increase," instead of saying: "You're not hacking it. No raise until you improve."

Learn to make your people aware of shortcomings in a constructive way. Work with them. "By their subordinates, ye shall know them" is often an evaluation criterion in promoting managers to higher office.

If a good person has shortcomings, grant half the usual amount. And explain why. As one veteran manager told me recently:

"You can't tell him he's got a problem and give him the same amount. He doesn't get the message. Money gets the message across quickly."

One Minute's Not Nearly Enough

In employee evaluation, I again challenge the practicality of Blanchard and Johnson's *One Minute Manager.*

In the first place, a busy executive should sit down with his subordinate for evaluation when appropriate. But it can't be done in one minute—that's silly. To even suggest this seems to indicate that you haven't been in true-life business situations.

The bigger problem is that managers are just plain reluctant to tell a subordinate he's done poorly. And to tell the truth, how far you can go in telling a strong subordinate "you really booted that one." If he's an aggressive go-go guy, he can bounce back and say:

"Well, you just don't understand the facts, boss. You just don't know this happened and that happened and the other thing happened."

This can generate a nonproductive cat-and-dog fight. A manager who gets this reaction once or twice may be reluctant to repeat it. So day-to-day instant reprimand has its down side.

On the other hand, the aspiring manager better learn how to deal with the unpleasant part of periodic reviews. If you need to talk to an employee about an important shortcoming, don't say: "I'll wait until Monday." It doesn't get any better. The passage of time makes it worse. Do it now. It's often not as unpleasant as you think. Often your employee will merely say: "Yeah, I see what you mean. I was wondering about that myself."

Instant reprimands separate the real managers from the so-so candidates for higher office.

"When you call in subordinates to discuss problems," a rising manager wanted to know, "do you handle it in a stern or light manner?"

Hew to your basic style. If you're a fairly easy-going person, handle it relaxed. If you're serious, this too is a serious discussion. Don't step out of character. But *handle* it. Ignoring the problem is no solution. Here, as in other areas, just remember you're dealing with people.

THE FORCES AGAINST OBJECTIVE CRITICISM

Admitting that you have an errant employee is difficult for other reasons, too. *Your* boss wants to hear favorable stories about your people. He doesn't want to hear grief that makes it sound like the department's in trouble.

Besides, your boss won't allow you to give Esmeralda a raise if you say "I've got doubts about her." So you put together a story to sell the increase. But once you get on the wheel of unrealism, there's no place to stop.

Evaluating your employee face-to-face requires courage and objectivity. Don't be like the proud mother watching her son's military parade: *"Everybody's* out of step except Bobby."

Contrarily, if you want to praise someone, use the telephone or, better yet, do it person-to-person. The letter you write may well turn up in strange and embarrassing places.

Even the people who work for you are mortal. Remember that. Your boss will.

Says William M. Ellinghaus, president of AT&T:

When you appraise your subordinates, you're appraising yourself. The person who has no one to recommend for promotion is leading an easy life. He or she isn't developing future management talent for the company. On the other hand, the person who recommends everyone for promotion isn't discriminating enough to move up to a job with more responsibility.

The Key Employee Quits

Every manager has key people—people you need to meet vital objectives. You're training others, of course, but right now you need Bill Jones.

The opening shot usually occurs when you're on your way to an important meeting. Bill timidly stops you and mutters: "Do you have a minute?" His message: "I quit." You look at him wide-eyed. Once you discover it's not money or perks, you often find Bill Jones really doesn't think his work is appreciated.

If you're human, your impulse is to escape to your meeting and mumble something about "talking things over later." But suppose Bill *is* quitting because he feels he's not important to you? Then rushing out will confirm his feelings. And he's gone, brother.

So, assuming Bill is a *key* person, drop what you are doing. Sit down and ask Bill why. Let him talk—Don't argue about anything. He's probably rehearsed his speech countless times. Don't lecture and don't panic. This is only the opening skirmish, not the war. You can't win the war here—but you can sure lose it. Your job is to prove he *is* important to you. And, of course, you must find out what else is bothering him.

In the end, you must go back to Bill Jones with a solution that addresses his real reasons for wanting to quit—a solution that will, in turn, benefit the company.

It's not easy. But you must try. Other employees respect Bill Jones. So the morale of other superior performers hinges on Bill's decision.

If you can present a solution that changes his mind, you've saved the day. If not, you've learned a valuable lesson: Make sure your people feel wanted and appreciated in the first place.

Improving What You Have

Okay. You've tried to get the best people. You know that doesn't mean ten superstars. You can't even handle six superstars. Better two stars and four workers. Superstars require more time and more attention. They've got all kinds of ideas and they require special handling.

But since you didn't get all stars, it follows that you'll get employees who need improvement. The world is composed of 80 or 90 percent ordinary people. The difference between the outstanding manager and the mediocre guy is the way he or she can get good results out of ordinary people. (John D. Rockefeller, Sr., the oil baron, saw it much simpler: "Good management consists of showing average people how to do the work of superior people.")

Sometimes you find a square peg in a round hole. The person has value, but not in that job. Make a shift.

Thaddeus O'Brien, industrial psychologist with Cleveland-based Rohrer, Hibler & Replogle Inc., tells of the middle-aged plant manager who found himself struggling. Everything about the job exhausted him. He hated facing the assortment of bumptious personalities. Production began to fall. The once-effective manager found himself on the carpet at headquarters.

He was basically a shy introverted person. Yet 90 percent of his job called for chewing people out all day. He hated the job, but was so ego-tied to being a general manager he couldn't easily accept his real feelings. A psychologist drew him out on why his performance was off. In time, he could accept it: He didn't like his job. He switched to a staff job and he's been doing well since.

Many an employee will realize he or she is happier on a plateau. We've all seen sales managers who had been excellent salespeople but were miscast as salesmanagers. They're happy and effective when they get back to selling again.

In other cases, the company expands around a person—say, growing from producing 1,000 units to 10,000 or 100,000 units. Many candidates are not suited for this vastly different kind of management. Jack Simpkins was such a case. The company had burgeoned all around him and pushed him up to production vice-president. He was miserable.

I went to see him. "You really shouldn't be in this job," I told him. "You ought to be vice-president in charge of traffic. You could do it. You'd like it."

He was greatly relieved. "God love it, Jim, I'm so frustrated I can't do these things, I can't keep up with them. I agree with you."

They gave him a lesser job. It worked better for him *and* the company. He became functional. All too often, the miscast just go on stumbling ahead. This is particularly knotty when nepotism is involved.

The founder of a financial firm was disappointed in his son—who had left the firm to become a professor of philosophy. Father to son: "Unless you come back, you're not going to inherit any of this." The son came back. He was absolutely miserable. He did his best but he was still a philosopher at heart. That's a double tragedy.

So before you axe an employee, ask yourself: What other way can we utilize this ability?

The Difficult Task of Firing Drones

The rottenest part of a manager's job is firing people.

If some slob has been goofing off, it's not so hard. But it's seldom that bad. Usually it's just persistent subpar performance.

Because firing is unpleasant, many companies stack up dead wood. This slowly lowers the standards. It keeps the chairs filled and discourages hiring motivated new people.

Ineptitude, like excellence, is contagious. Accept careful pruning as necessary. Weak limbs must be cut away so strong limbs can grow.

If you've honestly tried and can't make a future for an employee, have the courage to face him with the facts. In the long run, you'll both be better off.

People hate to fire employees so much they try to rationalize keeping them. A colleague asked me: "Jim, what do you do with an employee too bad to keep and too good to fire?"

Any employee not good enough to keep should be fired. There's no such animal as the marginal employee.

When an employee's not doing the job, try to help him or her learn how to do it. If, after a reasonable time, nothing happens, get rid of the person. That's all there is to that.

More managers run afoul of firing than any other problem. If a man or woman can't do the job, get them out—and get someone who can. Sure, it reflects on your original decision (no one likes to admit a mistake). But remember the words of one veteran manager:

"Doctors bury their mistakes. But business executives see them walking down the hall—grinning and chewing gum."

If you weed out dead wood at the right time, you'll be noted and applauded by top management. Most executives will keep a human mistake on the scene much too long. Don't put it off. Sit down and tell Johnny why he'd do better in another situation. Delay just makes it worse.

Management is not for you if you say: "Well, I really ought to make a decision about George—he's not doing his job. But he's been with the company 30 years. He's a nice guy and I'm just going to leave him alone." You can't think like that. If George is an obstacle, George has to go, period.

On this corporate climb, George is chained to the rest of us. If he's not pulling his weight, we're all working harder to no avail. As we go up the slope, although it's unpleasant and sometimes heart-rending, you must learn to cut the Georges loose.

Replacing an Existing Staffer

Suppose you want to replace a person. But to play it safe, you want to find the replacement first. "I'll conduct this search on the sly," you say. In most cases, you can't get away with it. Word gets around.

Instead, sit down with the existing job-holder. Tell him what you're doing. Otherwise, surer than hell, it'll get back to him from the outside. Then you've got a real can of worms.

This is true at the highest levels, too. One CEO once told me:

"He's got this whole division under his control and I don't want him disturbed. Besides, I'm not sure what I want to do. Once I look at the other candidates, I may feel we're pretty well off."

Even so, play it above board. The individual and the company benefit by knowing that management is looking. Tell the incumbent he has a shot at the job.

Sometimes management is casting for a higher job. Sometimes somebody drops dead and the company's got to decide whether to bring in an outsider or promote from within.

If you face a replacement decision about one of your own people, talk to *your* boss about it first of all. Square-shooting pays in all such matters.

So where are you in developing good people and unhooking the losers? Get the best people you can (but don't try to get all stars). Develop them. Set up an evaluation system that does *not* avoid the unpleasant but does communicate. Relate to people humanely, that is, with sensitivity for their feelings. Yet don't allow this to inhibit forthright discussions about faults. If you have a good person in a wrong job, try to save the person for some other task. If the person won't salvage, get rid of the problem without delay. Unhook the drones so you can add more contributors.

A tough assignment? Tough is the very word for it. But we never said it'd be easy.

CHAPTER 12

How to Manage Your People

Candidates for top jobs are often promoted—or derailed—depending on how they manage subordinates. After all, when you get to be CEO you must supervise *everyone*. Start learning now.

And make no mistake about it—management *is* the art and science of getting work done through others. It's that simple, and, to some, that complex. Basically, this means hiring the right people, understanding and communicating with them, motivating your crew to full potential, defending them, evaluating them, and knowing when to say "tilt!" and promptly getting rid of nonproducers or the ill-cast. When you get good people, turn them loose and let them do the job.

Like many simple descriptions, this assignment is complicated by the very factor it seeks to control—the human equation. However, the set of techniques can be learned and you can learn them. Many of your competitors have and will.

Too Many Stars Spell Trouble

Leo Johns, sales VP of a Midwest paper company, believed in hiring able people. His company (which is involved in about six different kinds of paper products) makes bread wrappers, glassine that goes around donuts, and wax paper. They also make boxes and cartons and milk cartons and all kinds of things.

Anyhow, six of Leo's eight product managers were very strong. They were stars. That was good. But they were also all prima donnas. Each wanted to gather credit so he could make bigger bonuses. They were constantly throwing stones at what the other divisions were doing. That was bad. One day Leo said:

"My God, someday I'm going to get out from under all this. Just give me one or two good fellows and just let the others be average."

Taking a leaf from Leo, in your hiring, get the best people you can. But don't get *all* stars. There are plodding jobs to be done, too. Besides, anyone can fire a person and hire another. It takes a real good manager to turn a mediocre performer into satisfactory manager.

But for every rule, there's an exception. In the late 1950s, IBM, for example, had an all-star salesforce. The strongest salesforce in the nation. And Vin Learson was one of the most powerful marketing heads I've ever met. Later he became CEO at IBM.

I was in Learson's office the day GE bought Stanford Research's Bank America machine. GE decided to go into computers, and banks were the first target. In retaliation, within 24 hours Learson assigned IBM salespeople to call on every bank with assets over $50 million to start selling IBM's new bank computer.

"If they were over a billion dollars, call on each bank every two weeks," he said. If they are from $50 million to one billion, see them at least once a month, and sell them on IBM's NEW BANK MACHINE!"

His salesforce did it. His word was law.

Then Learson called IBM's Research head and said:

"I've got to have a bank machine quick. Now, damn it, you get me one."

Against that power, GE didn't have a chance. Learson knew what he could do since no one could touch that salesforce.

That's an example of a cast of stars that was—and still is—a hell of a competitive advantage, rather than a disadvantage. So each rule has a counter-rule, although I believe IBM was, and is, atypical.

More common is the sales manager who told me:

"Give me ten hard workers and one or two superstars but don't give me an entire force of stars. They are eccentric, they have a lot of ideas, they require handling all the time."

So get the best people you can for the job to be done. Second, know what they can do and what they cannot do. Sure, you don't have a perfect person in each slot—but then again each slot wouldn't suit a perfect person. Finally, that's where real management comes in: getting work out of less-than-ideal people. So managing, by definition, means managing average people.

But here's where the most ardent capitalist can draw on Karl Marx: "Each according to his ability, each according to his need." A good manager will stimulate performance to whatever level the person is capable of—no one can do more.

If, on the other hand, this requires more time and energy than it's worth, then you face a personnel decision: Consider replacing the limited person altogether. But first ask yourself: Do I have *limited* functions that need performing—functions that will save my stars for star work? This is an important management decision.

Now you have person or persons reporting to you. OK. Sounds basic, but now you've got to tell them what to do and help them do it. You'd be shocked to know how many budding managers never really get over this crevasse. First thing you must learn: Both you and your subordinate are full-blown members of the Now Generation.

IMMEDIATE GRATIFICATION

This is the era of instant gratification, sociologists tell us. People don't want to wait for anything. "Now," they cry. No matter what the issue.

Well, this may not be good for society, but it's valuable in managing people.

The whole idea is that you establish clear-cut goals and then you sit down with the employee and you go over those goals. Then when they do a good job, you tell them they've done a good job. If they don't do a good job, you tell them that.

This makes good sense. (Although you cannot do it in a minute.) Most managers today don't do a good job telling people what to do and reporting back to them how they've done it. Instant gratification or instant reprimand: I buy that all the way.

The point of honest straightforward across-the-table communication with your subordinates—I can't argue with that. Do it on a regular basis. Those have been good principles since God knows when.

You're Not Dr. Freud

Don't try to be a psychologist in analyzing your people's problems. You're not in the head business.

When Hal Smitty was head of management development at GE, the company had a habit of extensively analyzing the characteristics a person needed to do a new job. They started with the job description and tried to reason out what characteristics were necessary. Then they'd go back to the candidate and decide if he had those qualities.

It didn't track. After four years, GE gave up the whole plan as impossible. They reverted instead to judging the candidate by how well he does his current job. Don't try to be a psychologist. That's not your role. You're not trained for it. If you get an outstanding performer, consider the candidate for the next job up the line. But don't hang out a psychology shingle.

Your Personal Rapport with Employees

Emotionalism and anger are luxuries the manager cannot afford. Yet you can and must be firm with employees in issuing instructions. Tone of voice is an extremely important weapon in your arsenal.

I was on a flight to Miami once with Leo (The Lip) Durocher, the famed Brooklyn Dodgers manager—certainly one of the most irrepressible of men (as many an umpire will attest). We ran into rough weather. The captain came on the intercom: "Please return to your seats and fasten your seatbelts." Lippy, wandering up and down the aisle, paid no attention.

"God bless you," he was telling a baseball fan praising The Bums. He ignored the captain's second request.

Then a 20-year-old stewardess who weighted in at 90 pounds soaking wet came up the aisle and said: "Mr. Durocher, go back to your seat and sit down. I don't want to have to tell you again!"

"Yes, ma'am," Lippy said, contritely. He went back and fastened his seat belt and did not say another word. The right tone can tame even the professional curmudgeon.

Angry bosses rarely get the best work from their staff, but neither do professional nice guys. The best way to motivate employees is by offering them earned recognition, achievement, growth, responsibility, advancement, and satisfaction in the work itself. The employer who depends on personal loyalty often causes discomfort and resentment.

Develop loyalty and responsibility to the company. Nice-guy employers often short-change their employees. Refraining from interfering with a subordinate in order to develop his initiative and skills is constructive and commendable. Refraining from interfering just to avoid trouble often brings on worse trouble.

Insensitivity to others may be a product of the person's upbringing. It may reflect the pressure he's under. Or the rate his career is progressing. But for whatever reason, some executives end up with an abrasive nature, an intimidating manner or a bullying style—or in some cases (God save the mark!) all three.

It's all too true. At least 75 percent of executives are *not* interested in bringing people along. They only use people to accomplish their objectives. They want to get a result. They want something done and they don't want to bother to explain it. They just say—"do it."

This is a widespread problem. For your career climb, if you can develop a sensitivity to others and still get work done through them, you'll have an important leg-up on your competition. Unfortunately, there are many bosses who are insensitive to people. They're rough and tough and don't give a damn. They ride roughshod. If you work for such a boss, you've got to plan your program.

And if you act this way with your own staff, better reform because:

- ☐ People will leave.
- ☐ You'll find events happening that nobody told you about.
- ☐ You'll find you're getting explosions from people.
- ☐ People will go around you to talk to your boss—or, more likely, to a third party who'll talk to your boss.

You *can* be demanding. Insist on high standards. But you cannot get away with acting like you don't care what happens to people. Being known as an S.O.B. too long and too widely will catch up with you one way or another.

"You can be *too* sensitive," a dissenter said. "You can work so hard at being popular you don't get work done. A plant manager in the housing field hired a new assistant. Later, he said he didn't think Paul would work out. We said: why? He said; 'Do you know that man's too *sympathetic* with his people!' "

Paul isn't a case of sensitivity—it's a case of politics, it seems to me. I'd be hard pressed to think of many *really* overly sensitive executives.

A natural leader's best role is bringing people along. That's the marvelous personal experience in management. Stop a few times a year to think about what the people under you are trying to do. What their frustrations are. Be sympathetic. Be helpful. That's a great thing. That's probably what your boss did and *does.*

Mail-order advertising, the experts tell us, is a constant process of testing. You may have utilized the medium for 25 years but you never stop testing: copy, lists, design, timing. There's no end to testing since there's no end to possible combinations against possible appeals.

Managing people is the same way: You never stop evaluating your people—one against another, this year against last, this assignment vs. another.

Evaluating and analyzing is a major part of each manager's job and don't ever lose sight of *that* fact, brother and sister climbers. But unlike mail order, with people you recount your findings to the subject in hopes that the subject can overcome his or her shortcomings. *That's* a tremendous difference. This requires promptness and candor.

Managing the Quality Circle

In recent years, the Japanese have stirred the world with management techniques centered on greater productivity of smaller groups working together like a family. Translated into Western mode, it really means a team getting together and motivating the group to perform as a unit.

On-the-job teams are like any other human relationships. To get worthwhile performance, you must work at building and maintaining them. Whether your team is a formal task force chartered to accomplish a specific mission or an informal work group with interrelated objectives, cultivating your team will increase both productivity and satisfaction.

When seeking players for your team, look for commitment and complementary capabilities. People put forth their best efforts only if they truly want to go where the team is going. Being on a team is like riding on a train: If you don't want to go where it's going, you either have to change your destination or get off. So be sure the people you assign to a project are committed to it.

Also, most projects require a set of specific skills. Seek out people who have strengths that complement one another—including you. If your communication skills are average, for example, try to find a player who is an excellent writer and speaker.

Once you get a team, keep it in top condition by exercising leadership. Each team must have a captain to maintain order, assign tasks, and cast the final vote. You're it. You, not a subordinate, must say "Okay, given everything we've said here, it looks to me like we should go ahead on this project."

Establish accountability. Encourage members to set their own standards subject to the needs of the group. Set deadlines and insist that they be kept.

Play to each member's strengths. The team as a whole can accomplish more than the sum of its parts. While one or two members may be in the limelight, the group makes achievements possible.

Each member of the group must derive satisfaction—via personal growth, opportunities for recognition, advancement—greater than the "costs" of participation. Find out what each member wants and help the person achieve it.

Watch the Squeaking Wheel

In administering your group, watch the clear and present danger of paying too much attention to complainers. As you've seen earlier, some squeaking wheels are quite articulate. But in listening, you often ignore the quieter types who need your help more.

Never react to a story laid down by one person. No matter how logical, convincing, or positive it is, wait until you hear "the rest of the story," as Paul Harvey advises us.

The FBI requires three different witnesses. That's a good practice. You'll find the stories are quite different.

If A complains about B, get both in your office and then let A repeat the allegation. Anytime an employee won't agree to an open meeting, "something's rotten in the state of Denmark," as Hamlet told us.

Another reason you can't listen to one side only: If you play favorites, people feel they're getting the short end of the stick. That's no way to get teamwork.

Defending Your People

Teamwork also requires you to defend your people against unwarranted attack. Suppose you and your crew have just come back from a convention. Your boss is also back, irate about one of your people—Coates Johns.

"He was there in the bar talking about company problems to a bunch of dealers," your boss storms. "I never heard anything like it in my life. That man's no good."

Under these conditions, it would be easy to agree with your boss—and condemn the man unheard. Easy but wrong. Better to say:

"I don't know what happened and I'll find out. But let's not judge him too quickly. He's got a fine record. He's handled a number of things well. Let me find out about this and get back to you about it. In most ways, I see him as a real asset."

Speak up when good people are under fire. That's when they need it.

And since preventive medicine is always better, defend your people *before* they're attacked—by thrusting them in the limelight.

Let Susan make the report or Mary make the presentation. Bring people along. There's enough credit to go around. After all, if she's under your tutelage, that's credit enough.

Handling the Boss's Son

There's tutelage and there's special tutelage. Suppose you're district sales manager and the president wants his son Ignace to get hands-on field experience. He calls you in and says:

"Because of your level-headedness and experience, you're the ideal person to supervise him."

Hmmm. Flattery will get you everywhere.

To start with, hold two or three good discussions with the president. Find out how he sees Ignace's shortcomings around home and other places. You need an evaluation of the Ignace's pluses and minuses early on.

Ignace doesn't have to do what you tell him. You know it and he knows it.

The boss's son is about as knotty a problem as you'll encounter. But if you've got the right kind of top man, he'll want you to instruct the boy on the straight and narrow. Tell him what he does right *and* wrong.

Obviously you can't yell at him. A light touch is best. Chide the son a little—to wit: "Do you feel sensitive about what your Dad would say in this situation?" It's a difficult situation. But a potential CEO can handle it.

Can You Fire Everybody!

A Container Corporation of America manager posted this sign on his wall:

A manager is a person who
Tells people what to do then
Checks to see if it's been done
Finds it hasn't
Listens to all the reasons why not
Gets the person started on it again
Finds later it still hasn't been done
Then catches hell from his boss for holding up production.
Why would anyone want to be a manager?

What this wall posting was saying is simple enough: Persuading subordinates to do their work is far more complicated than issuing orders. You must motivate, shame, persuade, cajole, even threaten.

And much more.

Sure, you can fire the real bad apples. And there are days when you want to fire everyone. But usually it's not possible or practical—as *Chicago Tribune* publisher Robert R. McCormick found out.

In the 1930s, waggish typesetters on the Paris edition of the *Chicago Tribune* composed a parody on the Prince of Wales' visit to France. The story concluded with the Prince asking a small boy his name.

"Go to hell," the boy said.

"Whereupon (the story went) the Prince took his gold-headed walking cane and bashed the little fellow's brains out."

This story, typeset for internal fun, somehow got into the *Tribune*. And McCormick read it in far-away Chicago. His cable to Paris was swift and characteristic:

"FIRE EVERYBODY."

But it didn't happen. If they fired everybody, who'd put out the next edition? So they didn't. Nor will you be able to throw people out in wholesale lots.

Sure, subordinates *theoretically* must do as you say. However, there are 1,001 ways they can drag their feet. And they often do.

So getting along with subordinates is a key quality. Your future depends on it. A corporate riser must have an effective team.

Why Manager Is Like a Coach

Andrew S. Grove, president of Intel Corporation, believes a manager is very much like a coach—encouraging competition.

"First, an ideal coach takes no personal credit for the success of his team, and because of that his players trust him," Grove wrote in *The*

New York Times. "Second, he is tough on his team. By giving critical feedback, he tries to get the best performance his team members can provide. Third, a good coach was likely a good player himself once. And having played the game well, he also understands it well."

Management is a team activity. But no matter how well a team is put together, no matter how well directed, the team will perform only as well as the individuals on it.

When a person is not doing his job, there can only be two reasons for it. The person either can't do it or won't do it. He's either not capable or not motivated.

For most of Western history, including the early days of the Industrial Revolution, motivation was based mostly on fear. In Dickens' time, the threat of loss of life got people to work. If people didn't work, they couldn't buy food. If they stole food and got caught, they were hanged.

Over the past 30 years or so, a number of new approaches have begun to replace older practices keyed to fear. Perhaps the emergence of the new, humanistic approaches to motivation can be traced to the decline in the relative importance of manual labor and the corresponding rise in the importance of knowledge workers.

Managers need to elicit peak performance from subordinates. Performance of the organization as a whole depends on skilled and motivated people within. Thus, your role as manager is, first, to train the individuals under our supervision, and, second, to bring them to the point where a drive to excel motivates them. Then their motivation will be self-sustaining.

"Why is it that a person who is not terribly interested in his work at the office would stretch himself to the limit running a marathon?" Intel's Grove asks. "He is trying to beat other people."

Competition, even subtle competition, is a great stimulator. Some years ago the chairman of an eastern railroad was striving to increase the productivity of rolling stock and yard crews. Time studies were made. Specific tasks developed. Programs laid out, but nothing happened.

Then he organized a biweekly meeting of his key managers, at which they posted results of their accomplishments against targets and previous periods. The worst performer had to talk first, explain why and tell about his future plans. Immediately performance improved.

It works.

THE NON-EASY WAY TO MANAGE PEOPLE

Bill Marsteller, the ad agency founder and savant, is a source of great common sense about managing people.

"Ability to manage is not inherited," Marsteller says. "Some *tendencies* toward being a good manager may be inherited, although I have never found out what they are. Mostly, being a good manager is simply discipline. That means that there is hope for all of us, however far we have already strayed."

If Bill Marsteller's talking about the average *manager,* I agree. If he's talking about leadership, I'm in fundamental *disagreement.* Based on observations over dozens of corporate situations and hundreds of executives, I believe that ability to lead people is a characteristic *some* people have but *most* people don't.

A real leader has a *genuine* interest in people. He or she gets satisfaction out of seeing people improve. The real leader encourages development and urges improvement in personal characteristics and appearance.

Most good managers, on the other hand, know how to *use* people effectively but are not interested in developing them.

So let's talk about managing people first, which is important and necessary. Then we'll move on to motivating people, which is harder, rarer, and very valuable indeed.

Looking at *managing* people as a full rung below *leading* people, I'm convinced these techniques make sense:

When you want somebody to do something, adopt a "let's-you-and-me" instead of a "let's-you-and-him" attitude.

People who work for you are often afraid of you. They often will not come to you with their problems. Get out to meet the troops in the field. Unless you circulate, good people will not bring problems to you. If you can set up an atmosphere where people *do* come to you for help, you are far ahead.

Consult with people. You like to be consulted. So do they.

All people want *consistency.* Morale is shattered by uncertainty. So, if you're an S.O.B., be an S.O.B. all the time.

A manager can't indulge in moodiness. If you get moody at times, stay by yourself until you get over it.

A big problem is favoritism. Real or imagined, it is lethal. Watch it.

People you like are not always right and those you dislike are not always wrong. The validity of an idea has little to do with the charm of its sponsor.

You can easily hire an office full of people who are good at meeting-going. But hiring people who can leave a meeting and get something done immediately thereafter, that's the trick.

Set your own high standards and establish with the people you supervise that you have a very low tolerance for the mundane. Praise makes good people better and bad people worse. Save praise for the truly extraordinary.

If you're still in the office on Friday afternoons or if you work the occasional weekend, you'll see its value. There is so much to see. Seeing who's there and who isn't. A time to contemplate your work, your job, your people.

Don't Neglect People-Mingling

When you get to middle-management, you must fine-tune the art of employee-mingling. Further up the slope, you're going to need it—as one short-lived CEO found out.

William A. Patterson, CEO of United Airlines, invited me to a gigantic bash at the Waldorf. It was VIP night. Music was lavish. Guests: his best customers, suppliers, lawyers, and friends—about 100 people all told. He brought chefs from all over—from San Francisco, from Honolulu, from Chicago. Each chef prepared a separate dish. Guests sat around a big U-shaped table to watch each chef come in proudly carrying his particular delicacy. A real gourmet experience.

At dinner, I sat next to an air force general named successor to Pat

Patterson (who was moving up to chairman). A number of speakers extolled the great job the general was going to do at UAL. At the table, I asked him about his approach.

"Well, I am not going to rush around the system," he said. "I'm not like the sales manager who frantically travels around the country. I'll respond to the people who come in. To me, a manager sits and thinks and never mind all of this flying around."

I explored that with him: Was he sure he'd get a feel of the market and the employees that way? He was sure.

A short time later he was off the job. Gone. He never got his teeth into it. He didn't meet the people in their own place of work (a serious neglect). He sat on his throne like an imperial Roman emperor awaiting tribute from the conquered provinces. In fact, he wanted to do just that—"get our country managers in periodically every few weeks."

"I'd a hell of a lot rather talk to them in their own setting," I told him. "Where they're comfortable. It is always good to go to a sub-manager's own setting."

But he wasn't buying this. Example of a CEO who never picked up his franchise.

YOUR JOB AS MOTIVATOR

Now let's get on with leadership. Up in Wisconsin, they tell of a lumberjack who came to town to visit the local call girl. When he got ready to settle his bill, she didn't want money—but asked him to buy her a pocket knife at the local hardware store. Wonderingly, he presented it to her, and asked why the knife.

"Well, I'm getting middle-aged now," the lady said. "And I might not be as attractive to the young bucks as I once was. But I do know that a Wisconsin boy will do most anything for a pocket knife."

The lady understood a basic principle of motivation: *Suit the incen-*

tive to the receiver—a lesson for the rising manger who, as a people supervisor, must also be a motivator.

Lee Iacocca motivates people and can make people play over their heads. In football, you get a team that's turned on, they just go like mad and you can't stop them. Same with business. Even if you're not an inspiring leader, evaluate the capabilities of people under you. Draw upon those people in exactly the right instance. Give them the right job, the right instructions. And get a good result that way.

I've known a number of noninspiring executives who do this. Many CEOs are good utilizers of people even if they aren't motivators.

The utilization of people works well with today's participatory management. The good leader knows what people buttons to push to really get them excited and go, go, go. Motivation is coming on more and more. You get people excited. Everyone works on a budget together. You build it up from the bottom. Everybody has participated.

It's their challenge and their property.

Trending Toward Participatory Management

At one time, the manager said: "Do this because I say so." Today we have participatory management. The manager gets people together, explains the problem, and seeks a solution from the group. Like many fads, *group-think* has gone too far right now. When the pendulum swings back toward the middle, we'll end up with a healthy trend.

I took a plane ride recently with a chairman who complained about a lack of urgency among his managers. He believes in participatory management to an extreme degree. So I said:

"Well, I guess that's one reason why they are lax in making decisions and moving out on things."

"That's one of the reasons," he admitted.

But the principle, kept within bounds, is good. The more you can get people to think about the whole world they live in and how their job functions within that world, the better. When it works right, A will make a suggestion about B's department—and vice versa—because they know what we're all trying to do and they are enthused about contributing to the overall picture.

Better get used to it. Participatory management is an idea whose time is here. Just keep in check and don't allow it to deteriorate into a debating society, or, worse, a committee. Like most good ideas, it skates on thin ice overlaying some bad ideas.

So what have you learned, fellow climber, about managing people? A few classic principles.

Get the right people on the job. Then insist on two-way communication. Be sure they know what they're supposed to do. Follow through to see that they do it. That's all there is to it. And that's plenty.

CHAPTER 13

Delegation: Getting Your Work Done Without Going Crazy

At Wright Field, Ohio, Colonel Winthrop Smith was in charge of producing P-51 fighter airplanes. He worked 24 hours a day, week in and week out, plus weekends—just ruining himself.

"Winthrop," I said, "you are never going to get this thing solved until you get these other guys to do the work."

"Well," he said, "then I have to do it over because they don't do it right."

He never did learn to delegate—to his downfall. They finally took the P-51 airplane away from him.

Delegation becomes particularly important the higher up you get. Finally it becomes vital. When you get 3000 employees, there's no way you can do it yourself. But you cannot do it all at any level.

When you hear a manager say, "I can't worry about getting other people to do things, I've got to do it myself," you're witnessing a flawed executive. There are not enough hours in the day for you to do every-thing yourself.

Working with people *is the job* in management. Floyd Lewis, CEO of Middle South Utilities, Inc., New Orleans, looks for this ability in middle-managers.

"I look for a lot of common sense," he says. "Perceptiveness in terms of appraising and leading people. Hard workers. An ability to get the big picture and achieve goals by working through people.

"I try not to get too involved in details that other people are respon-sible for. I believe in delegating responsibility and in giving sufficient authority. The only thing a leader in any sizable organization can do is to try to have the kind of people who can make things happen."

This is often hard to learn—particularly for entrepreneurs, once their enterprise grows. When a company is under $10 million in an-nual sales, the founder can know everything that's going on and make all the decisions. But once volume gets over that, he's got to work through others. There's no other way.

Delegation Begins with Attitude

Confidence is a vital factor in delegation. Acting like a leader—in ap-pearance, manner, and presence—is the first step.

Outward confidence is potent. When you delegate in a way that makes others *think* you *think* you can do it, they probably *can* do it.

Sometimes people fail to delegate—not because they're insensitive to others, but because they're inarticulate. They'd rather do it them-selves than try to explain it. Clue to climbers: If you're not articulate, spruce up. Take courses.

Delegation takes courage. Let George make his inevitable mistakes. Just hope the goofs aren't incorrectable.

Learn To Be a Good Teacher

A good delegator is an instructor. Teaching experience helps you to learn how. Coaching experience is also valuable. Explain to your subordinates what you want after you point out why it didn't come out 100 percent correct the first time. Next time they'll do it better.

Depending on the person, decide how much independent action you want and at what point he or she should report back.

Delegation requires authority. A former Houston field researcher was promoted to the New York office. His new job was not to do the work himself but to try to get others to do it. It almost drove him crazy.

"They don't want to work unless it's their idea," he said. At first, he was hampered by responsibility without authority. When he got that adjusted, he gradually learned to move from doing to inspiring.

Importance of Objectives in Delegating

Robert Townsend says only badly managed companies concentrate on management by objective. He's full of beans. Management by Objective is the only way to make things work.

Townsend says real managers delegate by frequent eyeball contact—evidently meaning half the meetings are held in the hall, the other half in the washroom. He's too simplistic. Sitting down and really laying out what a fellow is going to try to do—you can't do that on the fly. Then in six months, you need to sit down again and say: "Let's look at what we agreed to do and let's understand why we didn't get it done." Then you've got a basis of understanding.

Management by Objectives is just a way of formalizing common sense. You decide what you're going to do. You put it down in writing so everybody knows it and then you check to see if it's happening. You can't do that on a trip to the men's room.

(Of course, Townsend is a sensationalist. Sometimes his comments are entertaining—such as "don't hire Harvard Business School graduates." That's silly. Some of the highest quality trainees are coming out of business schools by the very selection process that accepts and winnows them out. A recruiter can find jewels there—but they are expensive.)

Townsend also says: "Fire the personnel department."

You can get rid of the personnel department—but you can't get rid of that delegated function. Somebody has got to do that work—hiring, paying, and training people. Sure, the boss of each department can do that, but if he doesn't have somebody helping him, it's going to detract from his other work. If a company is functioning effectively, perhaps, you don't see the personnel department. But you can bet somebody is performing the function.

Learning to Turn Loose

John Paul Jones, chairman of Servel, had trouble turning loose as he moved up the slope.

In Philadelphia, he worked on almost every machine in the plant. When the company moved to Evansville, he continued to assume he knew how to do every job in the plant. He didn't, of course.

He'd call the manufacturing people in and give them hell: "You're not getting enough productivity off that machine," he'd say, talking about a new machine he had no knowledge of.

His biggest weakness: lack of confidence in other people. He wouldn't assign a job and let people perform. (It's terribly important for a leader to delegate the job, give the employee the tools, and let him run it—even to the point of making mistakes.)

Jones would give out a job, tell the employee how to do it, and call a day later to see if he'd started it, and then give more suggestions. This got him in trouble.

Bradford Gates had a similar problem. When Gates reorganized his famous company into separate profit-responsive divisions, I said to him:

"You're going to have to learn to leave these people alone. You must delegate authority to division heads. You're going to have to be tolerant and let them make mistakes and hope to hell they don't make too many. Mistakes are not only inevitable but actually beneficial."

But Gates, with all his stature, was scared his subordinates were cutting the ground out from under him.

"But, Jim, the first thing you know, they'll be running things and there won't be anything for me to do—I'll be in terrible shape," he said. "They'll take my job away from me. The next thing that happens, I'll be out in the street."

"Come on," I said, "You *are* the company. You own a big chunk of the stock. You have people around you to do these things. You can't do all of them well yourself."

But he was hard to convince. Very hard. However, he did go ahead, setting up divisions and putting people (who made mistakes) in charge of them. But he didn't like it.

SOMETIMES DELEGATION IS FORCED

In times gone by, when the Norge division wasn't doing well, CEO Roy Ingersoll of Borg-Warner recruited Judd Sayre away from Bendix. Ingersoll knew Sayre was an accomplished appliance manager.

"I'll come but only under one condition," Sayre said. "You and your colleagues don't begin to understand consumer products. You've always been contract manufacturers, amortizing your total costs over each run of product. Norge needs consumer marketing and you don't understand that.

"If I'm going to run Norge, it'll be as a consumer product business. Cut out $15 million as working capital. Give it to me. Let's keep the books separately at Norge. You stay out of Detroit. Don't ever come into the Norge plant. I'll run Norge totally on my own."

Ingersoll agreed. He had to—to get Sayre. And Sayre did good things with Norge for three years. Sayre was no dummy. He knew how Ingersoll operated. He got himself a free hand before accepting the job. He forced delegation: He knew he had to have it to do the job.

Delegation Basics

High blood pressure is called the invisible killer because it works its evil without outward symptoms. Poor delegation works the same way— behind the scenes. I can't recall ever evaluating a person's ability to delegate *per se* in making judgments upon promotion. You *do* look at achievements and productivity. And these things can only happen if you know how to delegate and get things done through subordinates. It's built into the framework.

Don't ignore delegation. It's an invisible career-killer. An anti-delegator is sabotaging his own career climb.

Delegation requires communication between manager and subordinate. Expecting the assignment to be carried out is one thing. Building in essentials to enhance successful completion is another.

Many managers misunderstand delegation. You're not supposed to delegate your *job*. Delegate so you can *concentrate* on your job.

Define the tasks absolutely essential for you, tasks that *only* you can do effectively. Then assign things you do *not* have to do.

To delegate a job, define:

- [ ] The specific task.
- [ ] The items each subordinate is accountable for.
- [ ] The ways results will be measured.
- [ ] The deadlines and the way you'll measure results.
- [ ] The way you're to be kept informed and when.

That's all there is to it—in a lab situation. Putting it into practice takes doing and analysis.

Analyzing Delegation

You can't buy it by the pound. Nor can you find many books about it. But delegation is a commitment to turn over part of your duties and responsibilities to someone else. In managing your division or department, you've accepted functions and responsibilities and you're committed to objectives. Delegation is a process of dividing up parts of that job among subordinates. Delegation is not abdication. Far from it.

One beautiful May afternoon, a distraught woman walked into my office and said: "Mr. Newman, I have a major problem."

I listened to her story. She was a new CEO of the Lager Supply Company in Milwaukee. The 40-year-old company had grown steadily over the years, providing a good income for her husband and herself. Six months ago, her husband—who had been CEO—died. The attorneys arranged for her to be CEO.

As her first step, she called in Danton Long, the general manager (with the firm 13 years).

"I'm delegating to you responsibilities for managing the day-to-day business," she said. "But I want to be involved in all planning and policy decisions, plus any major problems that come up."

In addition, she wanted the lawyer and finance head to continue to report to her—could they all meet once a week to discuss all aspects of the business?

The first four meetings worked. Then things got tense. The general manager became sarcastic. He began to make it unpleasant for her to come into the office.

"I've developed an excellent solution," she said. "Today I don't go near the office. I haven't seen Danton Long for eight weeks. I've given up writing or telephoning. Let him go ahead and run the business without any help from me.

"But my problem is the business has not been doing very well lately. I don't know what to do about it."

Here was a woman who *abdicated* when she should have *delegated.* There's a big difference.

Sometimes abdication exists even in the presence of a large staff. In the White House, Eisenhower was criticized for overdependence on staff. Ronald Reagan has been hit with the same charge. (Of course, the White House staff is a prime example of elephantiasis. So is Congress. Neither ever gets smaller. Once you lay a function in place, it takes root and stays there administration after administration.)

Carter was going to cut out some of this bureaucracy, but since that proved impossible, maybe he should have utilized it better. While he assigned many projects to Cabinet officers or White House staff, he had no confidence in their work. One of his closest associates explained to me that practically every task that Carter assigned (from drafting new legislation to—flagrant example—freeing the hostages in Iran), he second-guessed the solution.

Each evening he took data and drafts to his quarters. There he'd think his own way to an ultimate decision which frequently differed from actions proposed by his supposed experts. Such a process doesn't divide the load. It only piles more on top.

PERILS OF PARTIAL DELEGATION

Splitting up the workload is a most essential necessity for any department or division head. There aren't enough hours in the day for one person to handle the workload. You must share the wealth with others.

Sit down with your subordinates. Review the work and its missions. Clarify the effort involved, the due date, and the desired end-product. Agree on yardsticks for measuring progress. Set times for progress reviews. Reassure subordinates that you're available for communication within reasonable bounds (but not recreational questions every hour!)

Delegate full authority to the people who need it and make sure everyone knows about this authority.

Many managers, obsessed with perfectionism, hand over tasks then pull them back partway. ("I've got to be sure it's done right!") Resist this temptation. A manager must pass on total responsibility. Cultivate a tolerance for mistakes. Nobody (but you!) is perfect.

Recognize that when projects are given out, invariably some part may be done wrong. They'll take too long. They won't be tied up in complete packages. The hardest thing in the world is to sit by and watch people make mistakes.

Yet it must be done. Not too many mistakes, mind you, but some. Then the real manager sits down with the faulter to go over what happened and why. While correcting, you must give the individual confidence to go on the next time.

Signs of Poor Delegation

Inadequate delegation soon becomes apparent. Among its symptoms:

- ☐ Putting out fires becomes a pattern.
- ☐ Work slows down to a standstill when the manager is away.
- ☐ Bottlenecks continue with nobody removing them.
- ☐ Deadlines are often missed.
- ☐ Inequitable workloads develop, with one level quite overworked, the other underworked.
- ☐ Good ideas accumulate, yet are never followed through.

☐   A rugged attitude develops toward mistakes.

☐   Key managers are unduly preoccupied with detail—for its own sake.

☐   Decision-making is slow, with too much authority clustered at upper levels.

☐   Committees and task forces are used excessively to bail out situations.

How smoothly is your team working? Are your people jaded and out of breath? Working all kinds of hours? Asking for more help? Sounds like they aren't delegating.

Preserve time to do what you do best. Farm out other tasks to staff. Trust an entire matter to another person—and give him or her sufficient authority to make it work. Keep hands off—even if the person doesn't approach the task the way you would.

Keep your eye on the main chance.

Make sure your people delegate authority to the people under them. Your message: "Wanting to keep a finger in every pie is human but you don't have enough fingers for all the pies. Besides, you crowd out everyone else who wants, or should want, to share the responsibility."

Do-It-Yourself is a great movement in home fix-up. But it's murder in management. The manager must let George do it—but he must make sure George does it right and on time.

Dangers of Perfectionism

When I worked for Lloyd Jasper, I put in nights and weekends getting out the most perfect report—100 to 120 pages. When I turned it in, Lloyd said: "Oh dear me." He cut it up. Next weekend I repeated the process with the same result. Finally, I took sections Lloyd had previously approved and incorporated them in new sections. He'd carve them up again. Finally, I said: "Lloyd, you ought to learn how to be sloppy. That's your biggest weakness."

In most cases, that's not the way to manage your boss. But Lloyd had an obsessive need for correction. He wasn't really making the product any better. He was concerned with *writing* when he should have been concerned with *content.* As a result, he was an anti-delegator (a serious career holdback).

Delegation, in short, is merely an intelligent utilization of the good help the company has provided or that you've provided yourself. You cannot do it all. You don't want to do it all.

Parcel out the work, use the extra time for planning and checking. Delegate with an explanation.

That's the drill. And that's *your* assignment. Please get started on it. We expect a progress report shortly.

PART ———— 5

Moving into Rare Air— How to Survive Storms and Avalanches

CHAPTER 14

Decision-Making, Cost-Cutting, and Problem-Solving

Lady MacBeth deplored "the milk of human kindness" as a weakness in the ambitious person. Yet in trying to expunge this trait, MacBeth lost his head to MacDuff. And Lady MacBeth went bonkers.

Many a corporate climber loses grip on the slope the same way. You cannot solve problems and make decisions like a medieval Scottish lord. You must maintain understanding and consideration in dealing with people.

The directors at a large Northeast metal fabricating company found this out—the hard way. Founder John Patron had built the company with strong employee empathy. He considered his employees' families. Each spring, he brought in truck loads of oranges. In the fall, employees helped themselves to bag of apples. The employees loved Mr. Patron.

One year, when traveling transatlantic on the *Queen Mary,* Patron heard an excellent shipboard organist. He hired the organist away from Cunard to play at lunchtime in the company cafeteria. Employees said: "It's marvelous."

But then: trouble in paradise! A board member recommended that a rank outsider, Brandon Gish, come in and take over as president, with Patron moving up to chairman. Everyone agreed.

Gish, who had never managed anything but government agencies, arrived and said:

"The first thing we've got to do around here is cut costs."

He axed the organist. He dropped apples and oranges. He tried by sharp analytical techniques to improve matters. But he became unpopular with middle management. The employees were extremely unhappy.

Jere Fisher, head of the Atomic Fuels division, was in constant touch with Admiral Hyman Rickover in Washington. Gish didn't like this (after all, *he* was the government expert), but he couldn't intrude into Fisher's domain. This rankled him, but he never said so to Fisher.

In the fall, when old John Patron went off the Bavaria (his traditional vacation spot), Gish presented the board with the problem: Fisher.

"One of us has to go," he said.

The board kept Gish and fired Fisher. This brought about a palace revolution. The supervisory staff wired Patron in Bavaria. He flew back and held a mass meeting in the cafeteria. Result, 154 out of 156 of the top managers resigned.

Obviously this wouldn't do. So the board had to replace Gish. Had Gish been as competent in handling people as he was at analysis—which he probably wasn't—he would have viewed apples, oranges, and lunchtime music as an excellent investment. As savvy managers know, it's not the cost that counts, it's the return on investment. And in employee relations, elimination of small benefits often foment large troubles—a vital consideration in decision-making.

THE JAPANESE CONNECTION

In managing employees, it's important to keep up with new trends in management—so you can adapt and adopt what's good for you. Participative management, for example, is all the rage today. The idea: Don't just *tell* them what to do. Discuss the problems and goals and let them help you *decide* what to do. (PM has merit if not carried too far. But watch it, or you get back to committee-itis again.)

New ideas often go *too* far—at first. Back in the 1920s, old F. L. Maytag—founder of The Maytag Company, Newton, Iowa—heard he ought to do something about employee relations (a new idea at the time).

He didn't much like the sound of it, but decided to try. In those days employees worked half a day on Saturday. So one Saturday afternoon, F. L. Maytag called for a military formation in front of the plant. He then marched the group over to the city park and said: "Have fun, God damn it." If they wanted employee relations, he'd give it to them.

Employee relations now is standard. So will PM be in time.

No discussion of participative management can be complete without the Japanese Connection. Says Thomas McGovern, director of Center for Management Control, Duxbury, Massachusetts:

> *Large segments of American business today are preoccupied with Japan, Japanese productivity, and worldwide Japanese economic penetration. In looking for solutions to industrial problems, Americans are focusing on the management, organization and production techniques that brought Japan from devastation to economic superpower in a generation.*
>
> *As a result, participative management is in. Quality circles—formal groups of workers and supervisors who work together for quality— proliferate.*

I agree with McGovern but I think the United States must consider these factors *before* hopping into the Japanese mode:

Participative management has logged only mixed results when tried in the United States, so far. Sometimes it becomes a divisive force instead of a force for close ties between workers and supervisors.

Quality-circle projects that do not recognize the special nature of the American workplace deteriorate into ineffectual gripe sessions— or become vehicles that allow rank-and-file employees to bypass supervisors and deal directly with management. This can lead to serious difficulties.

Americans are competitors. From our earliest years, we are encouraged to compete and are ridiculed if we do not. We believe competition is beneficial, productive, and necessary. Young people prepare themselves (as we point out in this book) by competing academically, athletically, and socially. Your competitive instincts move from the playing field into the board room. The score is tallied in terms of productivity and profit.

Nipponese culture is as unified and supportive as ours is individualistic and combative. A Japanese can therefore enter easily into cooperative effort at any level. There's no conflict between individual and group goals. The Japanese are accustomed to group effort, supporting those within the group, and competing only with the outside world.

Emphasis on group effort in Japan lasts a lifetime. A gifted U.S. child can skip grades or move into an elite group of exceptional children. In Japan, gifted youngsters remain with slower learners—using their superior skills to help their classmates. Attitudes and techniques of the quality circle are instilled from the beginning.

So you cannot lift the Japanese method up and use it blindly.

McGovern feels even stronger and I'll admit he makes a provocative point. Says McGovern:

The solution to American industry's problems of quality, customer satisfaction and productivity must begin in its executive offices.

Many American executives need to relearn, or at least take a refresher course in, guiding principles that brought their businesses and industries to the point where they were models for the Japanese in the first place.

COMMITTEES: THE BANE of Good DECISIONS

You must keep participative management from deteriorating into a committee for a simple classic reason: The committee is a lousy way to make decisions. As a communications device, the committee is fine. But as a decision-maker, it's a disaster, a perfect device for confusing responsibility.

Decisions must be made by an individual, not by a group. A group decision invariably ends up with the lowest common denominator. Again, you create the camel. Companies in the coal industry have created many problems via committee decisions. Remember Charles Lindbergh's comment when he stepped out of his plane at Le Bourget after his historic transatlantic flight: "It was easy, I did it *alone.*"

My friend David Ogilvy, the advertising genius, feels strongly about "group-think." He once appeared before an association committee as one of four agencies contending for the advertising assignment and recounted his experience.

Committee Chairman: "Unfortunately we have several applicants so each contender is limited to 20 minutes. When your time is up, we'll ring a bell."

Ogilvy: "Good."

Chairman: "Do you have any questions before we start?"

Ogilvy: "Yes. Who's going to judge the creative work the winning agency produces?"

Chairman: "Why, the committee sitting here of course, all 18 people."

Ogilvy: "Ring the bell, Mr. Chairman. I'm leaving!"

Since groups are a fact of life—and sometimes helpful to the manager—how do you avoid abusing committees? First, avoid 18 people. Try for less. And choose activists who really want to participate.

If you're mainly seeking a good cross-section of *opinion,* consider the "12 men good and true" that has evolved for juries. With less than 12, you don't get an objective community sounding. More than 12 gets unwieldy.

But in opinion-sounding with a jury-size group, remember the salient danger: One or two strong members tend to influence the rest. A forceful person with conviction and determination can bring others around—either because they're persuaded or because it's the easiest way—as in *Twelve Angry Men* with Henry Fonda and Lee J. Cobb. So you need a technique for polling the softer-spoken members too.

Of course the world's most notorious committee is the U.S. Congress. The public frequently admires individuals in Congress, but has little confidence in its deliberations-by-committee. As Will Rogers said:

"I understand that Congress opened up for the season last week. I was *afraid* they were going to do that."

In the movie *1776,* John Adams says in exasperation:

"One man is a lone incompetent. Two incompetents are a law firm. And three or more incompetents make a Congress!"

Today's Congress, committee action at its worst, has outlived its usefulness. It's a debating organization that has usurped powers of the two branches of government. Little is getting done. There were 20,000 bills introduced in Congress last year and only 500 passed. In state legislatures 7,000 out of 25,000 passed—one out of every four.

Sponsors of many federal "bills" are just grandstanding for voters back home and not sincerely seeking solutions. As a result, more issues are gravitating back to the states where they belong.

Moral: When a committee that is assigned an important function gets unwieldy, someone else must take over its work. Good lesson for the corporate climber.

The Taskforce

This is a valuable adaption of the committee idea. You avoid committee-itis by assigning a group of specialists to a problem. This is their full-time work—for the time it takes. Bethlehem Steel made good use of taskforces during the coal industry's legislative problems in West Virginia and Kentucky. One lobbyist and one ad man were assigned full-time to work in the coal industry while the problems existed. Later, they went on to other work.

Knowing when to abolish a taskforce is *the* key. Never allow them to achieve permanent status after the job is complete.

Several years ago General Mills placed Ed Rollins in charge of a management development taskforce—reporting directly to the CEO. His assignment: "Build the best managers possible."

A task assignment like that needs a built-in self-destruct button. (In General Mills' case, they promoted Rollins to president.) When a CEO isolates a real crying need, and assigns somebody to it, the problem gets a good airing. Predominant faults and needs come out in the open. Actions are slated to correct them.

But be warned: When temporary commissions *stay* in place, they develop their own bureaucracy and take on the same flaws they were trying to eradicate. The Committee to Abolish Paper Work in Washington finally got so loaded down with its own bureaucracy that it couldn't function in abolishing paperwork (to name one flagrant example).

Small task units are often good. Today the task-unit investigating computers in management systems are popular and often effective. But for Pete's sake, when it's done the job, close it down.

CUTTING COSTS

No one likes to cut back. Yet if sales are off, cost reduction is sometimes necessary. Don't take the usual route and order the departments under you to reduce costs by 10 percent. Try instead to eliminate work. That will automatically result in a rational reduction of the force.

Review what employees do. Determine what would happen if these things were not done. Again, eliminate functions, not employees directly.

Don't make business decisions for nonbusiness reasons—based on feelings, emotions, or pride. Pencil out how to bring the most down to the bottom line.

Nepotism decisions are often nonbusiness decisions.

A large eastern brewer was once quite successful. It had strong market position and sponsored New York Yankees' baseball. But as the company began to lose market share, it was hard pressed by Miller and others. It was losing its franchise in the New York market. Analysis showed the company lacked hard-driving executives at the next level down. Part of the reason for this: The chairman's son was the titular head of the organization. Consequently many able young people had left.

Engender Competition to Cut Costs

An excellent way to cut costs is to start a competition between employees. At the Bangor and Aroostock Railroad, after a study of each department, consultants outlined a number of specific actions to reduce costs. However, line heads weren't interested or couldn't read.

What to do? Bring out a tested weapon—competition. Get the president to hold a meeting. Everyone pledged allegiance, which was hardly enough to achieve results. But the meetings continued. Progress on a graph depicted how each of 14 department heads were doing in terms of cost reduction and employee reduction. Three department heads stood up at each meeting and explained why they were in the bottom three positions.

Competition was introduced. It worked like a charm. You never saw cost reduction take off so rapidly. Competitive incentives are powerful. Keep that in mind, voyager.

Preserving Time for Strategic Decisions

While you're doing all these things, try to preserve some time for long-range planning—for decisions that build toward significant change in your company and your industry.

Walter B. Wriston is an inspiration in this category. Standing tall in his corner office, looking down on Park Avenue from the 15th floor, Wriston, outgoing chairman of Citicorp, offered this comment regarding his 13 years on the job: "Whether you think it's good or bad, we've changed the environment."

The banking industry today (with notable exceptions, such as Citicorp) is a good heaven-forbid lesson to the corporate climber.

The financial services industry today is in perhaps the greatest state of flux since President Roosevelt engineered the bank moratorium and the splitup of banking services in 1933. Sears has bought into the banking business. Merrill Lynch has become a lender as well as a gatherer of deposits. American Express has added by acquisition a whole potpourri of financial services and hopes and plans that they may become melded into an efficient whole.

Against these forces, commercial banks have struck out in the opposite direction, with Citicorp as leader, buying savings and loans, getting into investment banking services, handling discount brokerage, issuing insurance, and endeavoring to cross state lines by buying banks in other states.

While all this is going on, most other commercial bankers persist in trying to conduct business as usual, trying to buy up one another, initiating political actions to block Citicorp and the nonbank bankers, apparently obsessed with that old adage: "The cobbler should stick to his last."

Today this short-sightedness is a sure road to disaster. Most bankers don't know what the words *strategic planning* mean. Presidents write about it, bank annual reports acclaim it, but few have done much research and analysis on what financial services should offer tomorrow, in what markets, and with what organizations. So, it's pretty much business as usual. Our old draft horses have just put on bigger blinders.

As you attain more responsibility, try to avoid fighting rearguard actions—hoping the sun won't rise or the tides won't ebb and flow. Take time out to think ahead. Stay in the vanguard of change. Be proud to say, as Wriston said, "I've helped change the environment"— for the better.

The CEO's Overall Role

Another way to keep time free for long-range planning: Avoid energy-sapping day-to-day crises.

"Ah, yes," I hear you saying, "but how?"

Good question. Understanding the CEO's multifaceted role will help. Except perhaps for a few very large corporations with long-established shares of their markets, the threat of crisis overhangs all big corporate decisions.

From the outside, the corporation appears to be a monolithic entity. Chief executives delegate most of the decisions that directly concern operations. The unique function of the chief executive is to resolve conflicting values.

The head of a three-billion-dollar corporation described it thus: "There are many claims on a business. I am at the intersection where you have to make decisions about them. My role in the corporation is a continuing thing, satisfying an ongoing river of claimants. We want to make all segments happy in the present but not sacrifice their future for the present."

The CEO is at once the head man of management and the fiduciary agent of the shareholders, responsible for the payoffs to both groups as well as to himself. To avoid corporate crises, the CEO performs a melding (a blend of melting and welding.) He steers the corporation in continuous movement over time.

"We invest in the future with charges against the present," said one president, "but the future payoff is viewed now."

Along with the intensified pressures of time and risk, the CEO melds into his decisions a number of other important values. Social values enter in. As the CEO of a paper and lumber company said: "Executives of well-managed companies do not have a single scale of values, but rather a mix, including duties, obligations as businessmen, useful services performed in a socially and economically acceptable way—all of these in relation to employees and their families and shareholders. The executive of a well-managed company wants both to be right and to seem right."

Finally, the CEO increasingly has to take account of social values pressing on the corporation from the outside. Said the CEO of a diversified high-technology company: "I long ago got over the feeling that a business exists only to make a profit. A corporation owes its existence to the state. The state licenses corporations and sets rules as a privilege. The state can be wise or unwise with respect to limitations. In other words, corporations are not God-given with rights like the human being.

"One rule is at least not to be harmful. At best to be constructive. In our case we drive to innovate, produce, and market useful products and services. In our society the profits are the privilege. That is, you have the privilege of making a profit if you serve. Lots of people say profits come first. But if you didn't live within the mores, no profit would be forthcoming."

Seemingly impossible job? Perhaps, but a few hundred men and women do it—usually with good results, and maintain mental health in the process. A few corner-office techniques will ease the pain.

Dissecting Problems

The ability to break things down, look at them one by one, and put them back together, is one such technique. Lois Dale, president of

Barter Advantage, New York's premier barter exchange, says: "Nothing is difficult if you divide it into small enough parts." Harry Lemmons, president of Saladmaster Corporation, Dallas, said: "By the mile, it's a trial. By the inch, it's a cinch." A manager who dissects effectively usually cannot be overwhelmed by the magnitude of problems.

Many otherwise effective executives can take things apart, but can't put them back together again. So-called progressive education is a culprit here. Schools teach kids to challenge everything—then they go home and forget about it. Student unrest of the 1960s was oriented toward taking institutions apart. They gave little thought to rebuilding.

During World War II, I saw this deficiency in a company producing fighter airplanes. There were many problems between plants. Designs had to be modified. The CEO identified them all—spread out on the table. But "all the King's horses and all the King's men, couldn't put Humpty Dumpty together again." What finally happened isn't surprising: A new CEO took over.

You just can't go on analyzing forever. After a point, action must take over. If you're a strong analyst and strategist, but weaker in tactics and implementation, get a number two person to fill that role. (When you do get such a person, by all means delegate.) The Eisenhower–Bradley combination in World War II is a good example of this principle in action. And the difficulties the strategist–politician (Eisenhower) and the tactician (Bradley) had working with a genius star performer (George S. Patton, Jr.) illustrates another kind of point.

Courage to Stick to Guns

When you do make a decision, stick with it. The effective climber must be able to make decisions and stick with them—in face of opposition from peers and bosses. Again, your record should prove you right—in most cases.

John Richman, originally chairman of Dart and later head of Dart and Kraft, Northbrook, Illinois, was originally advised not to merge Dart with Kraft, Inc. He believed the merger was good and kept at it. Critics said: "It'll be a drain on profits."

Richman did the merger. The Kraft division was a resounding success, accounting for $488 million of the firm's $860 million operating profit in a recent year. Richman's proposal didn't look so good to some people but he stuck with it—the mark of a successful manager.

Don't brood over the possible consequences of a decision. Imagine the worst-case scenario, the worst possible effect of your decision. This will place your fears in proper perspective.

Don't dismiss gut reactions. They could be telling you something.

Don't postpone. If you can't make up your mind, set a date for a resolution. By removing the immediate pressure, you will be able to judge the options.

Broaden the array of choices. Remember: There is seldom a 100 percent right choice in decision-making. You simply make up your mind, and then accept the consequences of your decision.

PLANNING: PLATFORM FOR GOOD DECISIONS

A good problem-solver often appears to snap off decisions by reflex. But in most cases, he's drawing on an accumulation of knowledge—carefully cultivated over the years.

Cultivation of knowledge, like a garden, requires advance planning. Planning is the rational determination of *where* you want to go and *how* you're going to get there. It is an on-going process—not an end result.

Planning enables you to determine what you must do *now* to be where you want to be next month, next year, or in five years. It identifies the lead time necessary to make things happen. Planning is concerned, not with future decisions, but with the future impact of present decisions.

"Planning doesn't eliminate risk but assures that the right risks are taken at the right time," one CEO told me. "It enables you to manage change and prevent crisis—rather than spinning wheels in reaction to change and crisis. It forces you to accept that the future need not be an extension of the past—or even the present. It can be what you make it."

I agree: Good planning must be objective-oriented—resulting in the identification and attainment of specific measurable objectives. See if you can make it factually based. This requires a thorough analytical review of history, profit and volume analysis, and assumptions. It involves subordinates—at all levels. Consider all available inputs. Allow a basis for control. Note deviations from the plan on a continuing basis.

Once you get your planning under control, you'll find that good decision-making follows the same pattern. As you have seen, a good decisionist has the ability to distinguish real from imaginary crisis. He or she can define the existing situation and decide: (1) Where are we going? (2) How do we get there?

The effective manager doesn't make decisions for subordinates until they have exhausted their own resources. Even then, ask what they recommend before offering your own opinion.

Above all, the good decisionist is willing to take risks. Do a risk/benefit analysis, then calculate the worst that can happen. Learn from mistakes but don't dwell on failures. You'll be too busy, much too busy, to brood.

CHAPTER 15

Developing the Global View

THE board was busy evaluating the two candidates for the CEO post. Both were well qualified.

"However," said the chairman, "since George Hanlon spent four years in Paris in charge of European ops, I do believe that makes a critical difference. After all, our international business accounts for 37% of volume now—with 43% projected for three years down the road. That European experience could mean the difference in earnings per share in the years ahead."

George Hanlon got the top job. This isn't an uncommon experience. Somewhere past midpoint in your climb, think seriously about getting some global experience if your company is so involved. (If not, is this an area you should develop?)

You've made your way up most of the slopes. You're one of the few left in the race. You're a division or general manager. You can even see the top peaks in the distance. Global experience might well be the last block you need to add. In fact, it might be a short cut that enables you to bypass a competitor who lacks international know-how.

Foreign experience is a vital necessity to many larger enterprises. Of the CEO's I know, 30 percent have spent time overseas, often three to seven years, and some longer. Most undertook programs to enlighten themselves on doing business overseas. They learned what was happening in developing countries. They became acquainted with foreign exchange and trading practices.

Start with Education

If you're previewing these up-the-slope specs early enough—a perceptive act!—you can plan your globalizing at the education level. If not undergraduate work at Cambridge or Oxford, then perhaps an advanced business program at Insead at Fontainebleau, outside Paris— probably the most renowned of all offshore business schools. Insead, difficult to get into, demanding in its trilingual requirements, is absolutely tops in quality of management education. Its graduates are in demand in Europe. Insead uses a number of Harvard's business professors and some of its case methods. (Other schools specialize in instructing American wives who sometimes get lost when they get overseas. And the way things are going, you'll probably be seeing classes for American husbands soon.)

In Switzerland, IMMEDE (under partial Nestlé subsidy) is another fine school—as the alumni association of European general managers will attest.

If you're still in school, by all means take a summer tour of Europe or the Far East. If money is a problem, perhaps you can line up short jobs in a country or two.

Back home, pick a country you'd like to understand better for independent study. Get books on its history and background. Experimenting in a foreign tongue is rewarding now and will pay big dividends later.

Reading *The Wall Street Journal* and *The London Times,* although important, alone won't do it. You must become involved yourself.

If you're just out of business school, you can seek out overseas with multinational firms. One of my associates in his early experience learned to live in tents with the Arabs. A mining engineer, in a recession, took up selling marine engines to Eskimos.

At your own company, find out which country is growing and how managers for these units are being selected. Seek out opportunities to become a branch manager or factory assistant in that country. Talk with your boss and the responsible division head. Outline your objectives. Ask for ideas and help.

EducatinG the Family

When you get a chance to get an overseas job, grab it. Your primary obstacles may exist at home! Your family may be concerned about leaving suburbia. ("Schools? The language problem?") These objections may be disguised as concern about overseas being a career sidetrack. That's just not so: not in today's global village with today's multinational company.

Besides, look at the benefits. First, there's money. You'll be able to save. Many expenses will be corporate out-of-pocket. One of our able young men went to work in Monte Carlo. Later I asked him why.

"I had nothing in the bank," he said. "I needed a nest egg. My target was a million dollars. I far exceeded that in the five-year period."

In addition to your living allowance, you can save because you'll get greatly reduced taxes (up to the first $85,000 is tax-exempt). In some places, you get a hardship allowance. You often encounter specific investment opportunities in foreign countries. Most international executives set aside greater resources overseas than are possible at home.

Further, living in a foreign country is a positive education for everyone—a seminar in how the world works, all at company expense. Studying geography and politics and economics is a chore for many. To experience these areas first-hand is an adventure of incalculable benefit in the years ahead.

Foreign experience is extremely invigorating. The French and the Italians have a distinct set of values, a vastly different culture, and a greater sensitivity to people. They attach great value to freedom of expression. The British, Germans, and Spanish have intriguing folkways and mores.

Not only will you enjoy learning other cultures, you'll need to understand how these people think, what their habits and customs are, and their likes and dislikes. All business begins in the marketplace with an understanding of how wants are created.

Breaking the Language Barrier

In taking on a foreign assignment, you and your family need to plan for a four- or five-year tour—particularly if you're going to a non-English-speaking country. The first year or two, you're learning to communicate. You can use interpreters, but it causes your opposite numbers to think you don't understand the problem. (And you won't either, without grasping the language.)

So get the language for yourself. Study language as a family. Struggling with a foreign tongue in the office and then speaking English at home doesn't make sense.

In the Berlitz total immersion program, you listen to tapes, you work with tutors in the day and night, you speak—at all times—in the language you're learning. This is a good foundation block.

Then you must make acquaintanceships, not just at the American Club, but among men and women from the country. You'll learn remarkable things about life as you try to understand their native values, namely, what they consider important, why they act the way they do. Soon you'll be able to evaluate the factors that motivate them. You'll find reasons for their happiness beyond wealth or status or position.

Oriental business people see English as a necessity. They learn to speak well, in many cases. But the words alone don't tell you the thought process. That requires considerable study.

An American company learned this in agreeing to sell lawn furniture made in Taiwan. After setting up the agreement, the U.S. firm's CEO got this telex from Taipei:

> We all appreciate ur pathfinding work n have got so much from ur persistence n courage of heroic quality to champion our new ventures.
>
> Now the road is clear.
> Let's go out n sell furniture, working 24 hours a day n travelling 200,000 miles a year in search of excellence.
>
> We can come together in faith n friendship to build a partnership relationship organization for our customers generations onto generations.
>
> We see in the crimson light of a rising sun fresh from the burning creative hand of God. We're never felt more strongly that best days lie ahead. We are a power force for good. With faith n courage, we can perform great deeds n take our next step.

Not exactly the language of two U.S. companies working out an agreement? No, but to the global manager, it's all in a day's work.

Check Your Words Going Overseas

It works the other way, too. Just because you understand something, don't assume it makes sense to another country. In fact, chances that it will are only fair. This is particularly true with product names.

"Domestic product names often take on unintended and hidden meanings when thrust into the global market," Dr. David Ricks, professor of international business at University of South Carolina, wrote in *Marketing Times*. "A soapmaker, considering a name for a new soap powder to be marketed internationally, ran a translation test of the prosposed name in 50 major languages."

"In English and most of the major European languages, the name meant *dainty*. But in Gaelic, it became *song*. In Flemish, it meant *aloof*. It said *horse* in the language of one African tribe."

When Coca-Cola was planning to sell in China, it wanted customers to use the English pronunciation—Coca-Cola. A translator developed a group of Chinese characters which, when pronounced, sounded like the product name.

These characters were placed on the bottles. But the characters translated to mean *wax-flatted mare* or *bite the wax tadpole*. Today Coca-Cola is again marketing in China. The new characters on the bottle translate to *happiness in the mouth*.

A vitamin firm introduced *Fundavit* in Latin countries. But it was too close to *Fundola* (Spanish for the rear of an attractive young female).

So what's in a name in the international market? Would you believe potential disaster? Check local meaning, symbols, and pronunciations—before you start out.

COURTESY COUNTS

Words are one thing. Actions are another. In most foreign countries, courtesy will long be remembered. For some months, we had been trying to see Gaevert, Europe's leading film manufacturer. I met Otto Straus, a principal, in a European hotel bar where I found he'd misplaced his shaving kit en route. I offered him mine. He was grateful.

On four occasions thereafter, in introducing me to his colleagues, Straus called my gesture "typical of Booz Allen's thoughtfulness." We got the assignment, largely due to his efforts.

And one-on-one courtesy, some say, becomes diplomacy when the factors become nations and the characters heads-of-state. When you're in another land, you automatically become an ambassador for both your country and your company.

Today's Headlines Tell Import

Today's headlines spell out the intense value of international experience. With all the hoorah about financial conditions in Mexico, Brazil, or Argentina, can you possibly discount the value of an executive who has worked in Latin America? To the true internationalist, these countries will be here tomorrow and, treated properly with the right consideration, will hold good markets for the future—*if the analysis is based on first-hand knowledge.*

When France volunteers to supply weapons to Jordan and Saudi Arabia after the United States declined, does this mean France is allied with the Russians and not to be trusted in business? "Not so," the global view says. "There may be other reasons for not doing business with France. But don't relate them to these events."

A major food company lost half of its expected worldwide earnings because of devaluation of the Mexican peso. Anticipatable? Maybe. Predictable? Probably. Production or marketing could have been structured to diminish the impact.

At many corporations, the bottom line is severely affected by overseas events. While no corporate plan can be foolproof, many safeguards can be erected through proper risk analysis. Many companies set aside adequate reserves from foreign earnings. Up-to-the-minute cash management of foreign resources is common, often hedged in foreign exchange markets.

When German and French products are imported into the United States in great quantities because of foreign exchange rates, be prepared to understand what is happening. Realize why U.S. goods cost so much overseas. Then decide whether to continue to do business in these areas or not.

In fact, you may want to ask your elected officials: "Doesn't allowing the United States to continue astronomical deficits make it perfectly understandable that foreigners want to come to the United States and buy some of this artificially inflated currency?" You'll find international responsibilities propel you more and more into public affairs—or should. It did with me.

When I was trying to get the chairman of India's supreme court to the United States on a lecture tour, I went to the Harvard Law School and Yale Law School. (This guy didn't have a rupee to his name. But he was yearning to come to America.) Well, Harvard was willing to advance a certain amount. Then I talked to New York Bar Association. Yes, they had a certain fund, but its use had to be cleared through the State Department. So I called up the State Department in Washington to check. A week later, they called back.

"We don't talk about this, Jim, but it'd really be better to put off bringing him here for a few years." At that time, the United States was siding with Pakistan and India with Russia. So global work involves you in public affairs.

Global View: Increasingly Essential

Right after World War II, with the pent-up demand for products and services, many management committees reasoned: "Let's stick to our knitting and not get involved with sales or production overseas. The U.S. market is huge and unsatisfied."

Many companies held to this strategy through the 1940s and 1950s. By the early 1960s, division managers were saying: "Europeans use razor blades, they drive cars, they use glasses and cosmetics. Why don't we ship our products overseas?"

The building of distribution organizations in Europe in the 1950s and 1960s led to Servan Schreiber's famous book *Le Defie Americain*. The thesis of this scathing volume was: The U.S. corporate power, having saturated markets at home, was now coming overseas to displace European manufacturers and to flood the continent with American products.

The premise proved to be entirely false. European manufacturers, it turned out, competed in world markets. Today the Fortune 500 lists a much smaller percentage of American companies. If anything, too many U.S. companies have had a head-in-the-sand attitude about global matters.

In the early 1960s, *Steel* magazine warned the industry: "Unless you get off your duff and get modern equipment, foreign competition will gradually take over U.S. and foreign markets."

At that time, the United States was importing less than 3 percent of its total steel consumption. Today, steel management and unions are trying to build trade barriers, screaming about foreign steel being dumped on the U.S. market and bitterly complaining about the subsidies other countries give their steel mills.

How did this happen? Because the Germans and Japanese developed more modern equipment. They invested in new continuous casting machines instead of following the old ingot blooming mill procedure. Their manufacturing techniques became technically superior. Will building protectionist walls save the industry? Never. It'll only cause reciprocal actions by other countries.

Ignoring what's happening in the rest of the world can be fatal. Today, happily, the steel industry is closing down unproductive mills, consolidating other mills, integrating the total steel process, and minimizing distribution costs. The steel industry is taking big strides to catch up.

You and your company must become involved in events around the world! Understand global resources, strengths, and weaknesses that affect your industry and your company. Be aware of the opportunities and the dangers of world marketing.

This world is getting so small so fast that other countries are becoming as important as U.S. regions once were. Many companies—Philip Morris for one—insist on international experience before you get too far up the slope. Dozens of multinational companies agree. In the years ahead, you'll find it increasingly difficult to ascend to the top in a large company *without* global experience.

All in all, going global is a great personal and career opportunity. Don't miss the boat that takes you up the slope.

CHAPTER 16

Productivity: Yours, Theirs, and the Nation's

Vaudeville headliner Eddie Foy once invited a showbiz friend to his Manhattan apartment. The friend was apprehensive: After all, the Seven Little Foys (later stage personalities in their own right) were widely known as hellions around the house. His visit was short.

"I wasn't too surprised to find the kids sawing the legs off the living room chairs," the friend said. "But I *was* shocked to see Eddie Foy down on the floor *helping them do it.*"

Portrait of a leader who understood two basic principles of productivity:

1. Never ask people to do something unless you understand it yourself.
2. When the boss pitches in personally, greater morale inspires greater performance.

The Eddie Foy story also illustrates the difference between *efficiency* and *effectiveness*. Foy's leadership was certainly *efficient* (accomplishing the goal of the moment) but hardly *effective* (Mrs. Foy questioned whether it needed doing in the first place).

This light home-management example shoehorns you into today's weightiest business concern: How can we get greater productivity?

Productivity is on everyone's red-alert assignment list these days. As Karen W. Anderson reported in *The New York Times:*

Solid, sustained productivity gains are essential if American workers are to have higher real wages and a rising standard of living, if American industries are to hold their own against foreign competitors.

Japanese and West German productivity gains have for years outpaced the United States. Though Americans still produce more than workers in other countries, the gap is closing, and quickly.

Now, before you shrug and say "that's too big a problem for me to handle alone"—stop and think. First, you *can* spruce up our personal productivity as an individual manager. Second, you *can* implement new ways to get your assigned employees to produce more—thus boost your company's effectiveness. And yes, you *can* contribute to productivity of the economy at large. In fact, as you rise in management, such a concern will be your decided responsibility. So gear up now.

PERSONAL PRODUCTIVITY: THE BASE

Boost your own productivity by accepting only do-able tasks. When the boss says "we've got to get these three things done by the end of the week" and you agree, then another boss comes in and says "we've got to get these two things done" and you say "yes," you're in trouble. You can't possibly do it all. You're programmed for failure. Yet this happens time and again.

When you get assigned more than you can do, say: "I'll be glad to work on that. But can you help me sort out the priorities versus these other four things I've got here? Do you think *that* should be first or should I do *these* first?

That forces the boss to establish priorities, either alone or in consultation with other bosses.

At Billings Corporation in Montana, John Cranepohl, the director of marketing, was retiring. His successor, Jens Mahoney, was being shifted from another job to take over the marketing post next year. Mahoney, a real riser in the company, started giving Janet Pegrim, the research director, *advance* instructions that conflicted with John Cranepohl's policies. She asked what to do?

"All organizations have a chain of command," I told her. "If somebody other than your direct boss asks you to do something, go ahead and do it. But tell your direct boss you've been so assigned. If there's a conflict, let them resolve it."

"Isn't this a sign of weakness?" she asked.

"Maybe," I said "But it's a 1000 percent less trouble, I'll guarantee, than you get into when you can't get conflicting tasks done."

One of our guys was commited to several assignments with only a week to do them. I was out of town. When I came back he didn't have the work done.

"I got sent to Geneva," he said.

"Did you make your existing commitments clear before you agreed to go?"

"No," he said. "I'd never been to Geneva and I wanted to go."

"Don't you do that again," I said. "Holding back pertinent information about existing assignments is irresponsibility. If you do this once more, you've used up all your tickets."

LEARN COMPUTERS—NOW

As you study productivity, learn the big picture—the right schedules, the right tasks for your people, effective incentives that get people to perform beyond task requirements, motivations that encourage reassignment of people-work to machines. At the same time, don't ignore the nuts and bolts of time management and work flow either.

Many people think productivity means working harder and getting more pieces off the production line. But, overall productivity—really hardly that at all—is (a) an amalgam of machinery and technical development that lets machines do things faster and gets machines to do things that people are doing and (b) the end result of incentives properly applied.

Thus, classic productivity is an overall scientific industrialized movement rather than an individual movement.

Of course, you need years of experience before you get involved in that kind of overall policy productivity. However, you can prepare now—no matter what your job—by becoming thoroughly familiar with computers.

Thousands of 10-year-olds have been studying computers in school for six years. Yet many executives haven't studied computers for six days. The times are passing them by.

I'm constantly amazed at what computers can do. Recently I needed a client's data compared with other companies in the same industry. In two days, our people put together charts and schedules and graphs that amazed me—showing clearly and exactly where the company stood in research and development and profits.

Computers, absolutely essential today, are being used to display great quantities of data that would have taken weeks to grind out before.

In the judgmental process, managers must constantly review options. You run an assumption through a model and preview the results. Pick any post for an aspiring climber—planning or working in the factory or production control or tracking costs—and the computer is vital to understanding what's going on. It helps you come up with the right answers.

If you've been out of school more than 10 years, you're behind in computers. If you're just out, you're going to be behind without regular updates. If you know computers, and your competitor doesn't, you're going to get the promotion—all other factors being equal.

PERSONAL TIME-MANAGEMENT

This is a powerful force (for good or bad) in your own productivity. Most time-management advice is common sense—which doesn't make it common practice.

Relaxation plays a vital role in productive time-use. Rest. Working for long periods without breaks results in decreased energy, physical stress, and tension. Take only emergency work home. After work hours, restore yourself. Relax with a book unrelated to work. Exercise to keep healthy.

Michael Cummings, president of British American Travel, said in *Marketing Times* that making lists is the difference between spinning wheels and confidently pursuing objectives. Lists point your direction. Make daily lists of tasks and activities. Include meetings, telephone calls, memos, letters, and chores.

Your lists are a blueprint of your long-range and short-term goals. Goals not clear? Here's the first item on tomorrow's list: Set goals for the week, month, year.

As you complete tasks, cross them off. The sense of accomplishment motivates and energizes. Lists are the first step toward becoming that noted busy person with time to solve problems.

Set priorities. Don't allow your daily lists to drive you crazy. There's always one more task to do. For reasons of physical health and sanity, you can't do everything. Time does run out. Your goal: a project that produces actionable results. (Said Winston Churchill: "PERFECTION-ISM is spelled PARALYSIS.")

So evaluate your list. What's most urgent? Next most? What relates and doesn't relate to goals? What can you put off until tomorrow? What can someone else do for you? Set priorities based on importance to goal-solving—*not* by which is easier. Then, and only then, have you roadmapped a productive day.

Carry a pocket calendar. Record day-by-day appointments. Note tasks you must complete—and when. Your pocket calendar is the story of your business life—past, present, and future.

Use block time. In planning your day, allocate time blocks for specific tasks. Block time allows you to prepare psychologically for the task. As assigned time draws near, you become equipped to devote enthusiastic attention to the job.

"Fill dead time," Cummings said. "Even the best planners face dead time—usually unexpected. Don't waste it. Keep less urgent but important tasks at hand to throw in the breach: letter writing, returning telephone calls, conversations with staff, homework for an upcoming sales presentation. Trains and airplanes are ideal for reading mail or important articles."

Use the telephone. Jacob Bronowski, in the famed *Ascent of Man* TV series, called the telephone "one of man's superb tools." Think twice about arranging fact-to-face meetings. Often the telephone is better. You get your person quicker. You get down to business faster.

Use the telephone to screen prospect meetings. In a few minutes, by listening to questions raised and objections offered, you can determine if it deserves a face-to-face meeting.

Use waiting time. Your out-of-office appointee is late. Cut your losses. Don't wait longer than 20 minutes. Leave politely and reschedule. Few meetings are worth more than 20 minutes wait.

Know who's on first. Schedule regular meetings with staff. Interchange ideas on tough problems. Conversations can reveal that work in progress is either unnecessary or wrong-minded. Cut losses. You often discover work you *don't* need to do—freeing time for something more urgent.

Personal Productivity

This boils down to budgeting your time the way you budget other assets. Decide what goals you want to achieve, then outline the steps you must take to get there. Focus each day's activities on these goals, rating every task according to its importance in relation to your goals and dealing with these tasks *first.*

Audit your personal activities for several days. It'll give you a better idea of where time is slipping away.

Learn from the mistakes of others as well as your own. Don't be a perfectionist. Most tasks don't require perfection. In many routine matters, you get the same result from an 80 percent effort as from a 100 percent one. Save your perfectionism for the really important tasks.

Don't get into the habit of taking work home. I'll grant it's essential— sometimes. But if you do it regularly, you can easily fritter away an afternoon telling yourself you're going to take the work home anyway.

Don't overcommit yourself. When you take on more than you can do well, you're going to do badly.

Value of Humor

Advice to managers sometimes sounds' grim and cold—with good reason, since leadership is a demanding science. However, a sense of humor about yourself and your follies is a valuable asset. When things get too uptight, think about this analysis from a retired dean of management named Murphy:

If anything can go wrong, invariably it will, and at the worst possible time.

Everything you decide to do costs more than you first estimated and every activity takes more time than you have.

Whatever you set out to do, something else must be done first.

If you improve or tinker with something long enough, eventually it will break.

By making something absolutely clear, somebody will be confused.

You can fool some of the people all the time and all of the people some of the time, and that's sufficient.

Nothing is impossible for the person who doesn't have to do it.

Anytime things appear to be going better, you have overlooked something.

Once a job is fouled up, anything done to improve it makes it worse.

Every discovered gain is more than offset by some undiscovered loss.

Never tell anyone your troubles. Half the people don't care. The other half are damned glad you're finally getting what's coming to you!

Encouraging Employee Productivity

With that wry perspective in hand, you'll be better able to upgrade productivity of people who report to you. A key question at the outset from a rising manager.

"I can do my work—or could. But I'm constantly interrupted by the people that work for me. If I'm stopped every five minutes, I can't do my own work."

·This problem bothers many. Don't let it be a serious roadblock. Your work and their work can—and must—coexist.

Sure, an open door policy for your people is good. But that shouldn't preclude block time when your door is closed—from nine to eleven each Wednesday and Friday, for instance. People will work around that commitment—just as if you were out of the office. (And time management specialists keep coming back to *block time* again and again as the cornerstone to getting things done.)

So make your open door policy figurative not literal until you get big enough to afford to sit around with your door open, inviting interruptions. (And if this ever materializes, it'll sound suspiciously like you're on a plateau—because top people don't do it.)

Doors are meant to be closed when you're planning or writing reports. "There is this crazy idea abroad in business today that you only shut your door when you are firing someone," says Bill Marsteller, the ad agency chairman. "Anybody who has invention as a part of his job description is entitled to periods of isolation."

Employee Feedback

This is an enormous aid to productivity—yet often the best feedback does not come through regular channels. Scott Nadler, a manufacturing company CEO, attends a luncheon with five or six randomly selected production employees each month. They talk about whatever bothers them about plant operations. Supervisors and production VPs are not present. Nadler just asks how things are going and what might they do better and, since Nadler has a common touch, employees are not afraid to speak out.

"Those employee sessions give me valuable input that wouldn't have filtered through immediate supervisors," he said.

"Well," I said, "this ad hoc lunch is good provided you observe two precautions: First look for the gems but realize three-quarters of what you get will have no value. Second: Devise some way of letting each supervisor involved know about each suggestion you implement—otherwise you destroy the command structure."

Nadler accepted both precautions.

"I also accept," he said, "the added bonus in employee *esprit de corps.* Each employee feels his opinion matters. ('I'm sure my suggestions are getting a hearing. After all, I told the CEO personally.') I accept the conditions because I'm downright enthused about the benefits."

Speaking of feedback, many organizations have a good rule: The boss *can* and *does* talk to any person. (Reminds me of the question: "Where does an 800-pound gorilla sit in a restaurant? Answer: "Any damned place he likes.") But if the boss talks to you two levels down, go to your superior immediately afterward and repeat what *he* said and what *you* said. Keep off personalities. Talk about methodology. (Even under the best conditions, such talk is implicit criticism of a supervisor for not having implemented the change already.)

Bob Masterson of Supreme Homes, was, by nature, outgoing. Yet he didn't relate easily to rank-and-file employees when he'd visit the plant in Bourbon, Indiana (a dry town, incidentally, not like Rye, New York, which is not).

"When I talk to production employees, I can't think of a thing to say," Masterson said. "I'm not shy, but I just freeze up. They talk about bowling scores and I just don't know how to react."

This is his handicap. A different person could have picked up insight about local problems on each trip.

In harvesting feedback, you'll find that the presence of middle-management at a complaint session can indeed inhibit free expression. One plant manager was happy to have you interview any employee—provided *he* sat in on the interview. Of course, the employee clammed up. So that was a waste.

When I was President at Exeter Academy in New Hampshire, we decided to give our trustees first-hand experience with students. We'd end the trustees meeting at 6 p.m. and send the trustees to a dormitory. They'd go down to the recreation room and ask students how they liked the school and the food, and listen to other complaints. To help the trustees communicate with the students, the dormitory faculty advisor sat in. The dialog:

Johnny: "Gee, that food we had last week was rotten."
The Faculty Advisor (for the next ten minutes): "What Johnny is talking about—what he really means . . ."

So we barred the faculty advisors.

Feedback sessions are often dropped in favor of more basic needs. But they must be put in again regularly. Knowing what people down the line are saying—even though you may not agree with it (*particularly* if you don't agree)—is an important factor in productivity.

Setting Goals for Employees

This is a key to productivity gains—but don't set them too high or too low. An effective target must be attainable but require some stretching. Set targets that involve moderate risk. When success likelihood is 65 percent to 85 percent, a person's inner sense of challenge is at its peak. As probability decreases or increases off this range, the motivation to achieve is reduced.

Make the risk too great and they see the target as unrealistic. Then if they don't make it, self-esteem is lowered. Set the risk too low and success is "a piece of cake," and they never go into overdrive.

For your own planning set targets at three levels: minimally acceptable, above average, and excellent. No need to discuss the minimal level: This is your own mental watermark for an employee to maintain employment. However, at the other levels make realistic but challenging targets very public. Then your employee can decide which level (middle or high) he or she will strive for. And you will distribute the rewards accordingly.

COMMON-SENSE PRODUCTIVITY

Not all productivity measures are computerized and complex by any means. CEO Bill MacDonald, walking through a mobile home plant with a poor productivity record, told the plant manager:

"Fix the cafeteria with no more than three or four seats to a table. They won't sit around so long that way. Try moving the bulletin boards out near the time clocks. After they check out, they can read. Make sure someone picks up magazines regularly in the lavatories. This isn't the public library. The first-line supervisors are too dressed up. Give them coveralls with the plant name on the pocket. When the men on line need a hand, they'll pitch in—they're dressed for it. Let's stop the reserved parking. The first to arrive get the best spots."

Common-sense productivity, he found, builds efficiency without any danger to morale.

WEEDING-OUT NONPRODUCERS

No productivity program is complete without a weeding-out process for employees who can't or won't contribute. This is probably the hardest part of a manager's job, as you've already seen, yet it must be done.

Do this in your own way. When Casey Stengel was manager of the New York Yankees, Bob Cerv, the outfielder, was sitting at one end of the empty dugout before a game. Stengel sat down near him, looked over at Cerv, and said: "Nobody knows this, but *one of us* has just been traded to Kansas City."

One veteran corporate manager goes further: "Fire five percent of your employees each year." His theory:

Every employee can be placed on a productivity curve: *Superior,* comprising the top five percent, then *excellent,* followed by the *satisfactory* majority, the *marginal,* and finally the bottom five percent that should be unhitched from the climbing team.

This evaluation, of course, must be based upon a fair and objective productivity measure. Standards known to all. Employees must know what is expected and how their work is judged.

"Doesn't this discourage people?" one seminar student asked.

"No," he says. "The morale of the good people goes up when they know they don't have to carry drones."

Even though this theory is cold-blooded (after all, don't lose sight of the human condition you're working with), it does give you an idea of your responsibility for constant evaluation of employee effectiveness.

On the positive side, you can improve productivity by promoting good people to better jobs. Look for men and women who assume responsibility *above* their assignment. Further, in these days of rapid technological change, look for people who (of their own free will) are improving their knowledge and skills by continuing education. Give them better jobs—this serves as a reward to individuals and a benefit to the whole company.

On another front, you often need to cut department costs. Sometimes this must be done fast. If you cut 15 percent across the board, the blood flows—you've slashed important organs. Then you've got to rehire and retrain. But three times out of four, cutting and adding back works pretty well.

Naturally when time permits, consultants can study each segment and tell you exactly how much to cut each place. But that takes four to six months. It's better than the blind 15 or 25 percent, when time permits.

When we were helping a major TV network cut overhead, we reduced 37 copying machines down to 13. The most important benefit—much more than the savings on machines and paper—was the saving of executive time in reading all that paper (most of it unnecessary).

Some people are absolute nuts about copies. They make copies and send them all over the place and it just clogs up everything. The copying machine is a mixed blessing. When you need copies, it's good. When you don't need them, many people make them anyhow. All new tools tend to be overused. ("The only difference between men and boys is the price of their toys.") Excess copying is a foursquare enemy of productivity.

Overall Industrial Productivity

Now you're ready to think about making your contributions to corporate and national productivity.

Essentially, productivity is nothing more than a way to measure how much output you get for every unit of input. Often you focus on the productivity of labor, a fundamental resource. An employee who produces 100 widgets an hour, for example, is clearly more productive than an employee who produces only 50 widgets an hour. Many factors can affect such figures: the machinery, the employee's education or skill, advances in technology, or the working environment.

Generally, output per worker hour plummets during a recession as production sinks faster than employment. (It usually rises following a recession as production increases faster than companies re-employ workers.) The minute you fall into a recession, volume falls. The company doesn't have as much work to do, so it cuts back. But never fast enough. If sales fall 30 percent, it might cut back 10 percent.

"John Johnson's a skilled die-maker," the foreman says, "and gee, if we let him go, we'll never be able to get a guy that good again."

So they keep Johnson. Productivity suffers. You're logging more worker hours than you need. Yet you're not getting the output—there isn't a call for it. In the meantime, productivity lags. Well, if this continues too long and the company's losing money, the CEO bites the bullet and fires those valuable old guys after all.

This sort of cutback happened to me at American Rolling Mill in Middletown, Ohio. ARMCO had excellent employee relations (so much so that employees kept running union organizers out of town). I was one of the 100 college graduates hired as trainees over a period of three years. A downturn came and we were told: "You've got to go.

After all, we can't terminate old timers who've been here for years."

When the economy improves (and things get better) and cuts are made, manufacturing firms go on overtime rather than adding people—overtime gives you greater productivity.

THE R & D FACTOR

John Kendrick of George Washington University says American productivity is coming back and the United States will be an outstandingly productive nation again—based on two factors: innovation and computer implementation.

He claims R & D expenditures have risen vastly—this will develop new products and new processes that will improve productivity. I take issue with him. Sure, R & D is popular measure (beloved by security analysts) for determining how well a company is doing. But it's not always an *accurate* measure.

In some industries, R & D is more important than others. In consumer products, R & D is often considered essential for coming out with new products, improvements on present products, or subtly copying products of competitors.

But in many industries R & D may be a false production measurement for two reasons:

1. Once management recognizes that the financial community uses R & D as a measure, they'll simply declare everything R & D—including the garbage collection. You can tell when this happens: Other costs go *down* while R & D goes *up*.

2. Not many managers know how to get optimum utilization from R & D. I've seen empire-building R & D departments add more and more people—and get less and less productivity. When not strictly controlled, research expenditures go up substantially. Departments get off into pure research (why safflower oil is

better than corn oil) because they think they can ultimately use that knowledge.

Basic research, best left to the universities, is almost always a bad idea in a company. I'm all for *applied* research. If you're in the hair care business, it's very important to understand how oil penetrates a hair follicle.

Du Pont's research approach has always been: "Our divisions must get out our new products, but not do fundamental research. We'll form a whole separate group under corporate management and let them stare at the sky and dream up the nylons." (In fact when nylon was first developed, Du Pont's operating division didn't want it. But they finally did accept it and the rest is history.)

One R & D roadblock is finding a good manager—as difficult as locating a good hospital administrator. In both slots, you're looking for a scientist with respect of colleagues and an administrator who can motivate people to produce results. In the research field, that's an almost impossible combination.

When a good research head *does* emerge, he or she gets pretty independent. They build empires. They go too far into basic research. They get into *applied* research, too, about how the consumer reacts—subjects properly left to the marketing department. Anytime R & D does marketing research, it's a mistake. Duplication is an enemy of productivity.

Evaluating R & D Productivity

Bill May, a trained scientist, came out of a university and spent ten years in R & D before he started up the slope at DuPont and American Can Company.

(From this research start, he rose to chairman at American Can. That's atypical. In most cases, being in R & D is not the ideal way to climb. First of all, the jobs don't pay as much. Compensation levels have a way of reflecting the market. Research people are not so much in demand, and they know it. So it's not the fast track.)

"I defy anybody to go into a smart-run research organization and tell how productive it is," May said. "It's just damn near impossible."

But you still must try. Start, as you must always start, by determining what the department's going to work on. And then keep it on those tangible goals. Avoid a scatter-shot approach. Build in fail-safe points. If R & D doesn't achieve your set goals in 60 days, throw the whole project out. Lay out your whole work plan over a 12 to 24 month period—with check points every so often.

The counter argument about tight research control runs thusly:

Researchers are stifled in too tight a milieu. One scientist started out trying to invent a new roach killer and, through serendipity, ended up with a fireproof rug. Put him in too tight a straitjacket and he'd never have invented the fireproof rug.

That's the argument. But I'm not buying it. Sure, sometimes serendipity strikes out of left field just like a group of monkeys at typewriters might turn out *Paradise Lost*—in time. But a good manager wouldn't bet company funds on it. Unless research is structured, scientists will come up with a super dog food that dogs don't like (which actually happened).

Integrate research into your business plan. Be cold-blooded. The new discovery might be wonderful. But if it's not what you're looking for, do away with it.

The Japanese Comparison

Robert Townsend pooh-poohs the whole idea of Japanese superiority in productivity. He says we're much superior to the Japanese if we'd just settle down. I don't totally share this view—I think we've got great power in this country if we'd organize it to do things.

But I think the Japanese have learned. It really stems from their philosophy of life. A job is lifelong job for a Japanese. Once they get a job they don't need to worry about being fired. Nor does the company need to worry about the complacency that so plagues U.S. civil service employees. The Japanese worker, as a point of honor and face, constantly works to make his company better.

And, of course, much has been said about the participatory management that gets ideas from all. You do get an awful lot of good ideas from workers. The problem is: The world is full of ideas. But only so many are practical. You've got to sort them out.

The Japanese do seem to have worked at getting optimum thoughts out of employees. We're learning to do that.

So, American workers don't have that group tradition beginning in grammar school, the way they do in Japan. Whether or not we can inculcate more group spirit at a later date is one of the issues in upgrading American productivity.

AMERICAN COMPANIES BOUNCE BACK

There are a number of good signs that American companies *are* doing something about corporate productivity—the kinds of steps that'll be your increasing responsibility as you move up the slope. Companies are adding new machines, cutting workers, and generally slimming down activities that grew fat during better times.

Intel Corporation, Santa Clara, California, discovered that 65 percent of its employees worked in administration and only 35 percent in manufacturing—the opposite of 10 years earlier. Intel responded by putting together a group of productivity experts to analyze jobs and simplify them where possible. These specialists have been trimming both paperwork and bureaucracy.

One billing process that formerly took 199 steps and 44 hours a month has been cut to 14 steps and 41 minutes. Ordering a $2.79 mechanical pencil once required 12 forms. Today, it takes one form.

Intel says corporate productivity is up 33 percent, while its administrative payroll has shrunk by $17 million a year to $225 million (mainly through attrition). The company expects to save about $60 million annually in the next three years.

The New York Times reports that at TRW Inc., Cleveland, the emphasis on productivity grew out of a desire to improve competitiveness.

At one 350-person plant, TRW put its hourly employees on a merit system and achieved an 11 percent productivity improvement. In its electronics and defense sector, the company found that moving computer software programmers out of a common bullpen and into cubicles brought in a 40 percent gain.

TRW's total productivity improvement the first year—about 1½ per cent—was below the national average of 3.1 percent. But the company expects a 2½ percent gain the second year and larger increases later.

"A 2½ percent improvement may not sound like much," said Edward Steigerwald, TRW's vice-president for productivity, "but on a $6 billion sales base, it's formidable. Besides we're really not talking about short-term changes."

At Boise Cascade Corporation, Boise, Idaho, the decision to try to raise productivity was prompted by the feeling that "if we didn't do something about the economy, we would all go down the tubes like Rome, and more recently, Britain," reported Robert Stolz, productivity director.

Boise Cascade managers have been encouraged—and trained—to be better communicators and less dictatorial. The company has added three new paper machines that can each handle 2,000 tons of product a day, double the previous capacity, but with the same size crew. The company's workforce was trimmed by about 7,000 from a total of nearly 36,000 four years earlier.

"There's no magic to productivity," said Stolz. "It's just a little different way of looking at things, keeping careful measurements, and a lot of hard work."

Thus the concern for better productivity will be with you at each level during your management climb. There's no bigger challenge. Inroads made in productivity will be decisive in your management career.

CHAPTER 17

SURVIVING and CONTROLLING CORPORATE INTRIGUE

WHEN Henry Ford II fired Lee Iacocca from Ford Motor Company, he told Iacocca simply: "I don't like you." This simple public announcement indicated tons of backstage intrigue, as you can well imagine.

Iacocca kept his own counsel for a number of years. But the story is coming out bit by bit. Iacocca recently called the Fords "wealthy snobs who practice the divine right of kings. The Fords wouldn't even socialize with you. You could produce money for them but you weren't about to hobnob with them."

Recalling his firing, Iacocca vows: "That's something I won't forgive. I told my kids: 'Don't get mad, get even.' I did it in the market place. I wounded him badly. It took five years."

The Ford–Iacocca case of corporate intrigue—long-running category—would need toning down to make it believable on *Dynasty*.

Learn to Cope with Intrigue

In your career climb, you're going to face quite a bit of intrigue. To ignore intrigue is to put your head in the sand. This doesn't mean you should become a full-time intriguer. But at the very least, be aware of it defensively.

Some people make a career out of politics. They advance by plotting to get around this guy or to sink the other fellow. Never allow intrigue to become a full-time job or sooner or later you will get caught in your own net.

You can't get by on intrigue alone. But you won't get by at all unless you are at least a defensive intriguer. Be careful at all stages. But when you get up near the top, politics becomes a much stronger force. Form your own evaluations of the plotters. Learn how close you can afford to be with one fellow versus another.

Power struggles are all around you. You often hear of people ending up on the wrong side of a fire-fight and, when the smoke clears, leaving the firm. When there's real competition for the division head's job, most people will throw their weight one way or another. And if you endorse late, you're in trouble.

Your best bet: Concentrate on your job. Talk with both candidates. Make your contributions to the Democratic as well as the Republican party. Maintain good relations with both. It's far from easy to do. But the effective people manage it.

Power: Tool of Intrigue

All intrigue isn't bad. Often intrigue is a tool the savvy manager deploys to get things done *without* using raw power. Raw power plays are seldom effective.

The good CEOs relax you, they talk, they persuade. Their main weapon is leadership, not raw force. They get people to *want* to do. They don't ride roughshod over subordinates.

Jimmy Walker, when mayor of New York, said: "Be nice to the people on the way up, because you are going to meet the same people on the way down."

Napoleon said: "Any leader who makes enemies of people he meets while gaining his leadership is a fool and will not be a leader long."

If you believe the way to the top is over the bodies of others, make a reappraisal.

Women normally are not taught about power. Most never played team sports where they had to take charge, interact under pressure, or lead a group. However, once women learn the fundamentals, they exercise power with as much proficiency and know-how as men.

An executive in a large computer company said: "If you can't get the people under you to do what you want them to do, even when they want to do something else, you don't belong in the executive suite and you probably won't get there."

At the same time, the effective intriguer knows when *not* to press his case—not until the climate is right and, on some subjects, never.

The Better Part of Valor

Many times, discretion is required to know when further intrigue is wasteful, even harmful. Gracefully retreat and plan to fight another day on another front. For example, you're not likely to win if:

- ☐ The CEO doesn't *really* like your idea.
- ☐ The chairman's wife had the same idea last week and it was turned down.
- ☐ Everybody in the company thinks they did it last year—and they all know why it didn't work then either.

☐   They really can't afford it.

☐   Somebody somewhere is using your idea as a way of testing his or her power.

☐   You don't address corporate fears—alway a good goal for any intriguer.

Running with the Ball

Taking the ball and running with it is nice in theory. In fact, you must find out *who* has the ball and is willing to run *with you.*

Effective intriguers maintain psychological barriers between themselves and co-workers, subordinates, and superiors. Most people around them know very little about their personal lives. They don't volunteer information.

Intriguers understand power is a habit. In all their relationships, they maintain little or no social relationships with subordinates.

If an intriguer has been lunching with the same four people for three years and then he becomes an assistant department head, he stops those lunches and starts lunching with other assistant department heads.

Real intriguers never associate with competitive insiders. Each gathers little groups of friends. They enlist the most able people and avoid the incompetents.

In relationships with subordinates, they continually reinforce their positions: "Move that chair over here, Tom." "Mary, please get me a cup of coffee."

If you work for a powerful boss and you try to play power games with him, you're likely to lose.

A top-100 corporation president says: "The most important thing you're going to have to do is bite your tongue and say, 'Yes, I made a mistake.' I had to eliminate two people for contention for top position in the past few years because I found them playing silly games. Come in with the idea of cooperating with the people in charge."

Position is critical to power. At meetings, if there is a stage, stand or sit on it. Height is not only power, it is also credibility. Stand when you speak.

"Skilled power players sit as near the prime power person as possible, preferably to the right," John T. Malloy says. "When you cannot sit there, sit next to another power figure."

Any powerful superior can intimidate by walking up behind a person, or sitting on his desk. This says: "I have the right to invade your property. It is my sign of power. You are almost impotent."

All animals, including the executive animal, defend territory with vigor. Territory (not just desk, office, or home) can be your restaurant or even your city.

But don't go too far. Don't go into another's office, throw your coat over his chair, spread your papers over his desk, and take over. These tactics are counterproductive. The officeholder becomes defensive or mad or both. Being pushy and being powerful are not the same.

Be careful how you use power in intrigue.

No: It's Not Fair

In Budd Schulberg's *What Makes Sammy Run?*, the protagonist says: "Fair? What kind of sissy word is fair?" The corporate climber asks: "Why can't I stay out of politics and be judged on the work alone?" Same answer. You're in the real world, old sport, and more people *want* top jobs than there *are* top jobs. Hence, the scramble is based on merit *and* politics.

No matter what anyone tells you, the thrifty, brave, and reverent don't reap all the rewards. Ad agency head Lois Wyse says:

Business, all business, is at one time or another exciting, overwhelming, tiring, interesting, fascinating, absorbing, exhilarating, joyous, a drag, thrilling, dazzling, preoccupying and boring.

But it's not always fair. And no one can promise you that it will be.

You will work very hard on a project, then watch someone else waltz off with the credit, recognition, and financial rewards.

You will give the best service and make the best product, then someone up there will make the wrong decision, and all your good effort will go for naught.

You will reward someone with your loyalty and your best work. Then someone else gets the promotion.

No. It's not fair. But it's not a bit fairer to your competitor.

Never Initiate Intrigue

Mike Barnett was doing a research study in an Illinois plant for a large steel company. Later, in reporting on findings to headquarters, Mike said to Jen Peterson, the general manager: "Did you know the assistant sales manager is going out nights with the receptionist? I'm amazed at the way they do things out in Illinois."

Peterson wasn't buying any.

"Barnett, God damn it," he said, "We hired you to do a study. Now, let's leave all that intrigue stuff alone and find answers to the questions."

You usually lose by initiating gossip.

The Hidden Microphones

Sometimes the CEO himself is an intriguer—and gets caught in his own trap. The chairman of a large trucking company put microphones in the conference room ceiling when the new building was under construction. He kept it secret—for a while. But when the telephone company came in to change wires, a juicy corporate Watergate erupted. Senior VPs resigned in protest. Later, after the hidden listening post had been dismantled, they came back. But much ground was lost as well as reputation.

Listening in on others is unthinkable. Nobody will stand for that. There are lots of times when you'd *like* to know what people are saying. But if you start eavesdropping, where will it all end? It's unthinkable.

You'd also like to know what your competitor is doing. The question is: How far can you go in finding it out? Competitive companies are often involved in a tremendous amount of corporate espionage. Schick was desperately trying to figure Gillette's move when the ribbon razor was still under wraps. They tried unsuccessfully to hire Gillette's people. Finally they contracted with a development engineering firm that had employed previous Gillette engineers. This is a ticklish area.

Will They Respect You in the Morning?

There are certain Marquess of Queensberry rules about going to work for competitors. On one hand, your knowledge and your acquired management techniques are really your stock-in-trade—your product when you're on the job market. You ought to be able to sell your knowledge on the open market as you wish.

However, like most coins, there's another side. If you're working for Zenith in TV set product development and RCA wants to hire you away, be cautious. I've seen many a candidate cast on the garbage heap after he's been pumped dry. So if they want you for specific competitor knowledge, the answer is: No, they won't respect you in the morning.

There's one industry where none of these rules apply: advertising. Advertising people move regularly around the circuit—from agency to a network to a corporate department. Competitor rules don't apply. Say you're working for an agency and produce a hot new campaign. But by the time you could possibly go somewhere else, that campaign is all over. Besides, it's published in newspapers or magazines or broadcast. So everyone knows what it is.

But in most industries, be chary of the job offer that appears predicated on specific insider knowledge. This will always be a controversial area. Our consitution allows people to go where they want. Lawsuits often follow. But I don't know any that ever won on this point. You can keep people from taking files, but you can't keep them from picking brains. Hence there's no way this can be stopped.

Some companies go too far by putting all wastepaper through shredders. This is unnecessary paranoia, and doesn't always work as has been demonstrated in Japan.

The Marion Harper Switch

In working with a consummate intriguer, be prepared for sudden shifts—and learn to recover quickly. Walter H. Johnson, Jr. found this out working for the legendary Marion Harper.

Harper, who blazed across the corporate sky like a comet, was president of Interpublic, the advertising conglomerate. Walter Johnson had been hired away from airline sales management jobs as Harper's executive VP.

One day Harper went into Walter's office on the 44th floor of the Time-Life Building: "I'm making a presentation to American Cyanamid tomorrow morning in New Jersey. Can you stay in town tonight and work on the presentation?"

No one ever said no to Harper. Walter phoned his wife to tell her he wouldn't be home that evening.

Walter discovered Marion hadn't even started on the Cyanamid presentation. It was 9:00 p.m. before he saw Marion again. The two went to work. Data from computers flowed in, and rough charts were sent to the art studio, on all-night alert.

By 4:00 a.m., the proposal was finished. The two men departed to hotels nearby.

They met at 8:30 a.m., the presentation in the limousine. As the car entered the Lincoln Tunnel, Harper said:

"I've changed my mind. You're going to make the presentation."

"Okay," Johnson replied, wondering about the last-minute change.

At Cyanamid, they went directly to the conference room. The screening people filed in and took seats at the other end. Instead of sitting beside Johnson, Harper sat with the Cyanamid people and chatted about New Jersey politics. When everyone was assembled, he nodded to Walter to begin.

As the presentation proceeded, questions arose—some critical and difficult to answer. Marion, too, asked questions—some of the toughest.

"Son of a gun," thought Walter. "He has joined the client as a critical observer."

The presentation lasted less than an hour. After a brief silence the chairman said: "Would you mind leaving us alone for a few minutes, Mr. Johnson, to discuss your proposal among ourselves?"

Johnson left the room, but Harper didn't move. About 15 minutes later, Johnson was recalled. They had the business. Harper had, in fact, joined the client and helped make the decision.

Moral: If a consummate intriguer thinks getting on the other side is the best strategy, he'll do it.

When Devious Is Good

In plays and novels, the villain is often described as *devious*. Yet in behavioral psychology, the white rat that's most inventive about getting around obstacles in the maze gets the highest scores. Ditto in management.

Effective CEO's have deviousness—they know how to get around problems, how to deal with the unorthodox. If they can't beat it head on, they'll find another way to deal with it. They don't accept defeat. They figure out a way it will work. Develop your deviousness. In your climb, it'll be helpful, indeed.

Employees Outpoint Boss

Intrigue works from the bottom up at times. At an insurance company, Gene Simat ruled the actuarial department like Caligula on his worst day. He imposed impossible deadlines. He never praised performance, no matter how good. He was a tyrant with a good record, even his critics admitted that.

"In fact," related Jackson Earthier, "we decided to use his record to get him out. We made up a beautiful résumé on him, chipped in to buy the best graphics, and mailed it to our competitors. Sure enough, he got a job offer and he accepted."

An impossible boss was gone—a victim (if you can call a better job being victimized) of employee intrigue.

DON'T ACCEPT BOOBYTRAP ASSIGNMENTS

You're assigned a job you know you can't possibly do. You suspect you're being assigned so you'll stub your toe.

If it doesn't look right, bring it all out at the beginning. The boss can't be critical of you for expressing realism at the outset. Perhaps a clever rival suggested this boobytrap job in the first place. Develop a sense for these inspired assignments. You know the six or eight key people you're in greatest competition with. If you don't have that ability, develop it. Always remember: They're out to get you. Henry James said it best: "Life is a slow reluctant march into enemy territory."

WHEN YOU'RE THE INTRIGUER

Remember to play by the rules. Use the stiletto, not the baseball bat. Don't overtly cut the ground out from under your rival's feet. Don't poison his coffee. You're expected to compete with your peers, but you can't hit them below the belt. Telling stories about a rival drinking too much is not cricket. Besides, it often backfires.

In picking a successor to the executive VP at a big package goods company, we narrowed it down to Henry and Justin.

Justin said to us: "Henry gets drunk and talks too damn much"— a story that made us wonder more about Justin than Henry. We found Henry didn't drink that much. He emerged as the stronger candidate and we picked him.

And while we're on drinking, it's a major factor in all sorts of intrigue—who drinks and who doesn't, who drinks too much. It's a common topic since business uses alcohol to evaluate people, to determine secrets, to convince ("Let's get him out for two or three drinks—he'll be more open with us"). If drinking makes your customer more receptive, that's good. If it makes your employee talk too much, it's bad.

In career advancement, drinking habits are always in the spotlight. And you *do* have a choice. In case after case I've heard people say: "I had to have a drink because"—but it really isn't so. You can always drink Perrier or wine or soda in any situation.

A climber is in much better control on the short side of drinking. The brain just doesn't work as well. You say things you forget. You say things you shouldn't have said.

Alcohol, as a social lubricant, is a double-edged sword. Watch it.

Value of Flanking

In developing corporate intrigue, remember the frontal assault is seldom as effective as the flank attack. (Study the Second Battle of Bull Run to see how Generals Lee and Jackson bamboozled Union General John Pope.)

Jeremy Dorr and Blake Waters, chairman and president of a large shoe company, were locked in a gigantic power struggle. In jockeying for position, Dorr told the board (and convinced Waters) they should re-hire Charles Moone, a 68-year old former board member to head up the company's retail chain. After Moone, a Dorr supporter, had been on the job for 60 days, Waters noticed Moone was bringing up subjects Waters had discussed only in private with Dorr.

Waters, certain Dorr was feeding Moone information, did not make an issue out of it before the board. He launched a flank attack by promoting George Schipper, a Waters supporter, from treasurer to financial VP. He then assigned Schipper to make a detailed cost analysis of Moone's division.

In four months, Schipper's evidence disclosed management decisions that proved Moone totally inadequate. Waters presented the findings to the board and suggested that Moone be replaced. The board agreed. Dorr, outpointed in a bloodless coup, spluttered but could do nothing more. He soon took early retirement. Waters' flank attack won the battle—and the war.

Calling Intriguer to Account

However, at times, the frontal assault *is* the proper weapon. Just make sure you get the high ground and have the firepower before you jump off.

Jose Securidad had both. Securidad had done a good job as manager of Brazilian operations for a global food company. But the chairman, John Streeter, didn't much care for Securidad. On a pretext, Streeter "promoted" Securidad back to headquarters and sent a protégé to take Securidad's place in Brazil.

In the home office, Securidad soon became suspicious because Streeter (a) gave him no job but merely assigned him to the chairman's office—without title and (b) removed him from any function that utilized his extensive knowledge of the South American market.

Securidad, unhappy, decided to resign and take a job with a smaller food firm that planned to use his experience. Here is where Streeter made his mistake: He cut Securidad's severance drastically "because you're going to a competitor," which he wasn't, really.

That did it. Securidad's Latin blood boiled. He drew up a detailed case of mistreatment and presented a copy to each board member. This caused a major rhubarb. The board reversed Streeter's decision. Streeter lost considerable face. Securidad won.

Don't Sign on as a Hatchet Man

Staying out of corporate intrigue altogether is good, if you can manage it. In any event, be particularly careful about taking a new job as hatchet man—in a situation where intrigue factions are already aligned. Ben Sharp, a brilliant and accomplished banker, was offered a post reporting to a bank chairman—but *without* specific responsibilities. Sub rosa, he was supposed to analyze what other department heads did wrong—and report back to the chairman.

Sharp asked me: "Should I take the job?"

"No, I said, "you're headed for disaster. Whenever a person is brought into the higher echelons of any business without portfolio, anything he does tends to be a reflection of his peers. You're setting yourself up for subtle attacks, false or distorted information. Soon your value will be diminished—even in the CEO's eyes. Ask for specific responsibilities or don't take the job."

Sharp decided he was smart enough to handle it. He signed on. Things started going bad right way. Soon he was target for brickbats from all around. The other top people united against him. Soon the chairman stopped his support. Sharp lasted four months—a real setback in his career.

Moral: No one likes a hatchet man, even the person that hands him the ax. No matter what money or positions are offered, don't go in a no-win situation.

Keeping Intrigue Manageable

As you gain altitude, you'll be more and more concerned with controlling intrigue. After all, it can be lethal. One prominent advertising agency had to close down as its only solution to *politicitis extremis.*

Here are rules for keeping intrigue at bay:

Never hire your friends. Never hire your own children, or the children of your partners, or client's children however able they may be. And never hire personnel from client or customer organizations.

Fire the worst of your politicians. You can identify them by how often they send you blind copies of posion-pen memos to rivals.

When somebody comes to your office and denounces his rival as an incompetent rascal, summon the rival and make the denouncer repeat what he just told you.

Crusade against paper warfare. Make your people settle their fights face-to-face.

One executive likened it to pest control: "Roaches have been with us since ancient Egypt. We can't get rid of them. We just try to keep them in check." Ditto corporate intrigue.

PART ——— 6

MEETING YOURSELF AT THE SUMMIT

CHAPTER 18

THE MANY FACES
AT THE SUMMIT

NOW you're nearing the top of the Matter-horn. The CEO, that distinct corporate animal, is clearly visible. In fact, you probably work with him regularly. Some day soon, you hope to move into the CEO's chair. Good time to get checked out on the job specs.

What are the characteristics of this near-mythical creature?

F. Scott Fitzgerald said: "The rich are very different from you and me." Ernest Hemingway said: "Yes, they have more money." Is this true of top managers? Sure, they're *different*. But different only in more power and status? No, top managers *are* a select breed—somewhat from the beginning, but mostly because of the constant sorting process as they ascend the slope. By the time they reach the rarefied pinnacle, they are quite different indeed.

Now what is a top manager?

The CEO's Go-Go Nature

The dedicated climber never stops—no matter what his achievement. My friend Ian McGregor was chairman of AMAX with a wall full of management trophies. Retire at 65? Not for a minute. He went over to England to head up British Steel. He took over a terrible situation. No profits. Falling sales. Battles with unions. He had to close plants and put people out of work. He fought the media and fought the Queen. He even fought with Maggie Thatcher. He took on all comers.

In three years, he got British Steel in fair shape, still losing money, but greatly improved. Now as the economy picks up, it looks like he'll get into the black.

Achievement enough, you say? Not for McGregor. He turned around and accepted the job of cleaning up the British Coal Board organization—responsible for 280 thousand miners. It's a no-win situation. Again his only choice is to close mines and put people out of work.

Ian McGregor eats problems for breakfast and calls for seconds. He's an excellent example of the corporate battler.

John DeLorean, on the other hand, is executive drive run amuck. But you need that kind of drive as part of your equipment. For every climber who exceeds the limits, ten don't reach the limits in the first place.

Lee Iacocca is an excellent marketer. An action-oriented guy. Go-go. He wants to get things done. He'd rather not debate the merits of something he instinctively feels he's right in doing. He has a great charisma—getting people turned on and excited about what he's doing, where he's going. He can bring people along and that's important. He deserves a tremendous credit for bringing Chrysler—a company everybody had written off—back into the real world.

The CEO's Killer Instinct

What the best managers have—and I'm not sure it can be developed—is sometimes called the killer instinct. It's the ability to blot out all the nonessentials and go for the jugular—on issues, on priorities, and at times on personnel that need weeding.

This instinct stems from insatiable curiosity—the need to understand everything you're exposed to and the ability to store up information and experiences that will later give you a reputation for gut reactions.

It *looks* like instinct. But it's *informed* instinct. An outdoorsman walking through the woods avoids snakes, seemingly by reflex. He says it's instinct. But analyze it: he's been through the woods hundreds of times with open eyes and ears. He learned to look for certain characteristics of terrain and foliage movement. He has a whole series of knowledge components stored away. He taps into this know-how with instant access—like using a computerized database.

Hubert Humphrey was a great extemporaneous speaker. Spoke for hours. No notes. What HH was doing was drawing on a lifetime of experiences. The extemporaneous manager with a reputation for gut-instinct decisions is like the woodsman and the speaker. If you have this gut instinct to start with, it can be developed by knowledge and experience—to give you management instincts.

The CEO as Inspirer

About Theodore Roosevelt, critic H. L. Mencken—normally no praiser of presidents—said: "He was excited about what he did. He had the ability to get others excited about his actions, too." In short, TR was an inspiring leader.

The potential CEO who can inspire others to top performance has a marked advantage.

Inspiration is a great thing—if you can engender it. But this quality is difficult to produce if it doesn't come naturally. Being an inspirational leader traces back to your childhood and your relationship to others and your ability to set the example. Did you become the model your classmates tried to emulate? Such is the effect of natural leaders on others (and a great characteristic to look for in people you're hiring as you go up the line).

If you yourself are not inspirational, try to recruit a number two who can inspire people. Make sure somebody fills this role. No one leader possesses all the desirable qualities. Seek complementary talents.

The CEO as Decision-Maker

As everyone knows, the sign above Harry Truman's desk at The White House said: "The buck stops here." As you get on up the slope, you've got to make clear-cut decisions without committees to lean on. Get the best knowledge available (even in the computer age, you never can have all the answers) and make *judgments.*

Often a young climber tends to be too cautious. He bucks decisions up to his boss that he himself ought to make. Some people want the boss's blessing on everything they do. But you cannot have it both ways. No guts, no glory.

There are also corporate politicians who buck decisions upward so the boss can be impressed with their *thinking.* Keeping the boss informed is healthy and necessary. But political grandstanding is a waste of time. And the savvy boss—of which there are many—will see through it quickly.

You're managing a midwest territory. There are three ways of informing your boss about an unusual move:

'I'm going to go to Kansas City tomorrow because I think that it's important that I work with Jim Henson." (*Strong.*)

"Do you think I ought to go to Kansas City tomorrow?" (*A negation of your responsibility.*)

"What do you think I ought to do about my problem in Kansas City?" (*Weaker still.*)

The potential CEO probably uses the first alternative on the way up.

The Yin and the Yang

"Jim," a colleague said, "you are always looking for the mean between two extremes. You frequently will point out the danger on the left and the danger on the right and you're trying to get things to work better in the middle."

That is a fair statement of my philosophy. I believe a professional manager should take his cue from the Chinese symbols Yin and Yang, which represent force and counterforce.

It's a product of experience and approach to problems. They're always two sides to every problem. I'm never content to hear one side unless I hear the other side. If somebody beats the drums on the merits of X, I automatically think about what's on the other side—the offsets to it.

The opposite side of the coin is always a good place to look because there's always an opposing view. This is very important for the CEO to understand.

The CEO as Scrapper

The CEO must be a scrapper, a real contender who enjoys the good fight. The comparison between athletics and business is not accidental. Nor is the great emphasis on money in both—compensation is the score that tells how well you're doing. In sports you are always trying to beat somebody or your own record—or both. The desire to be involved in competitive games is also another indicator you're a scrapper—that includes poker, chess, or whatever.

Management is like playing poker. The rules of the game are simple.

Almost everyone can learn how to play after a few hands. But no serious player ever so completely masters poker that he or she stops trying to learn more. Amarillo Slim, who frequently wins the World Series of Poker in Las Vegas, triumphs one year fully aware that someone can knock him off next year—as sometimes they do.

Management is the same way. No serious player ever masters the technique so completely as to stop trying to do it better.

Compensation experts know a score sheet is vital to motivation—and a key to the retention of workforce and executives alike. It's not that a top guy needs the extra $10,000. A person in that tax bracket doesn't get much of that extra $10,000 anyhow. So it's really a competitive thing to outdo his colleagues or his competitors.

So scrapping is certainly one of the characteristics of the potential CEO. If the person undertaking this climb doesn't like to get into the arena, that's a signal in and of itself.

The CEO as Philosopher

The potential CEO will be aided if he's a philosopher who sees humor in his own foibles and can look at the weaknesses of others in a sometimes entertaining, sometimes instructive manner.

Charles Brower, when president of BBDO, was such a person. Samplings of Brower philosophy:

☐   Honesty is not only the best policy, it is rare enough today to make you pleasantly conspicuous.

☐   The expedient thing and the right thing are seldom the same thing.

☐   The best way to get credit is to try to give it.

The CEO's Not an Operations Manager

Sometimes we find the CEO as both planner/pilot *and* day-to-day operations manager. Perhaps he carries the titles of both chairman and president. This is usually dangerous.

Unforeseen events (particularly executives jumping onto a faster rocket ship or sudden illness or a policy disagreement with the board) may cause vacancies that make it expedient for one person to cover two jobs *for the moment.* But you should start to correct the vacancy immediately.

"Now that the old CEO has been relieved, I'm going to operate the business without any marketing or manufacturing head for a few months while I get acquainted with the middle managers and see what they are doing," one chairman told me.

This move placed him directly in charge of three product sales heads, one advertising manager, two marketing managers, three factory managers, two engineering departments, plus the usual coterie of staff people—legal, finance, personnel, and new product development.

He kept the same structure for two years. Things began to fall apart. Result: Out went a great chairman (who'd tried to both coach and play all the positions). A replacement came in from the outside. Moral: There's too much to be done in overall policy and planning direction, on one hand, and operations, on the other, for any one man to handle both for long—even if he's a genius.

Importance of Confidence

The management mind is confident—willing to rise and fall on its decisions.

William F. Farley, sole owner of a Chicago-based conglomerate valued at $610 million, never doubted he'd reach his goal—to make a lot of money. He began his quest in 1976 with a confidence and single-mindedness that bordered on obsession.

"I simply decided I wanted to be independently wealthy," Farley told *The Philadelphia Inquirer.* "I knew I could do it."

Yet, Farley soon found himself personally in debt for $7 million one year after he purchased a troubled Ohio machinery manufacturer. Despite a legally bankrupt company, Farley quit everything else and began working 20-hour days. He instituted a cost-cutting regime, devised new marketing strategies, developed new customers—until the company was profitable.

"If you haven't had a major failure in life, you really haven't been tested," he said. "If I failed, it would have been the end of my career. But I couldn't accept that I would fail—and I didn't."

Because of this confidence, the achiever is continuously unhappy with past accomplishments—he or she always wants more. This often breeds frustration.

"All my life I've had the feeling that I'm running out of the woods and no one is following me. I'm constantly frustrated by delays," said Sheldon Weinig, founder of Materials Research Corp., an Orangeburg, New York, electronics company that he launched 26 years ago.

This frustration sometimes takes the form of anti-bureaucracy—as with William G. McGowan, the founder and chief executive officer of MCI Communications Corp., the discount long-distance telephone company. When he assembled his managers for brainstorming, he said: "I know that some of you, with your business-school backgrounds, are out there already beginning to draw organization charts and to write manuals for operating procedures. As soon as I find out who you are, I'm going to fire every last one of you."

He was kidding—or was he?

The CEO as Futurist

When Charles H. Percy (now U.S. Senator from Illinois) was CEO at Bell & Howell, he placed a sign over his desk that said: *My job is planning for the future.*

When a colleague came in with a question pertaining to day-to-day problems, Percy pointed to the sign.

Actually, Percy, like other effective CEOs, worked much in the present, too. But this was his way of keeping his focus on the forward-thinking part of his job. Unless someone is actually working on the future, there won't be any. And no manager can be a whiz at strategic planning if he's overly involved in solving nitty-gritty.

The CEO must sit back and think about where the company's going and determine what changes to make as the marketplace changes.

Not only must the CEO be a futurist for his company, he must be prescient in evaluating career opportunities. Donald F. Dvorak, partner-in-charge of Peat, Marwick, Mitchell's executive search, has this kind of insight in divining the kinds of managers most in demand in 1990s:

- ☐ We need more emerging New Entrepreneurs in the middle-management ranks.
- ☐ Executives with hands-on, analytical, and people-handling skills in the exploding field of information systems management.
- ☐ Managers with new abilities in participative management.
- ☐ Executives who can relate to the global marketplace.
- ☐ Executives who accept self-motivation as important despite a slow- or no-growth environment.
- ☐ Men and women who understand and accept the pay-for-performance management.
- ☐ Executives with proven track records of successfully balancing corporate goals with existing life styles with chosen forms of psychic income.

So the effective CEO has a handle on the future for his company and for himself.

The CEO as Work-Oriented

"If you hate Mondays and therefore hate work," a seasoned manager told me, "you ought to quit. You can marry rich or get by on welfare and begging. I have always looked forward to work. I've always had to work. Work is a fact of life. I like Fridays, but I also look forward to Mondays."

It adds up: the real potential CEO *likes* to work.

THE CEO AS REALIST

Sure, the potential CEO is a positive thinker, he doesn't give up easily, and he keeps at it. But at times he must know when to stop battering against the stone wall. Remember the doggerel:

Everyone said it couldn't be done, And the odds were so great, who wouldn't? But I tackled the job that couldn't be done, And what do you know—it couldn't.

The effective manager knows when to reassign his time to more do-able goals.

Thus as you can see the CEO is many different persons—rolled into one. When you view the post as a *whole,* by personality type, you get a still different view. Here personality type meshes with corporate character.

A non-nuclear public utility (running along and growing five percent per year) doesn't change too much. Such a post requires an *administrative CEO.* He keeps loose ends tied together and keeps everything on the track. He conserves existing assets. A caretaker.

A rapidly growing hightech business is quite a contrast. Here you need a *creative CEO* who thinks two jumps ahead of his competitors.

When you get the wrong CEO on the wrong job, the results are predictable. A few years ago, several large trucking firms decided to integrate backward to get a jump on the energy shortage and insure gasoline for their fleets. They bought up oil refineries and contracted for crude to make their own gasoline. But refining oil into gasoline is a science in itself. It didn't work. CEOs experienced in trucking it, it turned out, got all gummed up in oil.

Some regulated industries require a *political CEO.* The more the business is regulated, the more you must think politically about every move you make. You plot the strategies, deal with congressmen and senators or executive board members that control your future.

Some CEO posts require a *public spokesman*—and an emerging need all its own.

You've met yourself at the summit and dissected the CEO's job. Not a simple assignment, not an easy task, but you've known that all along. By now you know what you can do. But can you cope with the isolation of the CEO's post? That's another matter altogether.

CHAPTER 19

The CEO's Role: Command Is a Lonely Function

IN North Africa, during World War II, General Dwight D. Eisenhower replaced General Fredenhall with General George S. Patton, Jr. When Patton arrived, Eisenhower advised Patton on weeding out dead wood:

"You must not retain for one instant," Eisenhower warned Patton, "any man in a responsible position where you have become doubtful of his ability to do the job. This frequently calls for more courage than any other thing you have to do. But I expect you to be perfectly cold-blooded about it."

To his old friend General Gerow (training an infantry division in Scotland), Eisenhower expanded on the theme:

"Officers that fail," Eisenhower said, "must be ruthlessly weeded out. Friendship, family, kindliness and personality have nothing whatsoever to do with the problem. You must be tough. Get rid of the lazy, the slothful, the indifferent or the complacent."

For some, this advice goes against the grain. A good CEO is oriented toward developing talented people. Consequently, part of your character says "don't fire people—improve them."

Being a CEO *is* a lonely job. Nobody else can help. It's the endgame and you must say yes or no.

ALONE-NESS AT THE Top

By the single act of assuming the CEO's job, you have vastly changed your viewpoint. You now have a new set of internal responsibilities, an added public responsibility, and a concern about (a) where the *job* goes after you leave it and (b) where *you* go after you say goodbye to the job.

Sure, you're at the top. But it's damned chilly up there and, even though you can see for miles in all directions, you seldom see a confidant—such persons are off on their own peaks, coping with their own problems.

Your executives and board members are valuable advisors. But they're not confidants. There's quite a difference. In fact, as CEO you don't have anyone to talk to. As the climb has progressed, you've been leaving colleagues behind. Some have voluntarily unhooked. Others have been unhitched. Still others have settled on comfortable plateaus along the way.

So add it up: You cannot talk to employees about things that really matter. You talk, to a certain extent, to fellow CEOs—but you'd be surprised how few you know that aren't involved in entangling relationships (fellow board members, participants in joint ventures, serving on the same committee). These special relationships usually dominate the conversation.

You dare not go to your marketing head to talk about your financial VP or your manufacturing director. If you've got reservations about how old Henry is performing you can't go to ask Joe about it. If you're frustrated by the board, you don't go to Ray or Henry for help. This reflects weakness.

The board picked you to run the business and you'd better run it or they'll pick somebody else. You don't dare say to a board member: "I don't see how I can bring volume up another ten percent per year for the next five years. We're in a mature market and it's just impossible." So you can't talk to directors.

You can talk to consultants, whose advice is based on a wide range of experience. They must remain nonpolitical and confidential. Many CEOs use consultants as sounding boards for their concerns, fears, uncertainties, and sometimes even what amounts to psychological therapy.

After all, the most sophisticated machines in the world really only produce data. An experienced consultant can help you evaluate that data and keep your confidence in the process.

The CEO's Internal Responsibilities

One CEO took over his new post thinking "Ah, ha, now I'm the boss" and found to his surprise he had just *changed* bosses.

"Instead of an immediate superior as I've had all the way up, I now have 12 board members and 11,000 stockholders to worry about."

It's true. Everyone in life, it appears, must report to someone. Start with your largest body of bosses—the shareowners. Handling this population requires a high degree of skill. You decide on their dividends. You influence appreciation (or lack of appreciation) of their stock. You decide how much profit goes back in the business and how much goes into executive salaries—including your own.

Stockholders today are vitally interested in how their company is doing. CEOs once saw their job as maintaining bottom-line earnings and protecting themselves against being deposed. But today, recognition of the stockholder role is marked. Holders are more restive and more articulate. In this widely communicated society, stockholders are becoming extremely aware.

When a CEO does not think about what's on stockholder's minds, stockholders go to annual meetings and raise hell. Sometimes large-block stockholders—say, a pension fund group—start a proxy fight to replace management. At such times, help from a nonflappable public relations firm can be a life-saver.

Communications with stockholders is a prime responsibility of the CEO. One CEO, who had little communication with the stockholders, got into a proxy fight. Stockholders, who felt totally separated from the company, automatically voted for the insurgents. So not only must you be concerned about stockholders, you must be *visibly* and *communicatively* concerned.

Security analysts are also alert. Much of what the CEO does and says is reported. In fact, SEC's timely disclosure rules make it CEO responsibility to *see* that significant news *is* reported.

Resentment of Executive Salaries

Remember: Top salaries are most visible in proxy statements that go to stockholders. You're in a goldfish bowl. CEO pay, which has jumped faster than inflation and other measures, has become a *cause celebre* of late. Peter Drucker says if companies don't control themselves, Congress will set up restrictions on executive salaries. Labor unions are screaming about Lee Iacocca's compensation now that Chrysler's back in a profitable mode. *Time* reports that critics are assailing top management salaries as "an affront to the workers and as a threat to the economy."

One defense contractor lost 20 engineers who quit after only getting three percent salary increases when top management got 30 percent.

Some brickbats come from misunderstanding. *Time* reported that William Anderson, former chairman of NCR, earned $13.2 million in one year by exercising stock options he acquired over a ten-year span. But you can't really call that *annual* income. The whole purpose of options is to create a nest egg for the CEO. That's your retirement plan. It's created by giving you options that don't cost the stockholders anything. Only if the stock goes up are the options worth anything. Normally when you do exercise options, it's five or ten years later.

So dodging bricks regarding your pay is part of CEO training. (You also must dodge the IRS in all legal ways—to manage to keep quite a bit of this controversial gain. You'll need tax shelters that show a loss for four or five years until it gets into capital gains.)

I doubt if the CEO of a large company ever feels overpaid. He knows his worth. To get where he is required both talent and ego. He's not likely to be self-effacing. He knows how hard he's worked all these years.

What to do? The smartest CEO compensation structures do *not* come out in *Time* or *Forbes.* Compensation can be in the form of options, deferred income, the underwriting of real estate, equity in developing companies, or other things. Don't concentrate compensation in pure dollars.

Developing Board Relations

Those earthquake rumblings you hear may be restive directors. If they get too distraught, you can be deposed—an act that comes about with some regularity. You must work at relationships with your directors, who are unpredictable at best, downright surprising at times.

John Wagner had been number two at a communications conglomerate until a large oil company beckoned—they wanted him to come over as chairman. He signed on. The company had production (called *upstream* in the oil business) and retail outlets (*downstream*). Wagner's job: to continue strengthening the company in the oil scramble.

He didn't face any overwhelming problems on his new job. Nor was he saddled with a dominant director that required special handling (which you almost always find). Perhaps the *lack* of a large challenge lulled him to sleep.

He settled down in his golden chair on the top floor of his building— and looked out the window. He visited the oil fields. He spent time with retailers. But he had little contact with the board.

Prices of oil and gasoline fell off in the entire industry. His earnings fell. It was not a bad record, just a dip. But directors didn't identify with his administration. He hadn't kept them informed. So several directors got together and suggested that Wagner move on.

Wagner, a seasoned manager with a fine record, learned a lesson: You neglect the board at your peril. Directors must *feel* a part of—and *be* a part of—your program as CEO.

Board Politics

Board politics is politics at its peak. Who's a supporter? Who's an enemy? Where are the swing votes? You can wake up one bright morning and find the majority good and mad.

Now you may think: "If the board's this much trouble, I'll pick directors already on my side." Don't think it hasn't been tried, many times. (In the 1930s, FDR's decisions to "pack" the Supreme Court with allies is a case in point.) But when you pick supporters, you get a rubber stamp—and you can buy a rubber stamp at the office supply store. You need a group of seasoned advisors that can draw on their considerable experience to help guide this corporate animal.

The best bet, you'll find, is to influence board selection toward people you feel good about in terms of personal chemistry. Then you'll have directors that you see eye-to-eye with in general—but enjoy doing battle with on individual issues.

Executive Burnout

We've talked about how you can be deposed by stockholders and directors. You can also depose yourself—via poor health. As CEO, you must keep up your strength. Exercise. Don't get the idea you're God. Don't do foolish things. The sage advice of Satchel Paige applies to CEOs: "Don't eat fried meats. They angrify the blood. Take it easy on the vices. The social ramble ain't restful. Never look backwards. Somebody may be gaining on you."

Another baseball philosopher, Casey Stengel, also equated proper rest with performance. In commenting on ball players that chase women at night, he said: "It ain't getting it that hurts them. It's staying up all night looking for it."

Executive stress *is* an occupational hazard. There are days when you must make five large-scope decisions before 5 p.m. It's the highest form of pressure. Offset this with change-of-pace exercise, unrelated diversion, proper rest, and sensible eating and drinking.

I agree with David Ogilvy who says a CEO "must be a good leader of frightened people. He must have financial acumen, administrative skill, thrust, and the courage to fire non-performers. He must be resilient in adversity. Above all, he must have the physical stamina to work 12 hours a day, dine out several times a week, and spend half his time in airplanes."

This requires good strength. Sure, you can take a short stretch of days off. But realistically you cannot do this frequently—the time pressures are too strong. Note the attendance at seminars (of which there are hundreds). Generally the powerful executives aren't represented. They're back at the office doing the work. If *they* can't take the time, that gives *you* a clue.

Your Growth Assignment

As CEO, realize that both people and organizations must grow. You cannot stand still. If your company doesn't grow, sooner or later you will start to lose people. Talented folk want to be with a company that's going places. So a reigning CEO's got to look for more peaks.

You are also charged with maintaining what you have—and this gets tricky, since it means fending off takeovers. There are always sharks around that love to find a company where *investor perception* (reflected in stock price) is lower than *book value* (what the company's actually worth via assets). For this reason, keep 25 percent of your stock in friendly hands. You'll also need to order a good supply of shark repellent via new corporate bylaws to keep sharks at bay.

Whenever takeover attempts turn into proxy fights, you're in full-scale corporate war. Proxy battles are a type of heavy combat that make all other struggles up the slope look like a boy scout hike.

On the other hand, nobody ever said it'd be easy. As Dick Jacob, CEO of Dayco Corporation, Dayton, Ohio, said: "The most boring thing in the world is to run a company where everything's going well."

The CEO as Public Spokesman

The CEO is susceptible to jibes from colleagues who see this as an ego trip. The public-visibility manager—like Lee Iacocca or Frank Borman—become known to the general public by speaking out in commercials and in public issues of all sorts.

Obviously, CEOs-in-the-spotlight enjoy walking into a room where everybody knows them. But ego aside, when the company needs a public personality, using the CEO makes good sense. People like to feel they *know* the CEO. When he or she can communicate publicly and effectively, it's a valuable corporate asset. I can't think of a public spokesman-CEO who's been bad.

The Tylenol poison scare spotlighted the skills of Johnson & Johnson chairman James Burke. On a closed TV press conference networked to major cities, Burke's calm masterful handling of questions was widely hailed. (During the telecast, one J & J executive backstage whispered to a colleague: "They didn't teach him anything *this* valuable at Harvard Business School!") Without Burke's strong public presence, Tylenol's comeback could not have been anywhere near so rapid.

If the CEO does the other parts of the job well and is also an effective public spokesman, this is a plus. But a CEO who doesn't like to (or cannot) speak out should avoid it like the plague. If you're bad in your public pose, people will judge *all* aspects of your performance by the way you come across—just as they do for political candidates.

Broadcasting is only part of a modern CEO's public role. You must present company or industry views to government investigating committees. You must also indoctrinate and inspire employees. In this visibility/television age, the CEO who presents effectively will outshine the CEO who cannot.

Beyond the CEO Job

CEOs stay on the job an average of five years. So early-on, you must plan for a fitting successor.

Then what? Do you—like Alexander of Macedonia—sit down and weep because there are no more worlds to conquer? No.

There are *always* more worlds to conquer. Ian McGregor left AMAX to head up British Steel. He has since added several other top jobs. He wouldn't be happy any other way. So you *can* go after larger and more challenging jobs.

Jim McLamore on the other hand left Burger King and started leading what I call The Good Life. He's chairman of the University of Miami. He spends some time on his Montana ranch. He enjoys the fruits of his labor.

Taking on a public cause can be part of The Good Life. John Cowles, of the Cowles publishing empire, did that. He was a real believer in industrialized nations giving up material goods so developing countries can grow. So he spent his post-CEO time in global philanthropy.

Maybe you've said: "Government service might be interesting." But looking and trying are two different things. Dan Parker of Parker Pen went down to Washington, stayed for nine months, and walked away. "The most frustrating period in my life," he said. He felt he made no progress at all.

"People used to pat me on the back and say 'you're going in the right direction,' whereas I didn't think I was getting anything done at all," Parker said. So consider government, but realize it's another animal altogether.

Ambassadorships are another possibility. But this often calls for money contributions as well. The ambassador to the Court of St. James in years past has paid out $2 million a year and more in living and entertainment costs—out of his own pocket. (Of course, other posts are less costly than London.)

You've Arrived: What Do You Have?

Successors and The Good Life options are all in the future right now. You're the CEO. Less than one percent made it—but you're in that exclusive group. In many areas, you now possess all kinds of perks.

Your income places you in the upper one percent. You have unquestioned power. The number of people who work for you (1,000 to 100,000) is larger than many of Caesar's legions. A helicopter or airplane is at your command. To go anyplace, business or vacation, just say the word.

You're popular with the media (publicity's great for the ego). You are in demand as a speaker. You may even be asked to write a book (and not knowing how much work it is, you might say yes).

You're lord of all you survey. But "uneasy lies the head that wears the crown." You also have heavy responsibilities. You're managing the end-game. If you slack off, you know damned well certain things won't happen.

You wake up at three a.m. concerned about your pet enterprises. You think: "Jesus, is it worth all this!" (F. Scott Fitzgerald said: "It's always three o'clock in the morning in the deep dark recesses of the soul.") But somehow you get back to sleep. When you wake up at your normal time, you say, "I'll get that bastard this time." Nothing looks as bad in the sunlight as it does at three in the morning.

By morning your orderly persistence takes over. You outline the six things you've got to do today. By day-end, often to your surprise, you've made considerable progress. And most of the time, you wouldn't change places with anyone in the world.

You're drawing on skills you've learned during the long climb. It's been a difficult ascent full of *in*fighting (part of the way leaders are selected) and *out*fighting (warding off the saber-tooth tigers from the outside world).

You may not be aware of all your assets—many are reflexes by now. Yet if you analyze it, you'll find your abilities are most impressive. You handle social occasions well and use stress constructively. You're smooth and unruffled in tense situations. You rally groups to a common goal and you're comfortable when faced with diverse views.

In addition, you have a consistent interest in improving the way things are done. You initiate—with confidence in abilities and goals. You've learned to help others improve.

You're skilled in oral and written communication. You tend to put business needs before personal needs. You maintain objectivity in a dispute. You know your own strengths and weaknesses. You're adaptable and obviously you have the mental stamina to put in long hours.

That adds up to uncommon achievement, indeed.

So congratulations! You're a professional manager who has risen to the peak. Without ability and persistence, the object of your own quest surely wouldn't have happened. *With* this organized *willpower*, you've climbed the Corporate Matterhorn to make your personal dreams come true.

Epilog

If you decided to preview the final chapter *before* you get the CEO post, we're not surprised. Advance preparation is the fuel that has kept moving you up the slope.

Index